CELTIC WARFARE

For Sara

CELTIC WARFARE
1595–1763

JAMES MICHAEL HILL

JOHN DONALD PUBLISHERS LTD
EDINBURGH

ISBN 0 85976 151 7

Reprinted 1995

Phototypeset by Quorn Selective Repro,
Loughborough.
Printed in Great Britain by Bell & Bain Ltd.,
Glasgow.

Acknowledgements

The idea behind this book evolved over the past six years. During that time I have accumulated a tremendous debt to many people at the University of Alabama who have helped me to transform that idea into reality. My sincere thanks go to Bernerd C. Weber, Gary B. Mills, Howard Jones, Michael Mendle, Hugh Ragsdale, James Doster, William MacMillan, John M. Dederer, William A. Henderson, Catherine T. Jones, Mary Jane Craddock, Jonie Griffin, Rheena Elmore, Mary Marchant, Malcolm MacDonald, Ellen Shapiro McDonald, Ruth M. Kibbey, and Carolyn C. Sassaman.

The author also wishes to thank a number of institutions and individuals for permission to quote from manuscripts and documents in their possession: Council of Trustees, National Library of Ireland, Dublin; Manuscripts Department, Lambeth Palace Library, London; Department of Manuscripts, The British Library, London; Keeper of the Public Records, H. M. Public Record Office, London; Manuscripts Department, The Huntington Library, San Marino, California; Trustees of the National Library of Scotland, Edinburgh; Dr. J. T. D. Hall, Librarian, Edinburgh University Library, Edinburgh; Keeper of the Records of Scotland, Scottish Record Office, Edinburgh; Sir David J. W. Ogilby, Bart., for permission to use the Ogilby of Inverquharity Papers, located in the Scottish Record Office, Edinburgh; Captain P. L. Mackie-Campbell for permission to use the Campbell of Stonefield Papers, also located in the Scottish Record Office, Edinburgh; The Marquis of Graham for permission to use the Montrose Muniments, located in the Scottish Record Office, Edinburgh; Keeper of Western Manuscripts, Bodleian Library, Oxford; The Duke of Atholl for permission to use the Atholl Manuscripts, located in the Charter Room, Blair Castle, Blair Atholl; David R. Godine Publishers, Boston, for permission to quote from Julius Caesar, *The Battle for Gaul* (1980).

Thanks also go to: Sue McWhiney, Fort Worth, Texas; Joyce Batty, London; Lillian Baird, Edinburgh; the Saint Andrew's Society of Tuscaloosa; Daniel Gillis, The Iona Foundation, Prince Edward Island, Canada; Edmund and Mary Black, Ballycastle, N.I; Robert Hunter, Ballycastle, N.I; and John Tuckwell of John Donald Publishers Ltd., Edinburgh.

There remains a small group of people to whom I am particularly indebted: James E. and Marie Hollis Hill, my parents; my grandmothers, Annie Jaudon Hill and Virgie Lockhart Hollis; my late grandfathers, Ernest Hill abd Isiah Hollis; my sister, Pamela C. Hill; Tom Griffin; Warren A. and Rose S. Dundon, my in-laws; and Katherine Elizabeth and Emily Anne Hill, my daughters.

I owe special thanks to Forrest McDonald and Grady McWhiney of the University of Alabama and Texas Christian University, respectively, for reading several drafts of the manuscript during the past two years and for making valuable suggestions for its improvement.

Finally, I must thank Sara Dundon Hill, my wife, who has stood by me throughout the writing of this book. Her sacrifices are too numerous to mention. She has served as editor, critic, typist, and proofreader, drawn the maps and illustrations, and spent untold hours discussing with me the content of the manuscript. I owe her a debt of gratitude that can never be repaid. To you, Sara, all my love.

Though the efforts of many have made this book possible, any errors or shortcomings are the sole responsibility of the author.

James Michael Hill
Tuscaloosa, Alabama

Contents

Maps

Illustrations

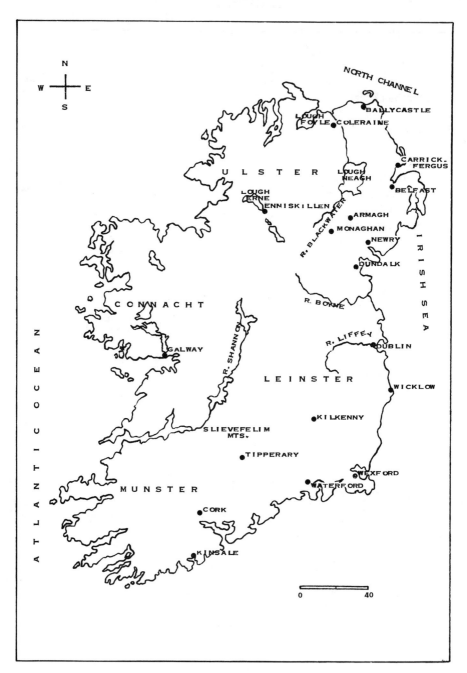

MAP 1.   IRELAND

MAP 2.   SCOTLAND AND NORTHERN ENGLAND

1
Introduction

The mention of Celtic warfare usually elicits from historians reflections on the Gauls' sacking of Rome in 387 B.C., the battle of Telamon in 225 B.C., or Caesar's Gallic Wars from 58 to 51 B.C; however, both the temporal and geographic scope of Celtic warfare is more extensive than is commonly realized. While it is widely recognized that the Gaels of the Scottish Highlands and Ireland are cultural and linguistic descendants of the ancient Celts, attempts to trace the continuity in Celtic warfare are lacking. The characteristics of the ancient Celts' military strategies, tactics, and logistics distinguished them from their Greek and Roman adversaries; these same characteristics are apparent in their Gaelic descendants' military system pitted against England from the late sixteenth through the eighteenth centuries. The purpose of this book, therefore, is to provide a sound, factual and analytical base that will help identify the continuity in Celtic (or more precisely, Gaelic) warfare from the Elizabethan conflict in Ireland in the 1590s to the French and Indian War in North America from 1756 to 1763. The author hopes the book will also provide a backdrop for further studies of Celtic warfare as it evolved on the American continent.[1]

The first and foremost element of continuity in Celtic warfare was the tactical offensive — the attack against all reason, against all odds. From the era of the ancient Celts to that of the Highland Scots and Irish, these primitive peoples relied on unbounded fury, strength, and dexterity to overcome a lack of military sophistication. The charge was the centerpiece of Celtic offensive tactics. Well documented from ancient times[2] to the mid-eighteenth century, the Celtic (or later, Highland) charge[3] derived its effectiveness from an initial impact that frequently overwhelmed stronger and better disciplined armies. The sword was the principal weapon used by the Celts in their impetuous assaults. An eighteenth-century witness described the Highland charge in terms that could be applied (excluding the reference to firearms, of course) across time and space to any Celtic army:

> Their manner of fighting is adapted for brave but undisciplined men. They advance with rapidity, discharge their pieces when within musket length of the enemy, and then, throwing them down, draw their swords, and ... dart with fury on the enemy through the smoke of their fire. When within reach of the enemy's bayonets, bending their left knee, they ... cover their bodies with their targets ... while at the same time they raise their sword-arm, and strike their adversary ... Their attack is so terrible, that the best troops in Europe would with difficulty sustain the first shock of it; and if the hordes of the Highlanders once come in contact with them, their defeat is inevitable.[4]

1

Numerous other observers have left us similar descriptions of the victorious Celtic charge, and such preponderant evidence of the Celts' success leads one to wonder how, with primitive tactics and arms, they won most of their battles against potentially stronger enemies.

The charge succeeded because of the emphasis that the Celts placed on individual prowess and accomplishment. They preferred individualized combat that highlighted the strength of each warrior. Once the attack began, each man forged ahead into what became for him an affair of personal honor, and when well armed and inspired, he was more than a match, one to one, for the best soldiers that Rome or England could muster against him. Armed with sword, target and, later, musket, the Celtic fighter was a self-contained combat unit. As long as the enemy fought according to the dictates of primitive warfare, the Celts would emerge victorious simply because of their individual abilities.

Because the Celts emphasized the individual warrior, they were at their best in the field when operating in small, mobile armies. A lack of organization and military discipline precluded an effective amassing of large bodies of troops. A Celtic general, often the foremost warrior of his tribe or clan, found it easier to command a small force because he led by example. He took upon himself the most dangerous and demanding tasks, thus cementing the all-important bond of trust and respect between him and his subordinates.[5] The general or clan chief and his lieutenants, as members of a warrior aristocracy, imparted to their men the importance of fighting for honor, reputation, and perhaps ultimately, secular immortality, as well as for the sheer love of combat. The larger his army, the more difficult the Celtic commander found it to conduct his irregular form of warfare based oftentimes on mobility and shock tactics.

A compact, mobile, and emotionally motivated army, though perfectly suited for irregular warfare on difficult terrain, fared poorly against the Romans and Anglo-Saxons in formal battle. Both the Romans and Anglo-Saxons had developed through long experience an art of warfare based on careful organization. Both were able to equip, feed, and move large bodies of troops in a coordinated fashion, thereby insuring numerical and technical superiority at the point of battle. Celtic generals usually lacked such organizational skills and therefore could not effectively handle large bodies of troops either before or during battle. If their initial attack failed, they lacked the tenacity to continue the fight, accurately assessing their inability to rally their dispersed forces. A mass — disorganized and largely undisciplined — best described most Celtic armies from the ancient era to the Jacobite rising in Scotland in the mid-eighteenth century. The Celts lacked the tactical organization of the legion or regiment, the auxiliary units that provided support services, quartermaster units that served logistical needs, and an officer corps that was capable of coordinating the overall military effort. In short, they lacked almost everything that was necessary for a regular army, and in the long run they were no match for the organizational genius of Rome and England.[6]

Since the Celts were vulnerable against regular armies on smooth terrain, they often employed guerrilla tactics within their own territory. Such tactics accounted for most of the Celts' successes against Julius Caesar during the Gallic wars of the first century B.C. as well as the victories of Hugh O'Neill over the Elizabethan armies of the late sixteenth century. Both the Gauls and the Irish used the wilderness as a valuable ally. They awaited unsuspecting enemy columns behind plashes (wall-like hedges fashioned from intertwined branches and thorns) flanked by deep ditches,[7] attacked savagely, and then disappeared into the safety of forest or bog. In this manner the Celts were able to use the tactical offensive — the charge — against an enemy who, despite his overall strength, was at a temporary disadvantage. Thus, offensive guerrilla tactics allowed Celtic leaders to arrange scenarios in which the shock value of their attack would fall with maximum force on the enemy with minimum risk to themselves.

Whether using guerrilla or formal warfare against the English, the Highland Scots and Irish from 1595 to 1689 relied on basically the same primitive strategy, tactics, logistics, and weapons as their forebears. During this period most Highland and Irish victories were based on variations of the Celtic charge, allowing the Gaels to pit their individual fighting skills against an enemy that had neither the training nor the nerve to stand up to them.[8] As long as the English and lowland Scots fought the Gaels in irregular, primitive warfare on harsh, unfamiliar terrain, the former enjoyed only limited success. But until the end of the seventeenth century the English and Lowlanders had few opportunities to fight them in any other manner.

Though for most of the seventeeth century the primitive Celtic or Highland charge dominated the battlefields upon which Celt fought Anglo-Saxon, the new British army developed effective methods of dealing with the Gaels after 1689. When the British began to apply technology and modern military science to the battlefield, a process that slowly depersonalized warfare, they gradually neutralized the strength of Gaelic warfare. The collective efforts of a modern nation-state produced engines and theories of war that overwhelmed the individual Gaelic warrior. The British developed a war machine that was better equipped, trained, and led, and the Gaels lagged behind because of their inability, or at any rate their refusal, to modify their primitive way of fighting. By the eighteenth century the non-personal or collective weapons and elements of warfare, namely mobile field artillery trains, warships, cohesive regiments, and supporting firepower, exacted a toll that the Gaels simply could not bear. Modern warfare had arrived, and the Gaelic peoples were not equipped to deal with it. They continued to view war as an art, while the British had begun to view it as a science. Against such opponents the Gaels bled themselves to death during the first half of the century.[9]

Though the Celts were neither the first nor the last people to practice primitive methods of warfare, their particular penchant for doing so is somewhat more curious than, say, that of the Afghan hill tribes, the Sudanese Mahdi, or any other primitive people. The Highland Scots and Irish, unlike most other primitive groups, lived in close proximity to the most civilized part of the world. During the century and a half of Gaelic warfare under study England and France emerged as superpowers in the naval and military spheres. Intercourse between Ireland and England, Spain, and France exposed the Irish Gael to the theories and implements of modern warfare. Yet the Irish, despite Hugh O'Neill's best efforts to the contrary, could not be made to accept them wholeheartedly in their wars with Elizabethan England. Likewise, the Scottish Highlanders had the benefits of even more immediate connections with these nations, as well as with Sweden, where many a clansman served under the tutelage of Gustavus Adolphus. Nevertheless, the Highlanders continued to employ the time-honoured tactics and weapons of their fathers. This aversion to modern military techniques is best demonstrated by the Gaelic attitude toward the use of artillery. As early as the wars of the 1590s the Irish had ready access to artillery, either provided by Spain or captured from England. But, as we shall see later in greater detail, the Irish made almost no use of it. The Highland Scots, particularly after Killiecrankie in 1689, attempted to employ artillery on a few occasions but failed because of their unfamiliarity with it.[10]

It may seem puzzling why the non-Gaelic military commanders who led the Gaels into battle (and there were many because the Highland chiefs refused to serve under one another) did not exert a firmer measure of civilizing control over their charges. Although these commanders either hailed from or had spent considerable time in more progressive areas, they still held martial glory in high esteem. Most of them were products of a high social circle that valued chivalric honor and principle. Though aware of the most advanced military therorems and technologies of the day, they were unable to shed notions of manly honor and glory on the battlefield. O'Neill tried to embrace modernism but ultimately cast it away for the traditions of Gaelic combat. John Erskine, Earl of Mar, bred up more to the pen than to the sword, proved too ignorant of any type of warfare to lead the militaristic Highlanders. The rest, all raised outside the Gaelic world, were drawn to that world and to its prospects for personal honor and heroism during a century in which the new world was eclipsing the old. Even had they sought to apply the lessons of modern war to the Gael as Mar so ineptly attempted in 1715, their plans probably would have been frustrated because of the nature of the Gaelic fighting man: he was an individual warrior motivated not so much by the ends of combat as by the means. To fight a good fight, win or lose, was often more important to him than to stain his honor by fighting in the distasteful fashion of his well supplied, but socially inferior, adversary. The lowest clansman proudly considered himself of noble standing, holding a respected position in his pastoral, primitive society.[11] This outlook undeniably contributed to the Gaels' eventual defeat. Their leaders, like the Gaels themselves, refused to accept practical expedients that conflicted with gallantry. As will be seen, the rashness and bravado of the Celts often won the day, but in the end much more was required to overcome the practicality and patience of the enemy.

Though the scope of this book is broad, it is not all-inclusive of Gaelic warfare in the British Isles. Several campaigns have not been dealt with. I should explain my reasons for these omissions. First, Hugh O'Neill's war with Elizabethan England was chosen as a starting point because the nature of that conflict represented an attempted break with the type of warfare fought in Ireland before the 1590s. The Desmond uprisings in Munster and the triangular struggles in Ulster among the

O'Neills, the MacDonnells, and the English were characterized by a type of warfare firmly grounded in the traditions of the Scoto-Norse *gallóglaich* (Highland mercenary families that settled in Ireland beginning in the thirteenth century) and redshanks (itinerant mercenaries from the western Highlands and Isles who commonly served Irish chieftains in the sixteenth century). These two groups dominated Irish battlefields after (and in response to) the Norman invasion of Ireland.[12] With the death of Sorley Boy MacDonnell in 1590 and the rise of Hugh O'Neill as the power in Ulster, the nature of Irish warfare was modified somewhat by the latter's conscious attempts to revamp the Gaelic military system in Ireland.

Second, several campaigns in Ireland subsequent to O'Neill's uprising are omitted. Ulster and much of the remainder of Gaelic Ireland, especially after the Flight of the Earls in 1607, came under unified control from England, a process that forever altered the foundations of power on the island and subjected the Gaels to the military influence of both Irish and continental captains who were schooled in the modern rather than in the traditional Irish mode of warfare. After 1607 the Gaelic areas of Ireland were no longer autonomous regions fighting to keep out the English invader, but were areas of mixed ethnicity and confused political loyalties seeking to expel the intruders who were now firmly planted throughout the island.[13] The battle of Benburb (1646), the greatest victory of Owen Roe O'Neill, illustrated the continuity of the tactical offensive in Gaelic warfare, but it was of little consequence compared to the Irish defeat at Kinsale a half-century earlier. Dungan's Hill and Knockanoss, both fought in the 1640s, were more significant in that they broke the back of the Irish Confederation and also demonstrated several aspects of continuity in Irish tactics. The fight on the Boyne (1690) and at Aughrim (1691) shattered Jacobite hopes in Ireland. As in so many other Gaelic battles, the Irish ultimately attacked the attackers.[14] Simply put, the Irish battles after 1607 frequently were no more than futile attempts to drive out an invader who not only had established a foothold in Ireland, but also had succeeded in subjugating a large part of the island. The post-Kinsale battles must be omitted from the present study, not because they fail to support my thesis — quite the contrary — but because they are of a different nature to those battles fought by the unadulterated Gaelic military system as it existed in Ireland before O'Neill's defeat at Kinsale in 1601.

Third, this study does not begin to cover the Scottish Highlands proper until the 1640s. Only then did the tactical refinements worked out in Ireland by Alasdair MacColla result in the Highland charge and mark a subtle but telling change in the Gaelic Scots' military system. The MacDonnells of Antrim, blood relations of MacColla, had taken center stage in the conflicts of both Ulster and the western Highlands and Isles. Clan Donald was the principal source of *gallóglaich* and redshanks who had established the military traditions dominating Gaelic warfare from the fourteenth century to the death of Sorley Boy. The subsequent reappearance in the 1640s of the Antrim MacDonnells and associated clans in the Covenanter-Royalist civil war in Scotland marked the beginnings of a 'Golden Age' of Scottish Gaelic warfare that lasted until Culloden in 1746. This century was a bridge in Gaelic warfare: from the *gallóglaich* axe and claymore to the broadsword, target, and musket, and from the Middle Ages to the modern world.

The inclusion in this study of the Highlanders' participation as British soldiers in the French and Indian War in North America is intended to impress upon the reader the fact that the Gaelic way of war did not die at Culloden but flourished and became a vital element of warfare in the New World.

The study of the warfare of such a primitive and anachronistic culture as that of the Celts is merited for many reasons, one of the most important being that Gaelic warfare played such a significant role in the development of the New World. Imagine for a moment what the demographics of North America might have been had Gaelic Ireland not succumbed to English conquest or had one of the Jacobite uprisings from 1689 to 1745 been successful. As it was, a floodtide of displaced Gaels went to America between 1700 and 1776 and eventually peopled the frontier areas of the South. Most of them migrated as a result of the upheavals that shook the Celtic fringe during the period under study. Historians ask many questions, not the least of which is 'what if?' It is therefore appropriate to wonder how the successful defense of the Gaelic world might have altered American immigration patterns. America might have remained predominantly Anglo-Saxon, perhaps avoiding the Civil War or at least altering its nature and time. If the Celtic South had never existed, the ethnic and cultural composition of the United States would have been more nearly homogeneous until demographic pressures forced Gaelic emigration across the Atlantic at a later time when orderly assimilation would have rendered sectional and cultural conflict unlikely.[15]

NOTES

1. For a controversial, ground-breaking study of how the Gaelic military heritage of the American South influenced the course of the Civil War, see Grady McWhiney and Perry D. Jamieson, *Attack and Die: Civil War Military Tactics and the Southern Heritage* (University, Alabama: The University of Alabama Press, 1982).

2. Greek and Roman historians — Polybius, Diodorus, Strabo, Livy, Appian, Caesar, and others — provided written records that give us valuable insight into the world of the ancient Celts. Their assessments we can accept in a general sense as accurate; however, their estimates of army sizes and casualties, among other specifics, are untrustworthy. We can glean important generalities from their work, particularly concerning the basic characteristics of the Celts. For perceptive studies on the credibility of the ancient historians, see Michael Grant, *The Ancient Historians* (New York: Charles Scribner's Sons, 1970); Hans Delbrück, *Numbers in History* (London: Hodder and Stoughton, 1913).

3. The Highland charge — a tactical refinement of the old Celtic charge — is thoroughly discussed in David Stevenson, *Alasdair MacColla and the Highland Problem in the Seventeenth Century* (Edinburgh: John Donald Publishers, 1980). For the role that the Highland charge played in the continuing tactical development of the Gaels and the part that it played in their defeat in the mid-eighteenth century, see below, Chapters 5, 6 and 8.

4. The Chevalier de Johnstone, *Memoirs of the Rebellion in 1745 and 1746*, 2nd ed. (London: Longman, Hurst, Rees, Orme and Brown, 1821), pp. 113–15.

5. Diodorus Siculus, *Diodorus of Sicily*, trans. C. H. Oldfather (London: W. Heinemann, 1933), vol. 3, bk. 5, sec. 34, p. 191. Viriathus, exemplary of the Celtic warrior-general in the ancient period, led his Lusitanian tribes against the Romans in the Iberian peninsula in the second century B.C. With a small, mobile army of 6,000 to 8,000 men, he fought five separate Roman legions to a standoff by combining guerrilla and formal tactics with harsh, mountainous terrain. Viriathus proved that the Celts could hold their own against the Romans when fighting within a simple framework that accentuated the strengths of Celtic warfare.

6. Hans Delbrück, *History of the Art of War within the Framework of Political History*, trans. W. J. Renfroe, Jr., 2 vols. (Westport, Connecticut: Greenwood Press, 1975), I: 508–13.

7. Julius Caesar, *The Battle for Gaul*, trans. Anne and Peter Wiseman (Boston: David R. Godine, 1980), bk. 2, sec. 17, p. 50; Captain Charles Montague's report, 16 August 1598, London, Public Record Office, State Papers, Ireland, Elizabeth, S.P. 63/202/3/20, i; Sir Francis Stafford to George Carey, 19 October 1600, S.P. 63/207/5/108, i (hereafter cited as S.P. 63).

8. Until roughly the period between the Stuart Restoration in 1660 and the Act of Union in 1707 the English and Lowland Scots fought a type of warfare firmly grounded in the military precepts of the pre-1600 era. While the continental powers devoted their time and energy toward new weapons and theories of war, the English concentrated on becoming a great naval power. Despite the efforts of such forward-thinking military men of the late sixteenth century as Thomas Digges, Sir John Norris, Barnabe Rich, Robert Barret, Sir John Smythe, Roger Ascham, Humpfrey Barwick, and Sir Roger Williams, among others, the English government paid slight heed to the call for a modernized army. For the next century the English and Lowland Scots found it difficult to subdue their Gaelic adversaries because of their neglect of their land forces. The result was rather primitive warfare between Gael and Anglo-Saxon, especially during most of the sevententh century. The Anglo-Saxon superiority in numbers, discipline, and weapons did not offset the savage fury of the Gaels. For scholarly studies of the development of English and continental warfare prior to 1603, see Henry J. Webb, *Elizabethan Military Science: The Books and the Practice* (Madison, Wisconsin: University of Wisconsin Press, 1965); C. G. Cruickshank, *Elizabeth's Army* (London: Oxford University Press, 1946); Charles Oman, *A History of the Art of War in the Sixteenth Century* (London: Methuen, 1937).

9. For the changing nature of the British military after 1660, see Frederick Myatt, *The British Infantry, 1660-1945: The Evolution of a Fighting Force* (Dorset: Blandford Press, 1983); Colonel H. C. B. Rogers, *The British Army of the Eighteenth Century* (New York: Hippocrene Books, 1977); Colonel Clifford Walton, *History of the British Standing Army, A.D. 1660-1700* (London: Harrison and Sons, 1894); Charles Dalton, *George the First's Army, 1714-1727* (London: Eyre and Spottiswoode, 1910-1912).

10. For further discussion of the Gaelic aversion to modern weaponry and tactics, see below, Chapters 3 through 6 and 8.

11. To the Highlanders the burghers and yeoman farmers who filled the ranks of opposing armies were a rude, vulgar lot, all the more so because they fought a type of warfare (especially after 1689) that detracted from personal prowess and accomplishment. For studies concerning the social structures and attitudes of the Scottish Highlanders, see W. H. Murray, *Rob Roy MacGregor, his life and times* (Glasgow: Richard Drew Publishing, 1982); John Prebble, *Glencoe: The Story of the Massacre* (London: Martin Secker and Warburg, 1966).

12. The history of the Scottish *gallóglaích* and redshanks and their influence on Irish

affairs in the sixteenth century are contained in G. A. Hayes-McCoy, *Scots Mercenary Forces in Ireland, 1565–1603* (Dublin: Burns, Oates and Washbourne, 1937); Andrew McKerral, 'West Highland Mercenaries in Ireland,' *Scottish Historical Review*, 30 (April 1951): 1–14. For further studies of sixteenth-century Irish warfare, see G. A. Hayes-McCoy, 'Strategy and Tactics in Irish Warfare, 1593–1601,' *Irish Historical Studies*, 2 (1940–1941): 255–79; Sean 'O Domhnaill, 'Warfare in sixteenth-century Ireland,' *Irish Historical Studies*, 5 (1946–1947): 29–54.

13. The Gaelic Irish effort to drive out the English invaders differed from their effort to expel the Normans in earlier centuries. The Normans who settled in Ireland beginning in the twelfth century came first to accept and then to adopt Gaelic customs and language. This Gaelicization process was fostered in large part by the taking of Gaelic Irish wives by Norman adventurers. The sixteenth-century English penetration of Ireland resulted in no such widespread assimilation process. The fourteenth-century Statutes of Kilkenny addressed the potential problem of the 'degeneration' of Englishmen who came into contact with the Irish way of life, and thus, among other things, forbade marriage between Anglo-Saxon and Gael. After the death of Elizabeth in 1603 Gaelic Ireland, especially in the north, was planted with Protestant settlers whose cultural, linguistic, and religious differences further complicated an already confused political situation.

14. An invaluable summary of these and other Irish battles is found in G. A. Hayes-McCoy, *Irish Battles* (London: Longmans, 1969).

15. Reference to the Celtic South is based primarily on the recent research of Forrest McDonald and Grady McWhiney. For a thorough explanation of their 'Celtic thesis' of American history, see McWhiney and Jamieson, *Attack and Die*; Forrest McDonald and Grady McWhiney. 'The Antebellum Southern Herdsman: A Reinterpretation,' *Journal of Southern History*, 41 (1975): 147–66; Grady McWhiney, 'The Revolution in Nineteenth-Century Alabama Agriculture,' *Alabama Review*, 31 (1978): 3–32; Forrest McDonald, 'The Ethnic Factor in Alabama History: A Neglected Dimension,' *Alabama Review*, 31 (1978): 256–65; Grady McWhiney, 'Saving the Best From the Past,' *Alabama Review*, 32 (1979): 243–72; Forrest McDonald and Ellen Shapiro McDonald, 'The Ethnic Origins of the American People, 1790,' *William and Mary Quarterly*, 37 (1980): 179–99; Forrest McDonald and Grady McWhiney, 'The Celtic South,' *History Today*, 30 (July 1980): 11–15; Forrest McDonald and Grady McWhiney, 'The South From Self-Sufficiency to Peonage: An Interpretation,' *American Historical Review*, 85 (1980): 1095–1118; Grady McWhiney, 'Jefferson Davis — The Unforgiven,' *Journal of Mississippi History*, 42 (February 1980): 113–27; Grady McWhiney, 'Continuity in Celtic Warfare,' *Continuity*, 2 (Spring 1981): 1–18; Grady McWhiney and Forrest McDonald, 'Celtic Names in the Antebellum Southern United States,' *Names*, 31 (June 1983); 89–102.

2

A Conflict of Cultures

The Celts who occupied the north-western fringes of Europe were forced to fight for their very survival against a series of invaders whose cultures differed considerably from their own. From the Romans to the sixteenth-century English, successive waves of conquerors sought to transform, assimilate, or eradicate Celtic culture. That the Celts successfully overcame these invasions until the Tudor dynasty is indicative of their adeptness at devising and implementing a military system that could counter a superior enemy. Though simple and primitive to outsiders, the Celtic military system reflected a culture that was viable and dynamic within its own bounds. The two cultures — Celtic and Anglo-Saxon — could have lived and prospered side by side but for the emerging English with their colonial aspirations. Against such a behemoth intent on conquest the Irish and Scottish Gaels had only one cultural advantage — their traditional militarism.

The cultural dichotomy between Anglo-Saxon and Gael that exists in the British Isles had its origins in the Roman occupation. When Julius Caesar landed in 55 B.C., the Romans began a long process of colonizing the lowland regions while the inaccessible highlands and Ireland remained free of the conquerors. In the occupied areas the Romans introduced their own system of land tenure, mined the natural resources, built roads and fortifications, and established political and economic contacts with the continent. The cultural assimilation of the lowland inhabitants into largely urban and commercial people at this early date marked the headwaters of divergent streams — those who later would call themselves Englishmen and those as yet undisturbed Celts to the north and west.

While life in the Celtic regions continued as it had for centuries, the invasions of the lowlands by the Anglo-Saxons and Normans reinforced the process of political centralization and urbanization begun by the Romans. Walled towns dotted the Wessex countryside, serving both as havens from the Danes and as centers for internal commercial activities. In the ninth century one of the hallmarks of the centralized state, taxation, was firmly established in the kingdom. From 802 to 955 the Anglo-Saxons brought under their control most of England and the Scottish Lowlands. Then the Norman Conquest markedly increased the degree of urbanization in the lowlands, and Norman feudalism strengthened rather than weakened the central government.[1]

From the thirteenth to the sixteenth centuries England developed most of the characteristics that would allow her to emerge from the ranks of a remote and insignificant feudal state to that of a nation of import under the Tudor monarchs: a strong kingship supported by an effective system of feudalism, internal and external avenues of trade, nucleated towns and villages, a strong manorial

9

community responsible for the preservation of social order, a tillage agriculture economy based on the three-field system, and an orderly transference of this landed wealth through primogeniture.[2]

After 1500 many Englishmen turned to the production and enjoyment of the wealth wrought by commercialization. At the same time a new breed of adventurer drew his blade and gazed northward and westward into the highlands and across the sea. Armed with sword, musket, and parchment, this conquistador soon undertook what his Latin, Anglo-Saxon, and Norman progenitors had failed to accomplish since the first century B.C: the total and irrevocable subjugation of the alien culture on his border. The conflict bore the mark of a crusade. Advancing civilization at the expense of the uncivilized weighs all too lightly on the conscience, and England stood unabashedly ready to enlighten the world. Her soldier-merchants had international wealth to gain. Her gaze fell upon Highland Scotland and Ireland — the Celtic fringe.

The Ireland that awaited the Tudor adventurers had long been a remote, largely inaccessible, and uncharted region. When what can properly be called Irish history began in the fifth century, the half million inhabitants of the island were Celtic in both custom and language. The Irish tribes lived and prospered free of the invader from the end of the Heroic Age in the mid-fifth century to the Viking invasions of the ninth, but to say that they lived peaceably is not entirely accurate. Internecine warfare was commonplace among the tribes, mainly to acquire or retain the two great measures of wealth: land and livestock. Across this landscape of mountain, drumlin, forest, and bog the Irish lived simple lives in close accord with nature. No towns or villages existed; only an occasional monastary rose against the sky as testament to Ireland's early Christianization.[3]

Ireland before the ninth-century Norse invasions was internally and externally dynamic. This was her real Golden Age, molded and shaped by priest, warrior, and poet alike. Christianity and bloodshed tempered one another to such a degree that nowhere else in western Europe can one find a society as paradoxical as early Christian Ireland. The poet's tale of violence and heroism stood unashamedly alongside the holy verse of the churchman. On the one hand warrior chiefs, compelled by prospects of honor and glory in battle, found a way to reconcile pride and ambition with a sometimes sincere religious conviction; on the other, the men of God with pleas for self-sacrifice and earthly suffering were not averse to promoting the ideals of heroic bravery. When the rest of Europe plunged into the Dark Ages, Irish monks helped to preserve the flame of knowledge and their flocks continued uninterrupted in their quest for mammon and secular immortalization. Ireland was half saint, half devil, her tranquil green fields stained with the blood of her sons. But until the first years of the ninth century it was only Celtic blood that flowed in endless internecine conflict; thereafter, the blood of the Gael would mingle with that of the Norsemen, Normans, and English.

The Romans and Anglo-Saxons of earlier centuries left Ireland untouched, but the Viking long boats that plowed southward through the tempestuous Herbridean seas in the ninth and tenth centuries were harbingers of a new age that would transform Irish society. The Vikings established towns along the seacoasts to facilitate trade with places as distant as Byzantium. Dublin, Waterford, Wexford, Wicklow, and Limerick all owe their existence to the Norse, who intermingled with the Celts throughout Ireland and the Hebrides. Norse language and customs found their way into Gaelic life.

But perhaps the most important effect that the Viking invasions had on the native Irish was to draw them out of their isolation and into the main current of European development. For over a century the invader forced many of the Irish tribes to unify and move eastward toward the Irish Sea. In a short-lived alliance under Brian Boroime (Boru), the self-styled king of Ireland, the Irish tribes defeated the Norsemen north of Dublin at the battle of Clontarf in 1014.[4] It was no coincidence that the first major contest with a foreign enemy during the millennium occurred in what is known as Ireland's 'eastern triangle'.[5] Bordered by Dundalk on the north and the Wicklow Mountains on the south, the triangle's flat, fertile valleys of the Liffey and Boyne are natural gateways to the interior. Here the Normans, and later the English, established footholds.

The Normans were invited into Ireland in 1166 to settle a civil war between a tribe of Ulster and one of Connaught, but they came as conquerors instead and redistributed much of Ireland among themselves. When the tide of civil war turned against the Ulster tribe, Dermot McMurrough of Leinster appealed to Henry II, the Norman king of England. Within the year energetic and land-hungry Normans led by Richard Fitzgilbert de Clare, Earl of Pembroke, marshalled for the journey across the Irish Sea. Pembroke, or 'Strongbow' as he is better known, landed near Waterford in 1169 with an army of 1,200 knights and archers.[6] In the following year he and McMurrough took Dublin and prepared for the arrival of Henry II. The king came and kept Dublin, Cork, and Limerick for himself, received homage from all the chiefs except those of the remote north-west, and made large land grants to the Norman barons. Strongbow, for example, enjoyed most of Leinster, while the 'kingdom' of Meath was created for another nobleman. Much of the remainder of Ireland fell haphazardly to Norman lords as local chiefs were dispossessed of their lands and fled into the forests and bogs. By the middle of the thirteenth century nearly four-fifths of Ireland had come under the dominion of the invaders, who must have thought themselves invincible within such fortress towns as Coleraine, Galway, Athenry, Drogheda, and Carrickfergus.[7]

The redistribution of landed wealth in Ireland was less important in the long run than was the establishment of a central government housed in Dublin Castle. Norman administrators established a system of taxation, minted silver coins, appointed sheriffs for the counties and liberties, introduced a court system and trial by jury, and summoned the first parliament in 1297. The areas that fell under Norman control no longer experienced the continual warring of the Gaelic tribes; instead, the natives were absorbed into a manorial economy run by Norman estate managers. But paradoxically, the resulting relationship between Norman and Gael led to the eventual Gaelicization of the former, until in the sixteenth century many families of Norman descent, such as the de Burgos (Burkes, or later

McWilliams), were said to have been more Gaelic than many families of native Irish descent.

The Normans' colonization in Ireland slowed by the mid-thirteenth century, and their population dwindled in the rural areas as sons went abroad for military service or moved to the towns to take up a trade. As the foreigner in their midst weakened, the Irish became emboldened and fought back. With the help of Scoto-Norse mercenaries (*gallóglâich*) from the Hebrides, the Gaelic Irish reconquered much of the countryside.[8] The Anglo-Normans retained their foothold in several of the towns, but much of Ireland reverted to its native owners. Even so, the Normans bequeathed to later generations of Englishmen a beachhead in the eastern triangle, the eventual Pale, and in Dublin Castle a first step toward political consolidation with the kingdom of England. In the sixteenth century England marched her legions through the gateway and her administrators into Dublin Castle. The Gaelic ascendency in Ireland would soon end.

Some of the same historical forces that molded Gaelic Ireland had their effects too on the Scottish Highlands and Isles. Just as the natural barrier of the Irish Sea separated Roman Britain from Ireland, so Hadrian's Wall testified to the Romans' conscious attempt to separate their southern provinces from the Highland hordes. The Gaelic stronghold in the western Highlands and Isles came under attack by the Vikings in the ninth century. Sailing outward from the Orkneys and Shetlands, the Norsemen so thoroughly conquered the Hebrides that the Gaels despairingly referred to them as *Innsigall*, the foreigners' islands, and to the inhabitants as *Gall-Gaidhall*, foreign Gaels, who were ethnic hybrids of Celtic and Norse blood.[9] Many Viking raiders settled along the west coast of Scotland, continuing to struggle with the Gaels until the thirteenth century. At its zenith the Norse conquest encompassed the east coast from Fife northward to Caithness, the Orkneys and Shetlands, and all of the Western Isles. Neither before nor since was as much Scottish territory in the hands of a conquering power. The Vikings' stranglehold was broken first by their defeat at the battle of Largs in 1263 and subsequently by treaty in 1266 that ceded the Hebrides to the king of Scots. Norse hegemony dwindled on the mainland and in the Northern Isles until in 1468 the last of the Viking possessions was pledged to the Scots.[10]

The Highland-Lowland split began in the eleventh century as the Scottish king sought to secure his power base in the Lowlands. As an Ulster chief would do in the next century, Malcolm Ceannmor (Canmore) established a precedent by kneeling before the Anglo-Saxon throne to enlist the king's power in settling Scotland's domestic squabbles. The resulting alienation of Canmore's Gaelic-speaking supporters marked the beginnings of the Highland-Lowland split that proved so fateful for Scotland. Meanwhile, the progenitor of Clan Donald, Somerled MacGillebride, laid the foundation for Gaelic dominance in the western Highlands and Isles. *De facto* Norse control of the Hebrides had weakened, and Somerled initiated open warfare with the Scottish crown, whose authority in the remote isles was nominal at best.[11] The rise of a semi-autonomous Hebridean kingdom in the vacuum left by the Vikings was, in part, a reaction to the increased Anglo-Norman influence in the south and east of Scotland. The MacDonald Lordship of the Isles[12] represented a Gaelic attempt to retain the territorial independence in the west begun by the old Dalriadic kingdom. To the Scottish kings, who during each successive reign became politically and culturally more akin to their Anglo-Norman neighbors, the western Highlands and Isles nourished an admixed race of savages who were not Scots and who displayed little interest in the emerging brand of Scottish nationalism.

Historians often have used the 'Highland Line' to delineate the separate spheres of Gaelic and Lowland culture, but this imaginary demarcation has only limited value. The line runs from the Firth of Clyde, through Stirling and across Atholl, northward over the Mounth, terminating at the Moray Firth north-east of Inverness. Historians have said that south and east of this line lay the Lowlands; by 1300 this area had already experienced a considerable taste of Anglo-Norman ambition. The Gaels supposedly lived to the north and west. It is more accurate to say that the real Celtic world existed only in the far west, across the craggy peaks of *druimm nAlban*, 'the spine of Scotland'. These were the people characterized by both the English and Lowlanders as half-savage brigands — 'wild Scots.' The ethnic and linguistic characteristics of these tribes are thought to have originated with early Gaelic Irish settlers in the second century. It is known that the Irish Celts (*Scotti*) of Dalriada in north-east Antrim established a Gaelic kingdom in Argyll around the middle of the fifth century. By 650 their descendants occupied the mainland coastal areas west of *druimm nAlban* as well as most of the Isles as far north as Applecross. East and south of this range that separated Scotland climatically as well as culturally lay a gray area of mixed Celtic and Norman influence tempered by remnants of ancient Pictish culture. For purposes of cultural or political analysis, then, the Highland Line is very inaccurate.[13] The heart of Gaeldom on the eve of the Wars of Independence lay on the west coast, in the Hebrides, and in rural Ireland.

The Scottish Wars of Independence served England's purpose of driving a wedge between the Gaelic and Lowland regions of Scotland as much as they served the interest of Scottish nationalism. Edward I's adroit diplomatic machinations — dangling the vacant Scottish throne before rival claimant families — were designed to bolster his influence in the northern kingdom by exacting acknowledgements of overlordship from the claimants and casting himself in the role of arbitrator. He openly supported John Balliol while he covertly sowed discontent within the camps of the rivals. From the half-century of confusion bred by Edward's plots emerged a destructive rivalry between the Balliols and Comyns on the one side and the Bruces on the other. These great families' connections with the clans west of *druimm nAlban* ensured Gaelic complicity in the struggles. For example, clans Donald of Islay and Dougall of Lorne, both descended from the lineage of Somerled, found themselves on opposite sides of the conflict. The MacDougalls aligned themselves with Edward I. The MacDonalds of Islay, the junior branch of Somerled's descendants, fought beside Bruce at Bannockburn in 1314. The fortunes of battle led to the MacDougalls' demise as the power in Argyll (territory eventually controlled by the pro-English Clan Campbell) and the MacDonalds' ascendancy as the Lords of the Isles.[14]

Though Bruce's rag-tag band of disaffected Lowlanders and Highland clans defeated Edward I at Bannockburn, the king accomplished at least part of his objective: he sowed the seeds of discord among the two halves of Scotland and played one side against the other with England reaping the fruits of discontent. Edward and his successors continually fueled the animosity not only between Highlander and Lowlander, but also between the rival western clans themselves. To gauge the success of this policy, one need look no further than the long-standing Campbell-MacDonald feud that raged in the Western Highlands for almost two centuries. Its sixteenth-century fruition was the culmination of a long process of Anglicization that forever divided Scotland and ultimately forced the obeisant Lowlander and the defiant Highlander into political unification with the south.

Scotland remained nominally independent of England until the personal union of James VI and I in 1603 and the later Union of 1707; in reality, the slow process of acculturation had begun 300 years before the first Stuart monarch ascended the English throne. Scotland was rent asunder and her south-eastern half was drawn, politically and culturally, toward England. By the mid-sixteenth century the Lowlands willingly yielded to pressures applied by the Tudor monarchs; the Gaelic west, however, fought to save itself.

The clan was the basic political, social and (above all) military organizational unit among the Scottish and Irish Gaels. The Gaelic term *clann* literally means 'children' or 'offspring', so the idea of the clan was based partially upon agnatic blood ties to the chief's lineage. But Gaelic customs such as fosterage, the raising of male children by a family unrelated to them by blood, did much to strengthen ties of fictive kinship within the clan system. In 1597 when James VI of Scotland forced all landholders in the Highlands and Isles to produce rights and titles to their territories,[15] it became clear to what degree the clans depended on bonds other than blood kinship. Since many of the clans held their lands by ties of fictive kinship, by force, or by invalid grants from the defunct MacDonald Lordship of the Isles, chiefs who wished to retain their holdings invented genealogical documents illustrating their rights and titles. The doubtful authenticity of many such claims demonstrated to what lengths the chiefs were willing to go to perpetuate the myth that clan organization was based primarily on agnatic kinship.[16]

The typical organization of this 'modern' clan system, particularly in Scotland, was based not on kinship, but on the plantation of septs by the main branch of a clan. The Lordship of the Isles was typical of the plantation process in the fourteenth and fifteenth centuries. After the demise of the Lordship in 1493 most of its septs had grown into powerful clans in their own right and half a century later were able to put hundreds of warriors into the field. It is obvious that not all of these men, who included a significant number of nobles, could have been relatives of the chief.[17]

By the sixteenth century clan organization was firmly grounded in the feudal lord-vassal relationship that was introduced in Scotland by the Normans in the twelfth and thirteenth centuries. Simply put, its central feature was the bond between the chief and those who swore loyalty to him. Many chiefs received feudal charters from the crown or from one another through which they greatly increased their territories and number of dependants. By absorbing the lesser clans or septs that occupied his new lands, the chief strengthened his power and influence. His new tacksmen provided military service in exchange for a portion of the clan's territory and in time of war provided the nucleus of the clan regiments.[18]

The chief's primary task was to lead the clans into battle. Below the chief the gradation of authority reflected the clan's military function. Subordinate to the chief and nominated to succeed him was the Tanist. In Ireland the Tanist *cum* chieftain ruled over a *tuath* (territory). Within these usually small territories (300 to 400 square miles) the *ceannfine* (chief) regarded himself as sovereign.[19] Many of the *tuatha* (tribes) were subordinate to a superior provincial ruler, such as the O'Neill of Ulster. The great lord himself held the title of *ceannfine*, and his subordinates were *urriagha* (sub-kings). Under Brehon law the *urriagha* were responsible for maintaining their chief's military forces by a system of *buannacht*, or a levy of money and food. In Highland Scotland the chief was followed by the heads of septs into which the clan was divided. The eldest of the chieftains or cadets sometimes served as the captain of the clan and in the absence of the chief led the clan in wartime. Next in the chain of command came the gentlemen, or lesser nobility. The holders of the offices descending from the Tanist to the gentlemen were collectively (and sometimes inaccurately) called the *daoine uaisle*, or the nobility of the blood. The remainder of the clan consisted of the general body, or those men who could claim no direct bond — neither agnatic, fictive, nor feudal — with the chief.[20]

The clan's emphasis on an efficient military organization resulted partly from the isolation produced by the remoteness of the Highlands and Isles of Scotland and much of Ireland. With each clan occupying its almost inaccessible territories among the glens, mountains, and bogs, it developed a high degree of self-sufficiency; it could count on little support from the Edinburgh or Dublin governments when threatened by neighbouring clans. Conversely, until the late sixteenth century the clans suffered only occasional interference from the Scottish Stuarts or the English Tudors.

The isolation of the Gaels led them to develop their own code of law that was mistaken for lawlessness by the Lowland Scots and English. Since no Scottish monarch ascended the throne as an adult from 1406 to 1625, royal authority did not extend into the Highlands and Isles. The governments in Edinburgh and Dublin listened helplessly to reports of livestock raids, feuds, and massacres. But in the late sixteenth century James VI of Scotland and Elizabeth I of England began a serious and coordinated effort to bring these wild Scottish and Irish clans under governmental control. The immediate object of James's attention was the Clan Donald, which for many years had caused problems for the central government in the western Highlands and Isles.

The MacDonalds, descendants of the twelfth-century Norse-Gaelic warrior Somerled, emerged in the mid-fourteenth century as the most dynamic clan in the western Highlands and Isles. As Lords of the Isles the MacDonalds ruled over a semi-independent state that at its greatest extent reached from Lewis in the north to Islay in the south. In addition to its Hebridean possessions, the Lordship also included territories on the Scottish mainland — Kintyre and Knapdale in the south; Morvern, Ardnamurchan, and Lochaber at the south-western end of the Great Glen; and the earldom of Ross farther north and east. The supremacy of the MacDonald Lords of the Isles continued over much of this vast area until 1493, when James IV of Scotland deprived John, fourth and last lord, of his lands and title.[21]

The collapse of the Lordship of the Isles was not followed by an immediate extension of royal power into the western Highlands and Isles. As a result Clan Donald split into several opposing branches that fought among themselves for territorial dominance. Other clans formerly subjugated to the Lords of the Isles threw off the yoke and emerged as powers in their own right. Remembering the frequent rebellions led by the Lordship, however, the Stuart kings of Scotland sought to prevent any single clan from again becoming too powerful in the area. Many of the clan chiefs formerly subordinate to the MacDonalds took vows of surrender and re-grant before the monarch in return for charters they had held previously. Parchment and Lowland law began to replace *coir a'chlaidiheamh* and the Highland code. Troubles between the various clans continued, and each sought to extend its territories at the expense of its neighbors.[22]

After several unsuccessful attempts to force law and order upon his Gaelic subjects, James revoked the charters granted to the clan chiefs and in 1499 appointed the Campbell earls of Argyll and the Gordon earls of Huntly king's lieutenants over much of the territory formerly held by the Lords of the Isles. By 1500 only Islay and much of Kintyre remained in MacDonald hands, and by the mid-sixteenth century the Campbells had become the most powerful clan in Scotland. Only one clan remained that could challenge the strength of the Campbells — Clan Ian Mor, or Clan Donald South.[23]

In the mid-sixteenth century Clan Ian Mor became the dominant branch of Clan Donald. It took its name from Ian, or John, Mor MacDonald (died 1427), a younger brother of Donald, second Lord of the Isles. The clan's strength was originally concentrated around Dunyveg Castle in Islay, but after Ian Mor's marriage in 1400 to Marjory Bisset, heiress of the Glens, its territories were extended into Antrim in north-eastern Ireland. Clan Ian Mor then became known as the MacDonalds of Dunyveg and the Glens, or of Islay and Antrim. Toward the end of the century the clan's power diminished because of external pressures from the Stuart kings and their Campbell allies and internal conflicts among rival MacDonald factions. In the 1560s Somhairle Buidhe (Sorley Boy) MacDonald (later MacDonnell), brother of James MacDonald of Dunyveg and the Glens, seized Clan Ian Mor's lands in Antrim and upon his death in 1590 passed them to his eldest son James (died 1601) and then to James's younger brother Ranald. Sorley Boy's seizure of the Antrim Glens marked the beginning of that branch of

Clan Donald South known as the Irish MacDonnells of Antrim or Dunluce. The MacDonnells of Antrim survived the English plantations in the early seventeenth century, and in 1620 Ranald MacDonnell was created first Earl of Antrim by James I of England.[24]

The split of Clan Ian Mor into Scottish and Irish branches reinforced cultural connections between these Celtic peoples. Redshanks continued to cross the North Channel in the late sixteenth and early seventeenth centuries, supplementing the already entrenched *gallóglaich* families: MacDonalds, MacLeans, MacSweeneys, and others.[25] By the beginning of the seventeenth century such ties among the Gaelic Irish and Scots tranformed the area into the heartland of Gaeldom and prompted a contemporary writer to observe that ' ... Scotland and Ireland are all one and the same'.[26]

During the first half of the sixteenth century the Tudor monarchs of England began the last (and ongoing) phase in the conquest and subjugation of the Irish Gael. Contemporary correspondence reflects the English opinion that the establishment of Anglo-Saxon predominance throughout Ireland was justified. Irish chieftains and their lieutenants were seen as unholy barbarians in dire need of the pacifying hand of civil government, while the lower classes were viewed as their helpless, enslaved subjects.[27] An English government official noted that

> The government of these princes was neither politique nor civil, but meer tyranical ... For the prince or Lord use at their pleasure their tenants, spend upon them with their trains, rule after their own lust, commanding all, and not to be gainsaid by any, so that the mightiest oppresseth the poorest, and justice is ministered according to the affection they bear to the parties offending or offended.[28]

From their foothold in the Pale other observers of Irish affairs reported to London a ' ... kind of government that draws all love and fear, and consequently all authority, from the prince and turneth it over to the great lord of the country ... '[29] The existence of a realm where great men openly defied English authority promised the Tudors a ' ... likelihood of continual war, which [would] be right hard to withstand ... '[30]

The English realized that to transform Ireland from a menage of petty, independent lordships into an exploitable appendage they had to replace the Irish herding tradition with tillage agriculture. The pastoral, transhumant way of life that nourished the Gaelic warrior prompted an Englishman to write that

> ... all countries that live by such sort by keeping of cattle ... are very barbarous and uncivil and also greatly given to war ... And therefore since now we purpose to draw the Irish from desires of wars and tumults ... it is expediate to abridge their great custom of herding and augment ... more trade of tilling and husbandry.[31]

The transformation would serve the dual purpose of eradicating the conditions that bred the hardy warrior class as well as bringing the country ' ... to yield the commodities that England doth both by sea and land'.[32] The implementation of this plan could only be accomplished by force of arms against the typical Irish warrior who was characterized as ' ... none of these idle milksops that was brought up by the fireside, but that most of his days he spent in arms and valiant enterprises, that he did never eat his meat before he had won it with his sword . . . '[33]

To bring Gaelic Ireland to its knees English armies would have to contend with the great and influential clan chiefs of the north and west. A contemporary scribe depicted the typical chief as

> . . . equal to the Hound of the Smith, for he never made an erring cast, and hardly ever did any one escape from him in deadly slaughter or red carnage . . . Moreover, he did not go into a fight or skirmish, into a dispute or struggle, that he did not wound someone somehow. He was a vindictive man and keen to avenge his wrongs . . . so that he was never taken unawares so long as he lived.[34]

One such 'Hound of the Smith' was Hugh Roe O'Neill, who wielded power over his people as 'The O'Neill'. Realizing the near-magical appeal of traditional Gaelic titles, English officials desired that ' . . . all the Oes and Macs which the heads of the septs have taken to their names . . . be utterly forbidden and extinguished . . . '[35]

England's problems with Gaelic Ireland began in earnest in 1595 when O'Neill disavowed his allegiance to Elizabeth I and acknowledged the beginning of the ultimate showdown between Gael and Anglo-Saxon. From 1595 until 1746 the Celtic fringe served as a battleground on which the forces of modernity sought to expunge the anachronism of Gaelic civilization.

NOTES

1. The culture of Roman, Anglo-Saxon, and Norman Britain outside the Celtic fringe is discussed in David M. Wilson, ed., *The Archaeology of Anglo-Saxon England* (London: Methuen and Company, 1976); David J. Breeze, *The Northern Frontiers of Roman Britain* (London: Batsford Academic and Educational, 1982); Thomas Wright, *The Celt, the Roman, and the Saxon: A History of the Early Inhabitants of Britain* (London: Kegan Paul, Trench, Trubner, and Company, 1902); Lloyd Laing, *Celtic Britain* (New York: Charles Scribner's Sons, 1979; London: Routledge and Kegan Paul, 1979); R. G. Collingwood, *The Archaeology of Roman Britain* (London: Methuen and Company, 1930); Peter Salway, *Roman Britain* (Oxford: Clarendon Press, 1981); Michael Hechter, *Internal Colonialism: The Celtic Fringe in British National Development, 1536–1966* (Berkeley: University of California Press, 1975); Colin Platt, *Medieval England: A social history and archaeology from the Conquest to 1600 A.D.* (New York: Charles Scribner's Sons, 1978).

2. Joan Thirsk, 'The Farming Regions of England,' in *The Agrarian History of England and Wales, 1500–1640*, ed. Joan Thirsk (Cambridge: Cambridge University Press, 1967), pp. 1–112. For further discussion of England's agricultural and commerical patterns during the period 1200–1600, see Dorothy Hartley, *Lost Country Life* (New York: Pantheon Books, 1979); Hechter, *Internal Colonialism.*

3. Francis J. Byrne. 'Early Irish Society,' in *The Course of Irish History*, eds. T. W. Moody and F. X. Martin (Cork: The Mercier Press, 1967), p. 44. For thorough analyses of Irish civilization before the ninth-century Norse invasions, see Alwyn and Brinley Rees, *Celtic Heritage, Ancient Tradition in Ireland and Wales* (London: Thames and Hudson, 1961); Stuart Piggott, *The Druids* (London: Thames and Hudson, 1968); Edmund Curtis, *A History of Ireland* (London: Methuen and Company, 1936); Karl S. Bottigheimer,

Ireland and the Irish, A Short History (New York: Columbia University Press, 1982); Ramsay Colles, *The History of Ulster from the Earliest Times to the Present Day*, 4 vols. (London: Gresham Publishing Company, 1919-1920); Robert Dunlop, *Ireland from the Earliest Times to the Present Day* (London: Oxford University Press, 1922); J. C. Beckett, *A Short History of Ireland* (London: Hutchinson and Company, 1958); John O'Beirne Ranelagh, *A Short History of Ireland* (Cambridge: Cambridge University Press, 1983); The Abbe Mac-Geoghegan, *The History of Ireland, Ancient and Modern, taken from the most authentic records, and dedicated to the Irish Brigade*, trans. Patrick O'Kelly (Dublin: J. Duffy, 1844; New York: D. and J. Sadler, 1845); Sean O'Faolain, *The Irish* (West Drayton, England: Penguin Books, 1947; New York: Devin-Adair Company, 1949).

4. William M. Hennessy, ed., *The Annals of Loch Cé, A Chronicle of Irish Affairs from A.D. 1014 to A.D. 1590*, 2 vols. (London: Longmans, Green, and Company, 1871), I: 1-15. For further discussion of earlier effects of the Norse on Celtic civilization, see J. H. Todd, ed., *The War of the Gaedhil with the Gaell, or the Invasion of Ireland by the Danes and other Norsemen* (London: Longmans, Green, Reader, and Dyer, 1867); Johannes Brøndsted, *The Vikings*, trans. Kalle Skov (Copenhagen: Gyldendal, 1960; Pelican Books, 1965); Gwyn Jones, *A History of the Vikings* (London: Oxford University Press, 1968).

5. J. H. Andrews, 'A Geographer's View of Irish History,' in *The Course of Irish History*, eds. Moody and Martin, pp. 20-21.

6. Hennessy, ed., *Annals of Loch Cé*, I: 143-45.

7. Ruth Dudley Edwards, *An Atlas of Irish History*, 2nd ed. (London: Methuen and Company, 1981), pp. 85-90; Kenneth Nicholls, *Gaelic and Gaelicised Ireland in the Middle Ages* (Dublin: Gill and MacMillan, 1972), pp. 12-17; F. X. Martin, 'The Anglo-Norman Invasion,' in *The Course of Irish History*, eds. Moody and Martin, pp. 123-43. Further effects of the Norman invasion on Ireland are described in A. J. Otway-Ruthven, *A History of Medieval Ireland* (London: Ernest Benn, 1968); Edmund Curtis, *A History of Mediæval Ireland from 1110 to 1513* (New York: The Macmillan Company, 1923; Dublin: Maunsel and Roberts, 1923); Robin Frame, *English Lordship in Ireland, 1318-1361* (Oxford: Clarendon Press, 1982); T. E. McNeill, *Anglo-Norman Ulster, the History and Archaeology of an Irish Barony, 1177-1400* (Edinburgh: John Donald Publishers, 1980).

8. For a fascinating and scholarly account of the role of Scottish mercenaries in the development of Irish history, see G. A. Hayes-McCoy, *Scots Mercenary Forces in Ireland, 1565-1603* (Dublin: Burns, Oates, and Washbourne, 1937).

9. W. R. Kermack, *The Scottish Highlands: A Short History, 300-1746* (Edinburgh: W. and A. K. Johnston, 1957), pp. 20-22. For further examination of the early history of the western Highlands and Isles, see W. F. Skene, *Celtic Scotland*, 3 vols. (Edinburgh: David Douglas, 1876-1880); A. and A. MacDonald, *The Clan Donald*, 3 vols. (Inverness: The Northern Counties Publishing Company, 1896); W. C. Dickinson, *Scotland from the earliest times to 1603* (London: Thomas Nelson and Sons, 1961); Euan W. MacKie, *Scotland: An Archaeological Guide from earliest times to the 12th century A.D.* (London: Faber and Faber, 1975; Park Ridge, N. J.: Noyes Press, 1975).

10. Discussions of the Viking incursions into the western Highlands and Isles of Scotland can be found in Kermack, *Scottish Highlands*; Brøndsted, *The Vikings*; Jones, *The Vikings*; A. Small, 'Dark Age Scotland,' in *An Historical Geography of Scotland*, eds. G. Whittingon and I. D. Whyte (London: Academic Press, 1983); Todd, ed., *War of the Gaedhil*.

11. W. C. MacKenzie, *The Highlands and Isles of Scotland: A Historical Survey* (Edinburgh: The Moray Press, 1937; reprint ed., New York: AMS Press, 1977), p. 96.

12. The history of the MacDonald Lordship of the Isles is set forth expertly in I. F. Grant, *The Lordship of the Isles, Wanderings in the Lost Lordship* (Edinburgh, The Moray Press, 1935; reprint ed., Edinburgh: The Mercat Press, 1982).

13. G. W. S. Barrow, *The Kingdom of the Scots: Government, Church, and Society from the eleventh to the fourteenth century* (New York: St. Martin's Press, 1973; London: Macmillan, 1973), pp. 362–66.

14. Relations among the Highlanders, Lowland Scots, and English during and after the Scottish Wars of Independence are discussed in William Ferguson, *Scotland's Relations with England: A Survey in 1707* (Edinburgh: John Donald Publishers, 1977); W. M. MacKenzie, *The Battle of Bannockburn: A Study in Medæval Warfare* (Glasgow: James MacLehose and Sons, 1913); G. W. S. Barrow, *The Anglo-Norman Era in Scottish History* (Oxford: Clarendon Press, 1980); Agnes M. MacKenzie, *The Kingdom of Scotland: A Short History* (Edinburgh: W. and R. Chambers, 1940); MacKenzie, *Highands and Isles of Scotland;* Dickinson, *Scotland to 1603;* R. L. Mackie, *A Short History of Scotland* (London: Oxford University Press, 1930).

15. Great Britain, General Register House, *The Acts of the Parliaments of Scotland,* ed. Thomas Thomson, vol. 4 (1593–1625), pp. 138–39 (herafter cited as *APS*).

16. I. F. Grant, *The Social and Economic Development of Scotland Before 1603* (Edinburgh: Oliver and Boyd, 1930), pp. 478–80; Skene, *Celtic Scotland,* III: 334–67.

17. Grant, *Social and Economic Development of Scotland,* pp. 484–86; Jenny Wormald, *Court, Kirk and Community: Scotland 1470-1625* (Toronto: University of Toronto Press, 1981; London: Edward Arnold, 1981), p. 30.

18. T. C. Smout, *A History of the Scottish People, 1560-1830* (New York: Charles Scribner's Sons, 1969; London: Collins, 1969), p. 45; Skene, *Celtic Scotland,* III: 318–25; Grant, *Social and Economic Development of Scotland,* pp. 487–502.

19. D. B. Quinn, *The Elizabethans and the Irish* (Ithaca, New York: Cornell University Press, 1966), p. 15. For further details on the Irish clan system, see Dublin, National Library of Ireland, MS 669 (herafter cited as NLI); San Marino, California, Huntington Library, Ellesmere MSS, EL 1701 (hereafter cited as Ellesmere MSS, EL 1701); Nicholls, *Gaelic and Gaelicized Ireland.*

20. For a detailed discussion of the Scottish clan system in the sixteenth and early seventeenth centuries, see Grant, *Social and Economic Development of Scotland,* pp. 472–550. For further study, see James Browne, *The History of Scotland, Its Highlands, Regiments, and Clans,* 8 vols. (Edinburgh: Francis A. Nicolls and Company, 1909); Frank Adam, *The Clans, Septs, and Regiments of the Scottish Highlands* (Edinburgh: W. and A. K. Johnston, 1908); R. R. McIan, *The Clans of the Scottish Highlands* (London: Ackermann, 1845; reprint ed., New York: Alfred A. Knopf, 1980); Donald Gregory, *The History of the Western Highlands and Isles of Scotland from A.D. 1493 to A.D. 1625* (Edinburgh: John Donald Publishers, 1881); A. and A. MacDonald, *Clan Donald;* Kermack, *Scottish Highlands;* MacKenzie, *Highlands and Isles of Scotland;* Wallace Notestein, *The Scot in History, A Study of the Interplay of Character and History* (New Haven, Connecticut: Yale University Press, 1947).

21. Great Britain, General Register House, *Accounts of the Lord High Treasurer of Scotland,* ed. Thomas Dickson, vol. 1 (1473–1498), pp. 238–39; Gregory, *Western Highlands and Isles,* pp. 9–10; Alexander MacKenzie, *History of the MacDonalds and Lords of the Isles* (Inverness: A. and W. MacKenzie, 1881), p. 122; David Stevenson, *Alasdair MacColla and the Highland Problem in the Seventeenth Century* (Edinburgh: John Donald Publishers, 1980), 99. 20–21; A. and A. MacDonald, *Clan Donald,* I: 36–37.

22. Gregory, *Western Highlands and Isles*, pp. 86–88; Stevenson, *Alasdair MacColla*, pp. 21–22; A. and A. MacDonald, *Clan Donald*, I: 286–87.

23. Symington Grieve, *The Book of Colonsay and Oronsay*, 2 vols. (Edinburgh: Oliver and Boyd, 1923), I: 261–62; Gregory, *Western Highlands and Isles*, pp. 94–95; Stevenson, *Alasdair MacColla*, p. 22; MacKenzie, *MacDonalds*, p. 126.

24. George Hill, *An Historical Account of the MacDonnells of Antrim: Including Notices of some other Septs, Irish and Scottish* (Belfast: Archer and Sons, 1873), pp. 120, 196–97, 231; Stevenson, *Alasdair MacColla*, p. 22; Gregory, *Western Highlands and Isles*, pp. 192–93; MacDonald, *Clan Donald*, II: 700–13.

25. Hayes-McCoy, *Scots Mercenary Forces in Ireland*, pp. 4–6; Stevenson, *Alasdair MacColla*, pp. 26–27.

26. Edmund Spenser, *A View of the Present State of Ireland*, ed. W. L. Renwick (Oxford: The Clarendon Press, 1970), p. 38.

27. Sidney to the Queen, no date, London, Public Record Office, State Papers, Ireland, Elizabeth, S.P. 63/19/43; Edmund Tremayne's Discourse on Ireland, 1573, Ellesmere MSS, EL 1701, f. 1; NLI, ms 669, f. 1v.

28. NLI. MS 669, f. 1v.

29. Ellesmere MSS, EL 1701, f. 1.

30. Articles from Sir William Darcy to the King's Council, 24 June 1515, London, Lambeth Palace Library, Carew MSS, vol. 635, pp. 188–90.

31. Spenser, *Present State of Ireland*, p. 158.

32. Ellesmere MSS, EL 1701, f. 2v.

33. Spenser, *Present State of Ireland*, p. 74.

34. Lughaidh O'Clerigh, *Beath Aodha Ruaidh Ui Dhomnaill, The Life of Aodh Ruadh O'Domhnaill*, ed. Paul Walsh (Dublin: The Irish Texts Society, 1948), pp. 53–55.

35. Spenser, *Present State of Ireland*, p. 156.

3

The Hounds of the Smith: O'Neill, O'Donnell, and the Irish Wars, 1595–1601

The Irish Gaels of the sixteenth century continued the military traditions of their ancient Celtic forebears by employing defensive strategy and offensive tactics. The Irish won most of their battles against Elizabeth's armies with a furious attack, sword in hand. Though the introduction of firearms marked the first refinement in modern Celtic warfare, Hugh O'Neill's Irish employed the musket only in the initial stages of battle, relegating it to a place of secondary importance at the climax. Using the charge to defend the rugged terrain of the Ulster homeland, the Irish often negated England's superior organizational and technological capabilities.

O'Neill believed that the Irish disadvantage lay in their inexperience in waging formal war. Traditionally, the Celts were not aggressors, but defenders, and their military strength was based on irregular tactics and a simple defensive strategy. To eliminate what he saw as a disadvantage, O'Neill attempted to revolutionize and modernize Gaelic warfare. On this score, however, he had to contend with Hugh O'Donnell, his chief lieutenant, and hundreds of other Gaelic fighting men who were adamant in their adherance to centuries-old military traditions. At Kinsale, the last battle in O'Neill's war with Elizabethan England, the outcome proved that the Irish could not carry out an effective strategic offensive. O'Neill wanted a disciplined, well-coordinated war machine. While England produced such a machine, Ireland produced individual fighters with individual wills, and nothing O'Neill devised could change the way they perceived war or performed on the battlefield.

O'Neill's and the Gaels' perceptions of the war itself were fundamentally similar. All believed that war with England was necessary and inevitable. It was the manner in which they acted on their perceptions, however, that was dramatically different. The following verse from a sixteenth-century Irish poet captures the typical Gael's attitude toward war and peace:

> Towards the warlike man peace is shown,
> that is a proverb which cannot be denied;
> throughout the beautiful forests of Banbha none
> but the fighting man finds peace.

> If anyone among the warriors of Bregia
> thinks it well to pacify the Saxons, this will
> be sufficient for his protection, so it is said,
> let him take a while to continually spoil them.

22

The Gaels of civil conduct will not find peace
from the foreigners, such is their warfare,
these most valorous, kingly hosts, theirs is
not worthy of a peace treaty ... [1]

Tadhg Dall O hUiginn,
untitled poem

But O'Neill himself was not a typical Gael. The natural forces that molded other Gaels into wild, undisciplined warriors were bridled in O'Neill by his exposure to modern ideas and the more orderly society of England, where he spent much of his youth. As a result, he led the Irish in a careful and calculated manner, while at the same time he recognized the force of Gaelic emotion and rode its tumultuous wave into war with England.

O'Neill's war to preserve Gaelic Ireland began in May 1593 when Hugh Maguire of Fermanagh attacked the English at Sligo and Roscommon. At the time O'Neill pledged his loyalty to the queen, and to prove himself to her he joined with Sir Henry Bagenal to defeat Maguire the following October. It was his last service for Elizabeth; his battle wound was a credible excuse to retire to his castle at Dungannon, away from the affairs of Ulster. Throughout the first half of 1594 both he and O'Donnell paid lip service to their royal commitments but covertly prepared for war. In June O'Donnell rose in rebellion. English suspicions of O'Neill's complicity increased, but he did not become openly active against the Dublin government until February 1595 when he forced the English out of their fort on the Blackwater river.[2]

Ulster's open break with England in 1595 ushered in war of a magnitude and type previously unknown in Irish history. O'Neill's kinsman, Shane O'Neill, had wrought a revolution in Irish warfare in the 1560s by mobilizing the entire population for war, and with the introduction of firearms into Ireland on a large scale around mid-century, both the size and efficiency of Irish armies improved dramatically. The principal firearm then was the arquebus, a primitive matchlock weapon, but the bulk of Shane's forces continued to employ *gallóglaich* axes, bows, javelins, and swords much in the tradition of their ancient Celtic forebears. With the advent of modern firearms — the musket and its smaller counterpart, the caliver — Hugh O'Neill fielded forces that generally were as well armed as the English. By 1595 he reportedly could muster over 4,000 shot.[3]

O'Neill and O'Donnell employed two types of Irish fighting men against the English. Many of the bonnaughts, or native Irish mercenaries, had received training in the continental wars of Spain. O'Neill maintained them by a system of *buannacht* (a levy of money and food) and used them as a national militia capable of mobilizing at short notice. They were his best troops. Sir George Carew, Lord President of Munster, marveled at a well-ordered Irish formation assembled near Kilkenny in April 1600, describing ' ... a troop of choice pikes ... of 500 foot strong and 20 horse, whereof 300 were bonnaughts, the best furnished men for the war ... as we have seen in the kingdom'.[4] At the time of his open involvement

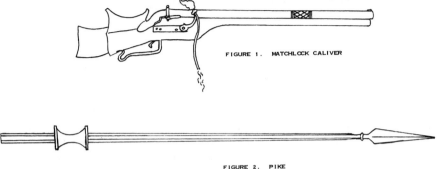

FIGURE 1. MATCHLOCK CALIVER

FIGURE 2. PIKE

against England in 1595, O'Neill commanded some 2,000 bonnaughts in Ulster.[5]

Most Irish warriors were *kernagh* (kerne) or lower class irregulars. Undisciplined and usually less well armed than the bonnaughts, the typical kerne was described as a ' ... footman, slightly armed with a skayne [a type of dagger], a target of wood, a bow and shefe or else 3 darts which they cast with wonderful facility and nearness, a weapon more noisome [annoying] to the enemy, especially to the horsemen than it is deadly'.[6] Nimble of foot and skilled in traversing the woods, hills, and bogs, the kerne served primarily as light skirmishers and scouts. They were perfectly suited for guerilla warfare, though of little use against heavily armed forces in open terrain.[7]

The increased efficiency of the Irish armies in the 1590s resulted primarily from O'Neill's organizational genius. Importing lead, powder, and firearms from Scotland, England, and the continent, he provided the necessities for training and equipping an army that he believed could stand up to the English. O'Neill converted the kerne to shot and retrained his Scottish troops, *gallógláich* and redshanks (who formerly had provided Irish chieftains with heavy infantry), in the use of the pike, a spear-like weapon twelve feet or more in length and ideal for close-formation defensive tactics. Under Shane O'Neill Irish soldiers had been segregated according to class; Hugh O'Neill blurred the distinction between the traditionally aristocratic warrior class and men of low birth by training them all in the use of arms. Thus by the beginning of his wars with the English, O'Neill possessed a well-equipped army that was trained in the use of the most modern firearms.[8] His forces were best suited for guerrilla conflict, but his imitation of English and continental armies suggests that he prepared for the possibility of formal battle. The English apparently respected the abilities of O'Neill's forces:

> ... they are very valiant and hardy ... great endurers of the cold, labour, hunger and all hardness, very active, and strong of their hand, very swift of foot, very vigilant and circumspect in their enterprises, very present in perils, very great scorners of death. Yea, truly, even in that rude kind of service he beareth himself very courageously, but when he cometh to a piece or pike, he maketh as worthy a soldier as any nation he meeteth with.[9]

English attempts to ring Ulster's southern border with a series of frontier outposts from 1595 to 1600 allowed O'Neill to employ strategic defensive measures most effectively. The Irish enticed the English into the fastnesses of Ulster where they were vulnerable to carefully planned ambushes. In the sixteenth century two main routes led into Ulster: in the west across the Erne at Ballyshannon and in the east from Dundalk through the Moyry Pass to Newry and north-westward to the Blackwater via Armagh. Between these passages lay the almost impenetrable center of the Irish line of defense stretching from Monaghan westward through Tyrone to Fermanagh, terrain described as ' ... very strong of woods and bogs, especially near the great Lough Erne'.[10] The only other passage into Ulster along this line lay near Enniskillen Castle, and the Irish blocked it in 1594. The English suffered one reverse in the relief attempt at Enniskillen in the same year and another at the Blackwater fort in early 1595; then, only two major outposts on the Ulster frontier remained as English possessions — Armagh and Monaghan. These wilderness garrisons, since they had often to be resupplied, placed the English squarely into O'Neill's hands and led to his first major victory at the battle of Clontibret.

At Clontibret O'Neill utilized the tactical strength of his Celtic warriors. The surrounding terrain was described as ' ... woods and thickets, deep and dangerous bogs, steep and craggy hills and mountains ... and ... straight and narrow passages ... '[11] O'Neill's Irish outnumbered the English roughly two to one and were positioned where ' ... a few muskets well placed will stagger a pretty army'.[12] O'Neill directed a continuous fire from concealed marksmen, while quick cavalry charges prevented the English from advancing far enough afield to disperse the pesky kerne. Intensive cavalry attacks forced Sir Henry Bagenal to deploy his men into a battle formation of pikes flanked by shot. This deployment would have been difficult enough for experienced troops on the best of terrain, and Bagenal's men were mostly raw recruits on a narrow track.[13]

O'Neill's guerrilla tactics led to the near-destruction of the English army at Clontibret. With a three-hour herculean effort, the English managed to push through the last Irish trap. They were low on powder and shot, exhausted, and demoralized. They dug in and awaited an Irish attack that never came.[14] Perhaps the Irish troops also faced a powder shortage,[15] or perhaps O'Neill wished not to annihilate the English, but to demonstrate his army's effectiveness in hopes of negotiating his objectives from a position of strength. He had beaten his arch-rival Bagenal, but he had not dealt the English army in Ireland a fatal blow. The English assessed their losses as thirty-one dead and 109 wounded, a casualty rate of only eight percent,[16] but the Dublin government later admitted that they suffered more casualties ' ... than was convenient to declare'.[17] The English also claimed to have inflicted several hundred casualties on the Irish,[18] but this estimate is almost certainly an exaggeration.

If Clontibret demonstrated what Gaelic armies did best, the skirmish that took place immediately afterward displayed what they did worst. As Bagenal's army huddled at Newry,[19] the Lord Deputy, Sir William Russell, journeyed north to stabilize the English presence on the Blackwater. O'Neill attacked Russell's 3,000-man force in open country as it marched back to Newry.[20] Though the

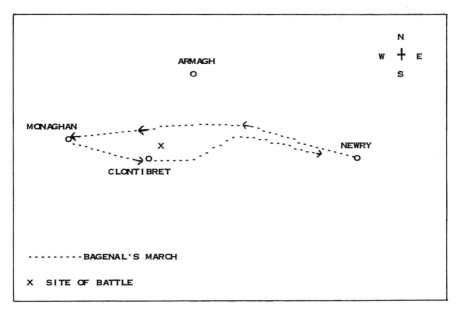

MAP 3.   CLONTIBRET   1595

assault was broken off quickly and was militarily insignificant, O'Neill's decision to take on such a strong force on unfavorable terrain may have signaled his recognition of the fact that sooner or later the old strategy and tactics, as well as the sheer force of Gaelic emotion, would cease to serve them so well.

The Blackwater valley including the nearby settlement of Armagh was the principal theater in which O'Neill carried out the tactical plan combining guerrilla warfare and the traditional Celtic charge. Armagh had received its first English garrison in 1551. Ten years later the cathedral was made into a fortress and became a hotly contested prize in O'Neill's day. Garrisoned again in 1595 by Russell, Armagh was for the English a stepping-stone for penetration into the heart of Ulster. Just north-west of Armagh lay the river Blackwater, O'Neill's first line of defense. English attempts to breach this line by the construction of a permanent outpost on the river prompted O'Neill's first overt hostilities when he attacked and destroyed the fort in 1595. Lord Deputy Burgh's construction of Portmore, or the second Blackwater fort, in 1597 led to the English defeat at Yellow Ford a year later.[21]

O'Neill made no attempt to keep the English out of the Blackwater valley from 1595 to 1598 nor to obstruct English efforts in building the second Blackwater fort. Despite a half-hearted try at scaling the walls of the new fort in early October 1597,[22] O'Neill probably was pleased to see the enemy once again making himself vulnerable to guerrilla attack on the frontier. He realized that the fort would have to be supplied periodically and that the relief columns would fare about the same as had the one at Monaghan. During 1598 the Blackwater fort remained so weak as to be almost useless. It was impossible to employ as a starting point for an attack into County Tyrone, and as a presence on O'Neill's southern border which would deter him from venturing outside Ulster it also failed. Drawing England's armies into the field every few months to feed it, the garrison on the Blackwater served O'Neill's purposes more than her own.

O'Neill quickly recognized the vulnerability of the second Blackwater fort and even helped the Earl of Ormonde, the new commander-in-chief of the English forces in Ireland, in ' ... the building up of the fort and bridge of Blackwater ... that her Majesty's garrison may be continued there without danger ... '[23] Ormonde resupplied the fort in December with cattle provided by O'Neill! But in early June, when the garrison once again needed supplies, O'Neill despatched part of his army to blockade it.[24] For the next few weeks the Irish lay astride the route to the Blackwater, spending ' ... the most part of that time in plashing of passes, and digging deep holes in the rivers, the more to distress the army that should come to relieve it'.[25]

The English apparently had learned little from Clontibret and planned another major effort to supply the Blackwater garrison. The first stage of the campaign involved the supplying of the fort, and the second stage a journey north to establish the long-sought garrison on Lough Foyle.[26] Ormonde protested the wisdom of the expedition, preferring instead to have the fort ' ... razed or yielded upon composition, than the soldiers to be left to the uttermost danger'.[27] But despite his objections the attempt to relieve the garrison went forward as planned. The English army numbered almost 4,000 foot and 300 horse when it marched northward in early August 1598.[28]

O'Neill confronted the English army with a tactical blueprint reminiscent of his efforts against Bagenal in 1595. The Irish slipped through bog and forest, raking the English column with a hurricane of crossfire. O'Neill had at his command ' ... as great an army as ever [seen] in the North ... '[29] As the English advanced over boggy ground, the approximately 5,000 Irishmen made no serious attempt to prevent their reaching the Callan stream. Both Irish chieftains — O'Neill from the left flank and O'Donnell from the right — utilized their superior mobility to strike the column repeatedly and then fall back to the protection of bogs and woods. The English army pushed ahead in the traditional vanguard, battle, and rearguard formations. The entire column extended about one mile from front to rear and one hundred yard intervals separated each regiment. Between the regiments were the horse, artillery, and baggage. O'Neill waited patiently for them to march into his trap.[30]

The field of battle of 14 August 1598 stretched from the outskirts of Armagh across a series of hills three miles away. The Yellow Ford lay beyond the Callan between the first and second hills and was not a ford in the strict sense but a marshy area that got its name from the color of the mire there. Between the second and third hills an open field flanked by bogs dominated the landscape. Here O'Neill constructed fortifications. His most formidable obstacle was a series of trenches described as ' ... a mile long, some five foot deep, and four feet over, with a thorny hedge on the top ... '[31] that crossed both the field and the bogs on either

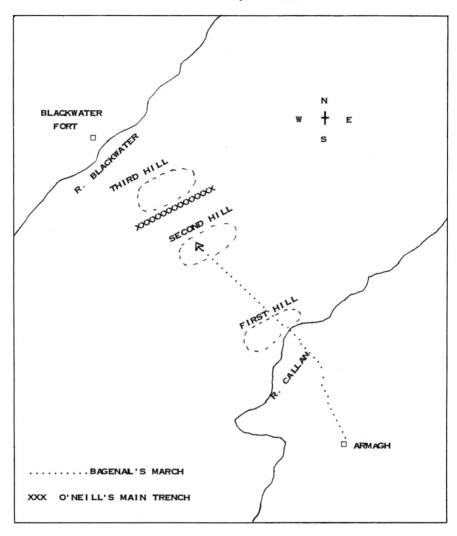

MAP 4.   YELLOW FORD   1598

side. The English would have encountered the obstructions whatever route they traveled, but O'Neill recognized the attraction of the passageway over the open field and elected to man it with his own Ulster veterans. Because of the nature of the terrain and O'Neill's preparations, an Irish victory was all but assured.

The enemy's original plan of march and deployment instructed the regiments to maintain contact; however, the terrain and constant harassment by the Irish caused an irregular pace and much wider intervals than their commander desired. Soon the three formations lost visual contact with each other, and Bagenal lost the ability to coordinate them. O'Neill took advantage of the enemy's situation by subjecting the lead regiment to heavy fire as it crossed the trenches and advanced up the third hill. The English penetrated no farther towards the Blackwater, and the rest of the day belonged to the Irish.[32]

Seeing his preparation and patience bear fruit, O'Neill unleashed his troops on the vulnerable English column. The charging Irish forced the enemy back, inflicted heavy casualties, and destroyed the lead regiment that they had allowed to reach the fortifications between the second and third hills. Meanwhile, O'Neill subjected the enemy detachment atop the second hill to heavy crossfire. Wave after wave of Irishmen rolled into the gaps between the English regiments. The cumbersome enemy columns were slowed by their artillery and supplies and fared poorly against the nimble, lightly armed Irish.[33]

A Celtic army's confidence often waned at the first sign of impending defeat; conversely, it waxed upon the verge of victory. When a musket ball caught Bagenal between the eyes, O'Neill capitalized on his warriors' confidence and chose to administer the crushing blow.[34] The Irish fell upon the enemy with 2,000 foot and 400 horse and stalled the English retreat. Then an explosion of three barrels of powder in the English ranks ' ... spoiled many men and disordered the battle'.[35] A pall of black smoke hung over the battlefield as the Irish hewed their way through the demoralized English pike formations and onto the now powderless musketeers. The English column narrowly escaped.[36]

At Yellow Ford O'Neill displayed a patience uncharacteristic of Celtic commanders in his careful selection of the time and place of lightning attacks that set up the English column for the final blow. The initial pinprick attacks by Irish sharpshooters were not intended to cause great loss of life, but to increase the distances between the English regiments. It was not that the English units lacked cohesiveness: their training and experience had not prepared them to defend themselves against the type of warfare fought by the Irish. Even the landscape aided the Irish; the hills not only obstructed the English view, but provided the Irish with staging points for charges that rolled down with tremendous impact upon the battered enemy. The English fought well at Yellow Ford despite Ormonde's scathing comment that they ' ... came away most cowardly, casting from them their armours and weapons as soon as the rebels charged them'.[37] Their losses were heavy, however, with twenty-five officers and 800 men killed, 400 wounded, and some 300 missing. Over 2,000 reached Armagh safely, and O'Neill's decision to allow them to escape provided them a nucleus around which future armies would be formed. Irish losses were lighter — 200 killed and 600 wounded.[38]

Even though O'Neill's influence in the wake of Yellow Ford was strong enough to bring much of Ireland into his camp, he ultimately failed to unify the disparate elements of Irish society. His familiarity with the continental powers made O'Neill acutely aware of the importance of nationalism to a major war effort; he alone among the great Gaelic and Anglo-Irish lords saw the inherent weakness of political fragmentation and its resulting localism. O'Donnell and the others saw only the necessity of preserving their independence as local chieftains. Whether imposed from within by O'Neill or from without by the English, centralized government was foreign to the Gaels. But O'Neill knew that to oppose the English successfully, he would have to transform Ireland into something of a modern nation-state where the conflicting interests of various localities would be subjugated to the will of the collective whole. That he failed in the long run to overcome the chieftains' deep-seated bias against a unified political system did much to nullify whatever military advantages he gained by the victory at Yellow Ford. Though O'Neill altered the appearance of Gaelic Ireland by implementing a military system that superficially resembled those of England and the continental powers, he could not erase a military tradition based more on emotion than on an orderly, efficient administration.

Yellow Ford was the zenith of Irish military success against the power of England; however, it was not the total victory that it might have been. The remainder of the army, some 2,000 men representing the flower of English military forces in Ireland, made its way to Armagh cathedral. The Irish leaders chose to allow its departure for Newry and then from Ulster itself. Among the possible reasons for O'Neill's leniency would be the expense of keeping his army together, his fear of an English landing to his rear at Derry, and O'Donnell's impatience to return to Tirconnell.[39] With only a week's supply of food and almost no hope of relief, the English troops could have been starved into complete submission.[40] Then O'Neill could have swept unmolested out of Ulster, ravaged the Pale, and threatened Dublin itself. The continuation of war outside the north would, of course, have necessitated a change of strategy, but O'Neill had earlier prepared for the possibility of a switch to the strategic offensive and actually did so in 1601.

The near-disaster in 1598 prompted England to take the Irish wars more seriously, though it was not until 1600 that the English were able to present O'Neill a serious challenge. On 26 February of that year Charles Blount, Lord Mountjoy, landed at Dublin as the new Lord Deputy accompanied by Sir George Carew as Lord President of Munster.[41] The new century dawned, and the Irish found themselves confronting four adversaries of a caliber previously unseen in Ireland: Mountjoy; Carew; Sir Arthur Chichester, governor of Carrickfergus; and Sir Henry Docwra, who soon would lead the effort to plant a garrison at Lough Foyle in the north.

Mountjoy began a thorough reorganization of the English army in Ireland based for the first time on an efficient military administration coupled with a new strategy. Drawing on the bitter experiences of past lord deputies, he decided that the English would no longer attempt to construct and supply widely separated forts that provided little mutual support. Thenceforth, Mountjoy determined to bring the Irish to formal battle by actively seeking them out and forcing them to meet him on his own terms. Better than any of his predecessors, Mountjoy knew of the enemy's dependence upon nature as an indispensable ally. He therefore determined to conduct his major campaigns in the winter, hoping to disrupt the Irish logistical system and render their guerrilla tactics ineffective. A contemporary English observer noted that

... in Ireland the winter yieldeth best services, for then the trees are bare and naked, which use both to clothe and house the kerne, the ground is cold and wet which useth to be his bedding, the air is sharp and bitter which useth to blow through his naked sides and legs, the kine are barren and without milk, which useth to be his only food ... [42]

The English also began systematic defoliation throughout the Pale, finding the forests ' ... ready hives to harbour Irish rebellions ... '[43] As Mountjoy traversed the countryside, particularly along the frontier, he stripped vegetation from the passes and defiles to discourage ambushes.

Central to Mountjoy's strategy was the disruption of Irish food supplies. To effect this strategy he sought to immobilize the *creaghts*, transhumant herds of cattle and their accompanying herders, that were the major food source for Irish forces on the move. The *creaghts* allowed the army to feed from cattle on the hoof and thus increase its mobility. Residing in the hills and mountains during the winter, the *creaghts* descended to the fertile pasturelands in the spring during the traditional campaigning season. A typical Irish army on the march might prearrange a meeting with a *creaght* in the immediate area and acquire food for several weeks. They would take with them a few hundred cattle to supplement their traditional ration of oatmeal and whiskey and found need for little else as they fed

... upon herbs and roots, their drink is beef broth, milk, and whey. They let their kine bleed, which being cold they bake in a pan, and spread upon bread. In haste they squeeze out the blood of raw flesh and feed upon it without farther dressing, which they boil in their stomach with Aqua Vita.[44]

When they stopped long enough to feed upon beef, the Irish normally killed the cattle and boiled the meat in the hides; thus, they did not carry utensils or cumbersome pots.[45] At the time of Mountjoy's arrival in Ireland, O'Neill, O'Donnell, and other chieftains fed a combined force of some 10,000 soldiers by use of the *creaghts*.

England's previous efforts in Ireland had been hesitant and often half-hearted; with Mountjoy's advent her policies were strengthened by conviction. Mountjoy's grim determination to wage and win an all-out war in Ireland is exemplified by the following report from the pen of Chichester:

We have killed, burnt, and spoiled all along the lough within four miles of Dungannon, from hence [we] returned hither yesterday; in which journeys we have killed above 100 people of all sorts besides such as were burnt, how many I know not. We spare none of what quality or sex soever and it hath bred much terror in the people who heard not a drum nor saw not a fire there of long time. The last service was upon Patrick O'Quin whose house and town was burnt, wife, son, children, and people slain, himself ... dead of a hurt received in flying from his house ... [46]

Mountjoy, like earlier lord deputies, found it necessary to penetrate the Ulster borders since disrupting Irish logistics and neutralizing the effects of the wilderness could not alone bring O'Neill's defeat. His purpose was not to resupply the exposed Blackwater fort, however, but to secure Armagh and actively pursue, corner, and destroy what he could of O'Neill's army. Mountjoy knew that he must disperse his forces judiciously to hold key points throughout the island while keeping pressure from all sides on Ulster. In the summer of 1600 the English army in Ireland numbered 14,000 foot and 1,200 horse.[47] Now, as Mountjoy prepared to assail the north with no specific geographical objective in mind, the Irish leaders had no way of determining where he might range. The carefully laid ambushes of the past would not suffice to defeat a force that might choose to march away from them. O'Neill decided to shift his efforts southward to block Mountjoy's passage into Ulster since the Blackwater was now an untenable line of defense.

Mountjoy chose as his point of entry to Ulster the Moyry Pass. Called *bealach an mhaighre*, or the gap of the north, the pass is located about forty miles south-east of the Blackwater and in the sixteenth century represented the only easily accessible pathway to Ulster from the Pale. A contemporary writer referred to the pass as a ' ... broken cawsey beset on both sides with bogs, where the Irish might skip but the English could not go ... '[48] O'Neill hoped that the ruggedness of the terrain and a series of elaborate field fortifications would serve to keep Mountjoy out of Ulster. O'Neill constructed five barricades across the pass, three of which lay south of the Three Mile Water. The two remaining barricades — which Mountjoy never reached — lay farther northward immediately south of the Four Mile Water.[49] The first three obstructions ranged from 100 to 150 yards apart and were fashioned ' ... in the manner of little sconces with great hedges upon the top ... '[50] An English officer declared that he had never seen ' ... a more villainous piece of work, and an impossible thing for an army to pass without intolerable loss ... '[51] On the rising ground to either side of the barricades the Irish blocked the way with wattle fences intertwined with twigs, thorns, and branches, similar to those employed by ancient Celts. Behind this barrier O'Neill waited with about 3,000 foot and 300 horse for Mountjoy's approach.[52]

While Mountjoy attempted to force the pass, O'Neill tried to lure the English into the maze of fortifications and attack them from all sides.[53] The Irish were so active that the climax of the battle on 2 October was described by Mountjoy as ' ... one of the greatest fights that hath been seen in Ireland ... '[54] The Irish stood their ground, ' ... ready to entertain skirmish on all sides, and not to give way, as their manner is sometimes to do ... '[55] For over two hours the battle raged. The English advanced a mile or so into the pass and drove the Irish from the first two breastworks, enduring ' ... terrible volleys of shot at the barricades ... '[56] Though in possession of the first two barricades, the English army could not remain in the pass; the Irish sharpshooters on the flanking hillsides made its position untenable. The English made what Mountjoy called ' ... a gallant and orderly retreat ... '[57] They nonetheless suffered heavy casualties as a result of O'Neill's charge which thinned their ranks as they sought safety at the mouth of the pass. An English observer reported that ' ... they do still remain ... in strength ... for Tyrone intendeth not to remove with his forces'.[58] The Irish leader's dogged resolve to hold the gap of the north reflected the danger he perceived should his newest adversary penetrate Ulster.

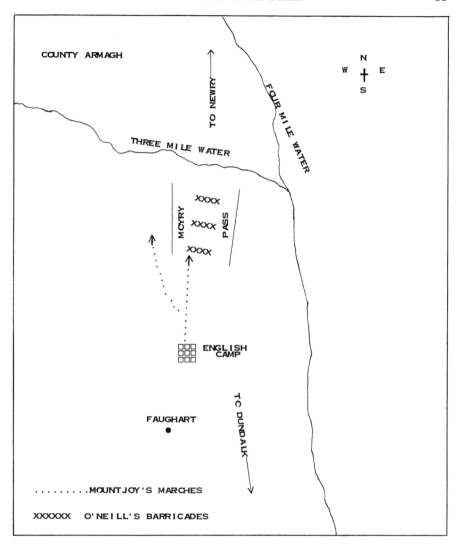

MAP 5.   MOYRY PASS   1600

O'Neill's success in denying Mountjoy's passage through the Moyry Pass was described in the correspondence of the English officers. One officer admitted the peril that faced the army during its second advance into the pass on 2 October: ' ... the carriages were seen to march away, they were so near to an utter overthrow'.[59] Another Englishman noted ' ... that if we fight after this rate but seven days more, there will be never a man left in the camp. There is no talk but of passing the Moyerie, or lying in the mire, which I think rather ... '[60]

Mountjoy's final desperate attempt to break through the pass exemplified the Celtic determination to attack even when they held a strong defensive position.

The English tried to outflank the Irish by climbing the heights on the left flank but were met by a wave of 300 Irish attackers who succeeded in breaking the impetus of the English advance and ending Mountjoy's hopes of forcing the gap of the north. This battle — the one commonly seen as typical of O'Neill's use of defensive tactics — thus ended, paradoxically, with an Irish attack. One of Mountjoy's officers admitted that it left the English army ' ... but where [they] were in the beginning'.[61]

Despite his success O'Neill's conduct at the Moyry Pass led to a rift between him and O'Donnell that not only was never resolved, but also grew wider as the war progressed. O'Donnell criticized O'Neill's handling of the affair and thought that O'Neill ' ... lay too long at the Moyerie, that he spent his munition, lost his best men, and wasted his victuals there to no purpose ... '[62] O'Donnell, whose beliefs represented the majority opinion among Gaelic warriors, preferred to allow the English passage into the fastnesses of Ulster, where their vulnerability to the weather and shortages of supplies would be aggravated further and where they could not easily withdraw to a place of safety. He obviously believed that Mountjoy would follow the example of his predecessors and plant further exposed frontier garrisons in Ulster that would necessitate periodic re-supply.[63] O'Donnell clearly misunderstood Mountjoy's strategies and underestimated his capabilities.

O'Neill's defense of the Moyry Pass marked a distinct break with the tactics employed at Clontibret and Yellow Ford and thus with Celtic tradition. The careless adventures of Bagenal were not repeated by Mountjoy, which meant that the Irish could no longer expect to pounce on exposed columns at the time and place of their choosing. As a result O'Neill relied more upon defensive measures at the Moyry Pass than he had before 1600. Instead of a loosely structured deployment, as at Yellow Ford, he began the battle for the pass with his forces set to carry out specific assignments, ' ... giving unto his especial gentlemen and captains their particular charge and direction where to fight and how to resist ... '[64] O'Neill controlled the field of battle at the Moyry Pass as masterfully as he had in 1595 and 1598; however, the offensive tactics of the ambush were replaced with a more controlled offensive–defensive effort that witnessed the Irish standing toe to toe with an unbroken English force. The strength of the pass must have emboldened O'Neill as he absorbed the full weight of Mountjoy's attacks and then mounted fierce counterattacks. That O'Neill succeeded in his objective at the Moyry Pass cannot be denied; but that success was of a very different nature to any of his earlier victories. The Moyry Pass was a repulse of the enemy — not a wholesale rout.

O'Neill grasped the changing nature of the war in 1600 as only he could and adapted his tactics, and later his strategy, to meet the change. The Moyry Pass was a transitional stage somewhere between the defensive strategy and offensive guerrilla tactics of the past and the offensive strategy and formal tactics that O'Neill would unsuccessfully employ at Kinsale. But despite his bending to the exigencies of warfare with a modern nation-state, O'Neill continued a tactical policy that stressed attack over defense. With the undaunted Mountjoy still determined to crack the Ulster defenses, however, the immediacy of stabilizing the borders took precedence over all else. Farther south Carew continued to subdue the local chieftains in Munster. More and more the Irish chiefs looked forward to the long-awaited fulfillment of Spain's promise to assist her fellow Catholics.[65]

'I have heard it from certain persons of knowledge and experience that it is a well known saying of old that every army which does not attack will be attacked.'[66] These words are attributed to the young and impetuous Hugh O'Donnell in 1592 as he embarked upon the first of many victorious campaigns. They may have passed from his lips once again nine years later as he watched the lightning flash across the sky, illuminating an unfamiliar Munster landscape far from the fastnesses of his native Ulster. As he sat in council opposite his confederate-at-arms, Hugh O'Neill, on that stormy night in 1601, O'Donnell cast his vote for the attack that would decide the fate of Gaelic Ireland, ' ... even if his death or destruction or the loss of his people should result from it'.[67] The cautious O'Neill urged patience. His experience suggested a blockade of the weakened enemy at Kinsale,[68] but in the end he gave in to the more primitive mode of warfare — the attack. At Kinsale the favored tactic of his ancestors failed and that one failure — his only serious reverse in nine years of war — was enough to destroy the old Gaelic order that he and O'Donnell had first risen to protect.

The landing of over 4,000 Spaniards at Kinsale in September 1601 marked the beginning of a critical phase in the Irish wars. Mountjoy must have known that the decisive moment had arrived, for he immediately began preparations to draw significant forces to Munster from all over Ireland. By late October Mountjoy's army near Kinsale numbered about 6,900 foot and 1,200 horse. Docwra retained 3,000 foot and 100 horse at Lough Foyle, while Chichester commanded 850 foot and 150 horse at Carrickfergus. The northern garrisons together accounted for only 800 foot and 100 horse. In the Pale and adjoining areas Mountjoy left just over 3,000 foot and 175 horse and in Connaught, 1,150 foot and about 160 horse. English forces remaining in Ulster, Leinster, and Connaught totaled 9,100 foot and 587 horse.[69]

The arrival of the Spaniards was even more crucial to the Irish in that they would now have to decide whether to leave Ulster and give up the strategic defensive that had served them so well. O'Neill reacted with extreme caution, but O'Donnell moved with characteristic impetuosity, marching his men south from Sligo in late September.[70] Mountjoy learned of his approach in early November and despatched a force to intercept him. The near impossibility of containing the elusive Irish prompted Mountjoy's secretary to comment that

> ... although they are as dangerous an enemy as any are in the world, when we are driven to seek them in their strength, or pass their fastnesses, yet are they the worst and weakest to force their own way, either upon the straights or plains, so that except they steal their passage (which I fear most) I make no doubt but my Lord President will give a very good account of them.[71]

English fears were justified. When they had blockaded O'Donnell's main route down the Suir Valley toward Kinsale, the only other passage to the south lay across the Slievefelim Mountains into Limerick, and this was impassable because of recent heavy rains. An unseasonable cold snap, however, froze the ground and allowed O'Donnell's 2,000 foot and 300 horse to march across Limerick and into Cork. The English commander watched helplessly as the Irish escaped his clutches by marching forty miles in a single day.[72]

O'Neill finally departed Ulster in early November with 3,500 warriors who carried only their weapons, oatmeal, and an extra pair of shoes. In early December he joined O'Donnell; their combined force numbered between 5,000 and 6,000. The Irish army neared Kinsale on 21 December. Most of the men had served throughout the Ulster campaign, and their presence *en masse* north of Mountjoy's camp posed a serious threat to the English position in Ireland. Their numbers matched those of Mountjoy, who mustered about 6,500 infantrymen.[73]

The strength of the English army deteriorated daily. A contemporary Englishman observed that ' ... the very trenches we made were continually filled with water, and the decay of our men was so great, by continual labour, sickness, sword, and bullet'.[74] Similar news reached O'Neill that ' ... the enemies are tired, and are very few, and they cannot guard the third part of their trenches ... '[75] When O'Neill received such reports he perhaps reasoned that the English could best be defeated by a simple blockade. Mountjoy must have recognized his vulnerability, for he kept his troops on continual alert for the attack that he probably hoped would come soon. His only chance was a test of arms as soon as possible, before his army ceased to exist.[76] While O'Neill pondered whether to attack or blockade the English, O'Donnell chafed at the bit, urging an immediate assault ' ... to maintain the honor of Irish arms ... '[77]

Shortly before midnight on 23 December O'Neill signaled to the Spaniards that the attack would begin at dawn. According to contemporary Irish observers, O'Neill set out toward the English with great reluctance.[78] But Mountjoy lay before him with the cream of the English army in Ireland. If O'Neill could somehow destroy this force, he would be master of the island and the long, grueling march from Ulster would be rewarded in a single stroke.[79]

O'Neill and O'Donnell quarrelled before the battle over who would have the honor of leading the attack and they therefore failed to coordinate their movements.[80] Relations between the two men had slowly deteriorated since the Moyry Pass, and it is likely that neither had full confidence in the other on the eve of battle. The night march on Mountjoy's camp demonstrated their lack of coordination; the formations reportedly lost their way and became separated. Consequently, when the enemies sighted each other at sunrise, the Irish were not yet deployed into battle formation. The Irish leaders' carelessness and slow deployment prevented them from denying the English passage over a bog that separated them from the Irish. By allowing the enemy to move first, O'Neill forfeited his one chance of victory — a wild, tumultuous charge against an enemy positioned on unfavorable terrain. Never before had O'Neill permitted the English to assume the tactical offensive. He did at Kinsale — and they never relinquished it.[81]

Confusion within the Irish ranks need not have been fatal, as their resistance

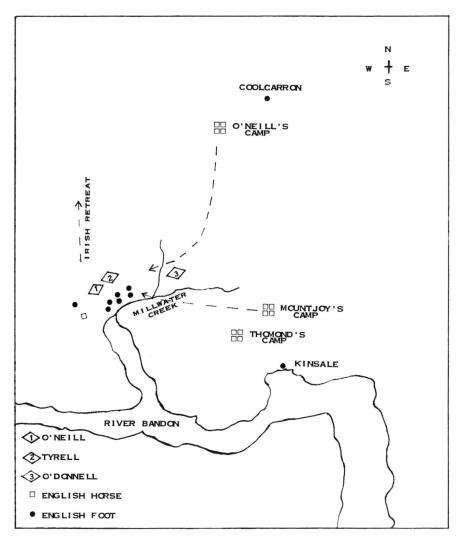

MAP 6. KINSALE 1601

stiffened when the English horse moved toward them. But O'Neill then committed a grave blunder: he deployed his men into a defensive formation similar to the Spanish Tercio. The pikemen formed a large square, at the corners of which lay small bands of shot, and skirmishers were deployed loosely along the wings. The square was cumbersome and ineffective; O'Neill's fighters lacked the discipline necessary to maintain it. By moving his troops into an unfamiliar defensive formation, he prevented them from reassembling into a line of battle and thus from employing any sort of offensive tactics.[82]

O'Neill's inability to control the Irish cavalry left his infantry unprotected and allowed the English horse to maintain the tactical initiative until the end of the battle. The light Irish horse could not fend off their heavier English counterparts, whose second charge caused them to break and flee wildly through the ranks of O'Neill's square. The confused departure of the Irish horse disordered the already shaky formation, and as the English cavalry and infantry closed in, the Irish foot took flight. O'Donnell's men were still not fully deployed,[83] and when O'Neill's fleeing division reached him O'Donnell urged them ' . . . to stand their ground . . . requesting his nobles to stand by him and fight their enemies . . . But, however, all he did was of no avail to him, for, as the first battalion was defeated, so were the others also in succession'.[84]

With the defeat at Kinsale, O'Neill, O'Donnell, and the other Gaelic chieftains lost the war to free Ireland from English domination. The reverse cost the Irish about 1,200 men, fourteen of whom were captains of various clans and families.[85] In terms of sheer numbers the loss need not have been fatal; however, O'Neill and O'Donnell suffered widespread defections not only among most of their lukewarm supporters, but even among their most loyal. O'Neill's military reputation was shattered and his personal charisma evaporated. He and his comrades returned to Ulster to regroup and salvage what they could of their homeland.

Success at Kinsale had undoubtedly been within O'Neill's grasp. Had he waited but a few more days before engaging the enemy, the English horse would not have been at the battle. An Englishman admitted that ' . . . it had been resolved . . . to send the horse from the camp for want of means to feed them, and if Tyrone had lain still, and not suffered himself to be drawn to the plain ground . . . all our horse must needs have been sent away or starved'.[86]

An even more interesting question is what might have happened had O'Neill moved into the Pale. An attack on Dublin in 1601 would have been a gamble, but no more than the attack on Kinsale. The Irish were reportedly fearful of and unable to use artillery and certainly could not have succeeded in attacking Dublin without facing it or employing it themselves. The Irish possessed several pieces, including a six-pound saker taken at Yellow Ford, even though the ruggedness of the terrain of Ulster and Irish guerrilla tactics did not provide a suitable environment for their regular employment. But O'Neill's connections with arms suppliers in Spain, Scotland, and even England and his experience with the most modern weapons then available discounts the belief that he did not possess the requisite knowledge to employ artillery. It was, to be sure, outside the traditional Celtic arsenal. Had the Irish chanced an all-out attack on Dublin and the Pale, their desperate venture at Kinsale might not have been necessary. O'Donnell's army would have sufficed to blockade Mountjoy while O'Neill struck in the eastern triangle. O'Neill did, in fact, delay his march to spoil areas of Leinster, but his efforts there were half-hearted. If O'Neill had made a concerted effort to ravage the Pale and threaten Dublin, Mountjoy might have found it necessary to despatch part of his army northward to protect England's interests there; the Ulster veterans would have severely tested the 2,000 English foot and horse left in Leinster.[87] And if Mountjoy still had refused to send troops to the Dublin area, O'Neill might have approached Kinsale from the rear, squeezing the English between himself, O'Donnell, and the Spaniards. By duplicating Mountjoy's moves and concentrating near Kinsale, however, O'Neill played into the hands of the desperate English commander. O'Neill's decision to march to O'Donnell was perhaps his greatest military mistake.

The objective that underlay the strategy of O'Neill and the Irish chieftains until 1601 was the defense of Ulster through the use of offensive tactics. The wars were fought largely within the borders of Ulster, and O'Neill's strategy was akin to that employed by the Confederate generals in the American Civil War. The Southern strategy was also based on the defense of the homeland against an invading army, and just as the Confederates marched from the familiar confines of the South to their defeat at Gettysburg, so too O'Neill and O'Donnell left Ulster and suffered irreversible defeat at Kinsale. It was not in the tradition of either to stand on the defensive, but neither was able to pursue an effective strategic offensive against a technologically and organizationally superior army. Both were forced to assume the strategic defensive, but neither the Irish nor the Confederates could keep to a purely tactical defensive. A proclivity for the attack was reflected in the tactics of both. In eight of its first twelve major battles the Confederacy attacked the invading enemy.[88] Similarly, the Irish attacked the English in Ulster in the first two major battles of the war, Clontibret and Yellow Ford, and ultimately attacked the attackers at the third, the Moyry Pass in 1600. O'Neill's successes before 1601 resulted from the application of a strategic defensive which employed offensive guerrilla tactics on favorable terrain, and his defeat at Kinsale stemmed from the abandonment of this policy and the pursuit of a strategic offensive that necessitated the switch from guerrilla tactics to formal battle.

O'Neill's ability in the early years of the war to arrange the type of extended battle that best complemented the training and preparation of his fighting men was unusual among Celtic commanders. His defensive strategy combined with offensive tactics was reminiscent of the ancient Celts' campaigns in Lusitania and proved that Celtic armies indeed could hang tenaciously to any enemy given the proper training and direction. But an English observer noted that while the Irish skirmished ' ... in passes, bogs, woods, fords, and in all places of advantage ... , they hold it no dishonor to run away; for the best sconce and castle for their security is their feet'.[89] O'Neill's practice of breaking off contact with the enemy and vanishing into the wilderness, also reminiscent of the ancient Celts, was not evidence of a lack of tenacity; rather, it was a premeditated plan to confuse the enemy and preserve his own troops for another day of fighting.

The Irish defeat at Kinsale was born of O'Neill's attempts to transform his bonnaughts, kerne, *gallóglaich* and redshanks from fighters into formal soldiers. For centuries the strength of the Celtic warrior had been his prowess in individual combat, but the unbridled temperament of most Celtic warriors was ill-suited for a highly formalized and disciplined mode of warfare that reduced the role of the individual. O'Neill, the first of the modern Gaelic captains, sought to restructure the Celtic military system in Ireland to such a degree that the collective whole overshadowed the individual. O'Neill's formula at Clontibret and Yellow Ford demonstrated the effectiveness of the Irish as fighters; Kinsale, however, pointed up their ineptitude as soldiers. O'Neill negated his prior advantages at Kinsale by fighting in a rigid manner far removed from Celtic military traditions.

What moved O'Neill to cast away the successful formula of 1595–1600 and march to Kinsale and overwhelming defeat cannot be known. He had the opportunity both then and after Yellow Ford to take the war into the Pale. But what surely would have deteriorated into siege warfare was not part of the traditional Celtic military repertoire; therefore, O'Neill's decision to stay at home after Yellow Ford in 1598 was certainly not timidity or a disdain for taking the offensive. Rather, it demonstrated his conviction that the key to success was an active pursuit of the superb offensive tactics practised at Yellow Ford. This, of course, renders his action before Kinsale all the more inexplicable. A rash adventure that would demand from his men more marching and waiting than fighting was apparently never seriously entertained in 1598. But in 1601, after the long trek to Kinsale that could have produced a great victory if he had passively awaited the demise of Mountjoy's army at the hands of the elements, O'Neill succumbed to the Celtic practice of risking all on a single throw of the dice. His men were truly 'hounds of the smith' spoiling for battle. They had actively sought the enemy and O'Neill could not restrain them further; a failure to attack would have disgraced and humiliated his warriors. Another possible explanation for O'Neill's decision to attack at Kinsale is that he knew that, without the wholehearted support of O'Donnell, the Gaels would reluctantly follow his lead in blockading the English. And O'Donnell wanted to attack at all costs. Rather than sacrifice the frenzied emotionalism of the Gael at war, O'Neill bowed to his lieutenant and to centuries of offensive, emotional warfare.

Despite O'Neill's efforts to mold the Irish Gaels into a modern army, they exhibited several military traits that suggest a high degree of continuity extending from Celtic practices of earlier ages. First and foremost was a love of combat made necessary by a culture that depended on it for survival. And it was a love of offensive combat, particularly, as is demonstrated by their four major battles from 1595 to 1601. Although they were generally as well armed as the English, the Irish did not depend on a complex logistical system. Just as their forebears had, they learned as young men of the deprivations common to the military campaign and of the necessity of traveling lightly to outmaneuver a better supplied enemy. Their close proximity to nature allowed them not only to live off the land but to utilize natural fastnesses further strengthened by the age-old practice of plashing, or constructing walls of branches and thorns. The use of all that nature provided to counter an enemy who relied mainly upon his technological and organizational superiority underlay Celtic warfare from the ancients to O'Neill and beyond.

The Irish wars marked a watershed in the evolution of Celtic military practice in that they witnessed a melding of the traditional with the modern. O'Neill, a student of the new English and continental schools of warfare, attempted to apply such lessons to Ireland, and consequently rendered his struggles with Elizabethan England conspicuously different from the type of Gaelic warfare that both preceded and followed his military career. A prerequisite for successful formal war in the sixteenth century was the supporting technological, political, and administrative machinery of the modern nation-state. Despite O'Neill's best efforts to transform Gaelic Ireland into such an entity, the conception of the island as a nation was foreign to the greater part of his lieutenants, including O'Donnell, who rarely looked beyond the borders of their own territories. His attempts to mold a nation and a modern army from such material ultimately failed. His sincere efforts to change what he perceived as an anachronistic and outmoded military system could not have succeeded as long as the Gaels remained Gaelic. Thereafter, his successors, perhaps less farsighted but more realistic in the short run, returned to a more primitive mode of warfare.

NOTES

1. Author's translation of an untitled Gaelic poem by Tadhg Dall O hUiginn, London, British Library, Egerton MSS, MS 65771, f. 91.

2. Cyril Falls, *Elizabeth's Irish Wars* (London: Methuen and Company, 1950; reprint ed. New York: Barnes and Noble, 1970), pp. 175-82; Tyrone's Grievances, 14 March 1594, London, Lambeth Palace Library, Carew MSS, vol. 617, p. 205; John O'Donovan, ed., *Annala Rioghachta Eireann, Annals of the Kingdom of Ireland, by the Four Masters, from the Earliest Period to the Year 1616,* 5 vols. (Dublin: Hodges and Smith, 1848), V: 1951.

3. G. A. Hayes-McCoy, *Irish Battles* (London: Longmans, Green and Company, 1969), pp. 74, 77, 93, 110.

4. Carew and Earl of Thomond to Privy Council, 18 April 1600, London, Public Record Office, State Papers, Ireland, Elizabeth, S.P. 63/207/2/115 (hereafter cited as S.P. 63).

5. Hayes-McCoy, *Irish Battles*, pp. 106-10; Falls, *Elizabeth's Irish Wars*, p. 68.

6. Dublin, National Library of Ireland, MS 669, f. 11 (hereafter cited as NLI).

7. Falls, *Elizabeth's Irish Wars*, pp. 69-70.

8. Hayes-McCoy, *Irish Battles*, pp. 93-94, 110-12.

9. Edmund Spenser, *A View of the Present State of Ireland,* ed. W. L. Renwick (Oxford: Clarendon Press, 1970), p. 72.

10. NLI, MS 669, f. 48v.

11. Sir James Perrott, *A Chronicle of Ireland, 1584-1608,* ed. Herbert Wood (Dublin: The Stationery Office, 1933), p. 92.

12. Thomas Gainsford, *The Glory of England* (London: Printed by Edward Griffin, 1618), p. 144.

13. Sir Henry Bagenal to Lord Burghley, 29 May 1595, S.P. 63/179/95.

14. Ibid.

15. Bagenal's service in the relieving of Monaghan, Carew MSS, vol. 612, p. 21.

16. List of English casualties at Clontibret, S.P. 63/179/95; List of English casualties, S.P. 63/180/6. The Irish sources give only non-specific information regarding Irish casualties.

17. Sir Ralph Lane to Burghley, 28 June 1595, S.P. 63/180/57.

18. Bagenal to Burghley, 29 May 1595, S.P. 63/179/95.

19. Sir John Norris to Sir Robert Cecil, 4 June 1595, S.P. 63/180/9.

20. Sir Geoffrey Fenton to Burghley, 7 September 1595, S.P. 63/183/9; Bagenal to Burghley, 9 September 1595, S.P. 63/183/19.

21. G. A. Hayes-McCoy, *Ulster and other Irish Maps, c. 1600* (Dublin: Irish Manuscripts Commission, 1964), pp. 5-6, 14.

22. Fenton to Cecil, 5 October 1597, S.P. 63/201/7; *Four Masters*, V: 2035.

23. Matters for Ormonde concerning Tyrone's submission, 5 December 1597, S.P. 63/201/95, i.

24. Fenton to Cecil, 11 June 1598, S.P. 63/202/2/62.

25. Fenton to Cecil, 24 July 1598, S.P. 63/202/2/110.

26. Falls, *Elizabeth's Irish Wars*, pp. 211–12.

27. Loftus, Gardiner, Ormonde, and Council to Privy Council, 17 June 1598, S.P. 63/202/2/72.

28. Hayes-McCoy, *Irish Battles*, p. 16.

29. Extracts from a letter to Fenton, 20 July 1598, S.P. 63/202/2/110, i.

30. London, British Library, Additional Manuscripts, 4763. f. 151 (hereafter cited as Add. MSS); Captain Charles Montague's report, 16 August 1598, S.P. 63/202/3/20, i; Declarations of captains Ferdinando and Kingsmill, 23 August 1598, S.P. 63/202/3/34. i.

31. Captain Charles Montague's report, 16 August 1598, S.P. 63/202/3/20, i.

32. Add. MSS, 4763, ff. 151–151v; Montague to Ormonde, 16 August 1595, S.P. 63/202/3/28, ii; Lieutenant Taaffe to H. Shee, 16 August 1598, S.P. 63/202/3/28, iii; Declarations of captains Ferdinando and Kingsmill, 23 August 1598, S.P. 63/202/3/34, i; Hayes-McCoy, *Irish Battles*, pp. 120–22.

33. Captain Charles Montague's report, 16 August 1598, S.P. 63/202/3/20, i; Montague to Ormonde, 16 August 1598, S.P. 63/202/3/28, ii, Lieutenant Taaffe to H. Shee, 16 August 1598, S.P. 63/202/3/28, iii, Declarations of captains Ferdinando and Kingsmill, 23 August 1598, S.P. 63/202/3/34, i; Declarations of captains Percy and Devereux, 2 October 1598, S.P. 63/202/3/94, i.

34. Lieutenant Taaffe to H. Shee, 16 August 1598, S.P. 63/202/3/28, iii; Declarations of captains Ferdinando and Kingsmill, 23 August 1598, S.P. 63/202/3/34, i; Opinion of Colonel Billings, August 1598, S.P. 63/202/3/56; Declarations of captains Percy and Devereux, 2 October 1598, S.P. 63/202/3/94, i; Declarations of captains Willis, Alford, and Pooley, 2 October 1598, S.P. 63/202/3/94, ii; Declaration of Captain Parker, 2 October 1598, S.P. 63/202/3/94, iii; Add. MSS, 4763, ff. 151–151v.

35. Declarations of captains Ferdinando and Kingsmill, 23 August 1598, S.P. 63/202/3/34, i.

36. Opinion of Colonel Billings, August 1598, S.P. 63/202/3/56.

37. Ormonde to Cecil, 24 August 1598, S.P. 63/202/3/36.

38. Hayes-McCoy, *Irish Battles*, p. 127.

39. *Ibid.*, pp. 127–28.

40. Montague to Ormonde, 16 August 1598, S.P. 63/202/3/28, ii.

41. Fenton to Cecil, 28 February 1600, S.P. 63/207/1/133.

42. Spenser, *Present State of Ireland*, pp. 100–01.

43. NLI, MS 669, f. 2v.

44. Spenser, *Present State of Ireland*, p. 59.

45. NLI, MS 669, f. 1.

46. Chichester to Mountjoy, 14 May 1601, S.P. 63/208/2/91, i.

47. Fynes Moryson, *An Itinerary Containing his ten Yeeres travell through the Twelve Dominions of Germany, Bohmerland, Sweitzerland, Netherland, Denmarke, Poland, Italy, Turkey, France, England, Scotland and Ireland*, 4 vols. (Glasgow: James MacLehose and Sons, 1908), II: 59.

48. *Ibid.*

49. Captain Nicholas Dawtrey to Cecil, 28 October 1600, S.P. 63/207/5/123.

50. Sir Francis Stafford to Cecil, 4 October 1600, S.P. 63/207/5/79.

51. Stafford to Sir George Carey, 19 October 1600, S.P. 63/207/5/108, i.

52. Sir Robert Lovell to the Earl of Essex, 5 October 1600, S.P. 63/207/5/80.

53. Journal of the Lord Deputy's proceedings from 20 September to 3 October 1600, S.P. 63/207/5/74.

54. Mountjoy's Journal, 28 October 1600, S.P. 63/207/5/122.

55. *Ibid.*

56. Lovell to Essex, 5 October 1600, S.P. 63/207/5/80.

57. Mountjoy's Journal, 28 October 1600, S.P. 63/207/5/122.

58. Stafford to Cecil, 4 October 1600, S.P. 63/207/5/79.

59. Mountjoy's Journal, 28 October 1600, S.P. 63/207/5/122.

60. Lovell to Essex, 5 October 1600, S.P. 63/207/5/80.

61. Fenton to Cecil, 9 October 1600, S.P. 63/207/5/87.

62. Advertisements out of Fermanagh sent to Fenton, 22 October 1600, S.P. 63/207/5/120, i.

63. *Ibid.*

64. Stafford to Cecil, 4 October 1600, S.P. 63/207/5/79.

65. Carew to Privy Council, 17 June 1600, S.P. 63/207/3/113; Carew to Privy Council, 18 July 1600, S.P. 63/207/4/26; Docwra to Privy Council, 23 April 1601, S.P. 63/208/2/19; Sir Henry Docwra, *A Narration of the Services done by the Army ymployed to Lough Foyle under the leadinge of me SR Henry Docwra, Knight*, ed. John O'Donovan (Dublin: The Celtic Society, 1849), pp. 250–51.

66. Lughaidh O'Clerigh, *Beath Aodha Ruaidh Ui Dhomhnaill, The Life of Aodh Ruadh O'Domhnaill*, ed. Paul Walsh (Dublin: Irish Texts Society, 1948), p. 45.

67. *Four Masters*, V: 2281–83.

68. Moryson, *Itinerary*, III: 80–81.

69. *Ibid.*, pp. 11–14.

70. *Four Masters*, V: 2275–77.

71. Moryson, *Itinerary*, III: 34.

72. Though O'Donnell's march was remarkable to the English, similar feats were commonplace among Celtic armies from Caesar's Gallic wars to the Scottish rising of the 'Forty-five. O'Clerigh, *O'Donnell Life*, p. 323; Falls, *Elizabeth's Irish Wars*, pp. 296–97; Hayes-McCoy, *Irish Battles*, p. 156; *Four Masters*, V: 2277–79.

73. Hayes-McCoy, *Irish Battles*, pp. 156–58; Moryson, *Itinerary*, III: 42–43, 75–76.

74. Moryson, *Itinerary*, III: 28.

75. *Ibid.*, p. 73.

76. *Ibid.*, p. 74.

77. *Four Masters*, V: 2283.

78. Power to Cecil, 27 December 1601, S.P. 63/209/260; *Four Masters*, V: 2281–83.

79. *Four Masters*, V: 2231.

80. *Ibid.*, p. 2283.

81. Power to Cecil, 27 December 1601, S.P. 63/209/260; Mountjoy and Council to Lord Chancellor and Council, 1 January 1602, S.P. 63/210/1/ i; Moryson, *Itinerary*, III: 76–77; *Four Masters*, V: 2283–85.

82. Power to Cecil, 27 December 1601, S.P. 63/209/260; Moryson, *Itinerary*, III: 78–79; Hayes-McCoy, *Irish Battles*, pp. 163–63; Falls, *Elizabeth's Irish Wars*, pp. 305–06.

83. Moryson, *Itinerary*, III: 79–81; Power to Cecil, 27 December 1601, S.P. 63/209/260; Sir Edward Wynfield to Cecil, 25 December 1601, S.P. 63/209/255; Carew to Cecil, 26 December 1601, S.P. 63/209/256; Hayes-McCoy, *Irish Battles*, pp. 165–67; NLI, MS 669, f. 11.

84. *Four Masters*, V: 2287–89.

85. Falls, *Elizabeth's Irish Wars*, p. 307; Hayes-McCoy, *Irish Battles*, p. 168.

86. Moryson, *Itinerary*, III: 81.

87. *Ibid.*, pp. 11–13.

88. Grady McWhiney and Perry D. Jamieson, *Attack and Die: Civil War Military Tactics and the Southern Heritage* (University, Alabama: The University of Alabama Press, 1982), p. 7.

89. Captain Thomas Reade to Cecil, 9 January 1599, S.P. 63/203/7.

4

Montrose and MacColla and the Civil War in Scotland, 1644–1647

During the civil war in Scotland between the Royalists and Covenanters (1644–1647) three factors emerged that would exert a tremendous influence on Gaelic warfare in the next century. First was the escalation of a long-standing feud between the MacDonalds and Campbells; second was the widening gulf between the military practices and organization of the Gaels and their English and Lowland enemies; and third was the introduction of the 'Highland charge'.[1] Alasdair MacColla, the champion of Clan Donald and the most remarkable Gaelic warrior of the century, was instrumental in all three. Allied with James Graham, Marquis of Montrose, the Royalist commander-in-chief in Scotland, MacColla and his Gaels defeated the Scottish Covenanting armies in five major battles and twice ravaged the home territories of Clan Campbell. From a tactical standpoint these successes were based on the Highland charge conducted against an enemy just beginning the transition from primitive to modern warfare. In the 1640s the Royalist clans held every conceivable battlefield advantage. They were led by the MacDonalds (the implacable enemies of the Campbells), who represented the strongest power bloc in the Gaelic world. They faced a Lowland enemy who could not compete with them in irregular warfare and who had not yet mastered the art of modern conventional war. In addition they had devised a new tactic — the Highland charge — that the enemy could not defend himself against.

The Gaelic civil war between MacDonald and Campbell that raged within the larger framework of the civil war in Scotland had its immediate roots in the policies of the Stuart kings of Scotland from 1597 to 1620. As early as the fifteenth century the Scottish kings had attempted to extend royal influence over the Gaelic regions by enlisting the aid of the Campbells. In 1597 Archibald Campbell, the seventh Earl of Argyll (the MacCailein Mor), used his influence with James VI to advance his territorial claims against Clan Donald South. He received the former MacDonald lands in Kintyre and Jura in 1607 on condition that these holdings would not be re-leased to any members of that clan and was created king's lieutenant in the southern Isles to forestall a MacDonald attempt to regain them.[2]

James VI exacerbated relations between MacDonald and Campbell in 1608 by kidnapping several pro-MacDonald chiefs and forcing them to comply with nine reform measures called the Statutes of Icolmkill (Iona). Through these statutes the government hoped to transform Highland society into something akin to the society of the anglicized Lowlander. The measures, among other things, forced a chief's eldest son and presumed successor to take his education in Lowland schools where he would be taught the English language.[3] Despite the government's best administrative efforts, the statutes were never fully enforced, but the Edinburgh-Campbell alliance kept Clan Donald South at bay from 1608 to 1614.[4]

In 1614–1615 Clan Ian Mor, the dominant sept of Clan Donald South, rose out against the Edinburgh-Campbell alliance, prompting King James to suppress the uprising. In 1616 the Privy Council of Scotland began invoking certain provisions of the Statutes of Icolmkill. The government now relied upon its own military strength combined with the power of the Campbells to enforce the measures. The MacDonalds and associated septs were forbidden to carry firearms or to consume large amounts of whisky, and every clan was required to turn a sizeable portion of its pasture land into arable. In addition, further steps were taken to eradicate the use of Gaelic. The government's overbearing military presence and the temporary enforcement of these and other provisions resulted in the destruction of Clan Ian Mor by 1617. For several years thereafter many western chiefs came to accept royal interference in their personal affairs, since clan violence and rebellion were forbidden on pain of summons to the council in Edinburgh. James's repressive attempts to integrate Gaelic society into Lowland society, however, had only temporary and superficial effects on the Highlanders.[5]

Though Clan Ian Mor was crushed, the rising of 1614–1615 was only the beginning of Clan Donald's struggle to regain its lost patrimony and re-establish its dominance in the western Highlands and Isles. In 1617 several important MacDonald chiefs and their clans lived in humiliation as Campbell tenants on land that once had belonged to them. MacCailein Mor's power in the south-western Highlands could be checked now only by royal authority, and James VI had long realized the danger of permitting one clan — even the loyal Campbells — to become too strong. So in 1620 he took steps to create a balance of power in the area between MacCailein Mor and the MacDonalds. Several MacDonald chiefs received royal pensions, and more importantly, Ranald MacDonnell was created first Earl of Antrim. Most clan leaders made no attempt to increase their influence in the west; Antrim's son Ranald, however, second Earl and first Marquis of Antrim, sponsored the Irish MacDonnell effort led by Alasdair MacColla to destroy the power of the Edinburgh-Campbell alliance during the civil war in Scotland.[6]

MacColla's landing in Scotland with 2,500 Irish veterans in July 1644 signaled the start of an all-out effort by Clan Donald to destroy the Campbells. MacColla attempted to recruit in the Highlands, but because of the clan chiefs' tradition of not serving under another of comparable rank, he was unsuccessful. It was only after Montrose joined MacColla that the Highland chiefs would consent to join the cause. Montrose, as commander-in-chief of the Highland army, was not so much concerned with revenge on Clan Campbell as with their role as supporters of the Lowland Covenanters. Naturally, a disagreement between MacColla and Montrose surfaced concerning the objectives of their union: MacColla had come for Campbell blood; Montrose demanded a fight against the Covenanters. Though most of the clans were probably of the same mind as MacColla, they were forced by the peculiar circumstances of their alliance to follow Montrose's directives. But the Gaels saved their best efforts for Clan Campbell.[7]

When MacDonald faced Campbell, both sides fought a primitive, irregular type of warfare; when the Royalist Gaels faced the Lowland Covenanters, however, considerable military differences were apparent. Lowland Scotland and England stood on the verge of what proved to be a gradual, but often erratic, alteration of their land forces. During the Thirty Years' War (1618–1648) Gustavus Adolphus of Sweden introduced a number of sweeping reforms in the areas of tactics, organization, and equipment that enhanced both mobility and firepower as well as troop morale.[8] But since the death of Elizabeth I the English had lagged behind the continental powers in adopting such improvements. James I (1603–1625) showed little interest in military matters. His son Charles attempted to revitalize the army, but was unequal to the task. So for much of the reigns of the first two Stuart kings of both England and Scotland, the realm's military forces fell into a state of disrepair.[9]

When civil war broke out in the 1640s, the nation still had no standing army or coherent military policy or organization and was forced to depend upon inadequately armed local militia for domestic defense and upon hastily raised recruits, usually of poor quality, for foreign expeditions. There were, of course, many Lowland and English gentlemen who took up the sword as a livelihood, but among the citizenry military service was generally unpopular. Personnel problems were further complicated by deficiencies in equipment and organization. Though the continental powers made progress in the area of field artillery, the English and Lowland Scots rarely employed anything more imaginative or effective than cumbersome siege guns. Nor did they imitate the Germans and the Swiss by organizing engineer units, divisions under the command of a permanent general officer, or field armies that contained and could coordinate infantry, cavalry, and artillery. They had no officer corps that was systematically trained to lead armies in modern warfare. Simply put, the English and Lowland Scots in 1640 had yet to cultivate a military system that was capable of fighting in the conventional manner of the day.[10]

The primitive warfare of the Gaels made the slow modernization of the English forces more of a liability than an advantage to them. The Covenanters had come to consider firearms as the primary weapons for infantry and dragoons, displacing the blade weapons of the recent past. They possessed artillery and were familiar with it, even though it played a negligible role in the campaign. Lowland armies were led by commanders who increasingly considered their proper place on the battlefield to be behind the front lines where they could coordinate the movement of the troops. In contrast, the Gaels considered firearms a poor second choice to the sword, thought artillery an unnecessary burden, and were led into battle by warrior-captains to whom drawing first blood was a point of honor. The old Celtic charge without refinement would have been enough to render ineffectual the Covenanting army's relative modernism. Their firearms were too inaccurate to break the charge's impetus and were useless in close combat. They relied too little on the blade weapons which could have given them parity with the Gaels in the hand-to-hand combat that followed the charge. In addition, the inexperienced forces probably could have benefited more from a general who led by example than one who directed them from the rear.

The refinements that MacColla brought to the charge probably had little impact on the outcome of the campaigns of the 1640s but would contribute hugely to the successes of the next century. The first refinement was the use of firearms, and the second, a change in formation after the charge began. The troops would array themselves in line of battle, fire a volley when within twenty or thirty paces, fling away their muskets, and then quickly deploy into clusters of twelve to fourteen men each. Each cluster would advance through the musket smoke with the new single-handed broadsword or the ancient claymore, and seek to pierce the enemy line at a particular point. The initial volley was intended not to cause great loss of life, but to disorganize the enemy and also to provide the black smokescreen from which the charge was staged. The formation change was meant to concentrate the onslaught of the charge and to provide more safety in numbers than there would be in a single line.[11]

The effectiveness of the Highland charge was demonstrated at Tippermuir, the initial battle of the war. The Royalist army easily routed a force about twice its size. The Covenanters had at least 5,000 to 6,000 foot and 700 horse but were poorly trained and led.[12] The Covenanting commander apparently did not expect the Royalists to attack because of their inferior numbers and lack of cavalry and firearms, so he sent forward his dragoons. The Gaels, however, met the charge with one of their own. If the Gaels had acted according to the dictates of contemporary tactics, they would have fired and reloaded for another volley. Then the Covenanters could have rapidly despatched their foot before the Gaels were ready to fire again. MacColla's Irish and the Highlanders, however, were not bound by textbook tactics. After firing their customary volley, they flung away their muskets and came on sword in hand. The counterattack shocked the Covenanting rank and file of burgesses and shopkeepers, and they suffered tremendous casualties. Over 1,000 Lowlanders fell in the three-mile flight from the battlefield to Perth.[13]

Tippermuir and the subsequent battle of Aberdeen helped to dispel the myth that the Celts could not stand up to cavalry attack. MacColla's Irish regiments disposed of the enemy horse at the outset of the battle by opening ranks and allowing the Covenanters to penetrate. They then quickly closed ranks, and surrounded and annihilated them. They were so (uncharacteristically) well trained that they had little difficulty in regrouping to stage the Highland charge and routing the inexperienced Covenanting infantry.[14]

Victories in the autumn of 1644 illustrated the brute strength and savagery of the Highland and Irish army. One chronicler noted that the Highland charge affected ' . . . both horse and foot men so desperately as they fell first into confusion and disorder . . . '[15] After neither battle did the Irish give quarter to the enemy. Instead, they pursued the Covenanters into Perth and Aberdeen and unmercifully set upon the townsfolk of Aberdeen, plundering and slaughtering for three days. The ransacking of the town was described by an observer who witnessed MacColla's men ' . . . hewing and cutting down all manner of man they could overtake within the town, upon the streets, or in their houses . . . ,' causing ' . . . pitiful howling, crying, weeping, mourning through all the streets'.[16]

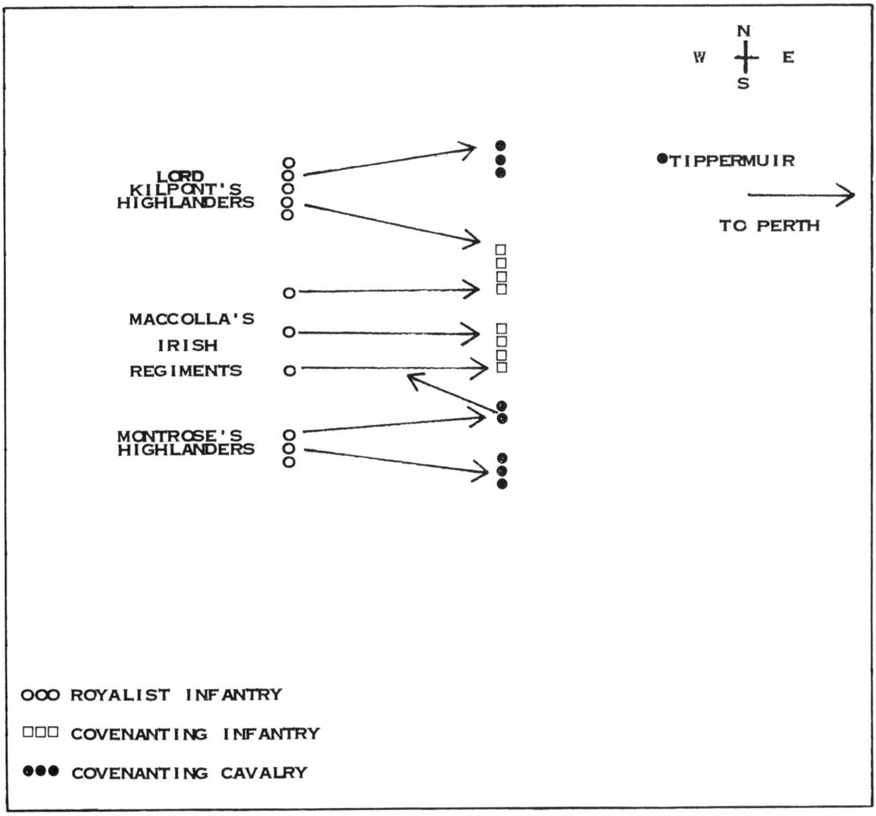

MAP 7. TIPPERMUIR 1644

The Covenanters' inept military performance contrasts with a contemporary's exaggerated description of an Irish soldier after the battle who was observed

> ... trailing his leg, so shattered at the thigh by a cannonball that it hung by a mere thread of skin. Observing his comrades somewhat dismayed at his misfortune, he hailed them with a loud cheery voice, 'Ha, comrades, such is the luck of war; neither you nor I should be sorry for it. Do your work manfully. As for me, sure my Lord Marquis will make me a trooper, now I am no good for the foot.' With these words he coolly drew his knife, without flinching cut away the skin with his own hand, and gave the leg to a comrade to bury.[17]

It is not an exaggeration to say that the Highlanders and Irish were heroic and that their actions ' ... raised the courage and spirit of the Gael from that [time] forth, in so much that they did not turn their backs to the enemy, either on even terms or under a disdavantage ... '[18]

Despite their initial successes, MacColla and Montrose faced the task of keeping together a considerable body of fighting men as the clansmen moved farther from their own territories. Since their union on the heather-strewn braes of Atholl, they

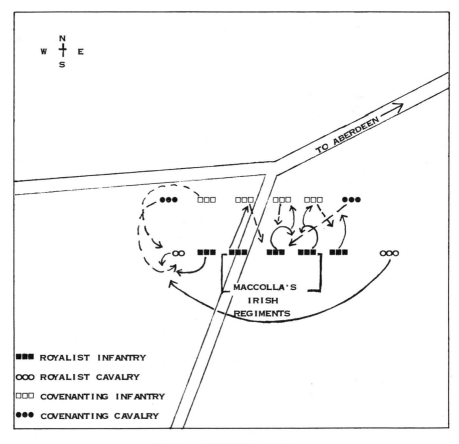

MAP 8.   ABERDEEN   1644

had suffered frequent desertions, and the Royalist generals were unable to count on the steady support of the Highlanders because of their erratic comings and goings. For several months after Aberdeen, MacColla and Montrose had to abandon the initiative and scurry to and fro through the glens in search of recruits. Their success can be partly attributed to the promise of plunder (and not from the Highlanders' loyalty to the king) and partly to the prospect of revenge on the Campbells.

MacColla knew that to maintain the army in the field he must persuade Montrose to sanction a campaign into Argyllshire in the winter of 1644–1645. The MacDonalds had not faced the Campbells either at Tippermuir or Aberdeen, and after two easy victories they were spoiling for a fight with the Argyllshiremen. When the plans became known throughout the Highlands, the Royalists' recruiting problems were temporarily solved.[19] The assault on Argyllshire in mid-December was a way for the MacDonalds to reclaim their lost possessions and avenge past humiliations. No Campbell prisoners were to be taken. The Royalist army of 3,000 men gained entrance into Argyllshire with the aid of Clan

MacNab and swept down on the Campbell capital of Inveraray, forcing MacCailein Mor to flee for his life, and then burned and looted its way back northward through Lorne.[20] One of MacColla's Irish officers wrote that ' . . . throughout Argyll, we left neither house nor hold unburned, nor corn nor cattle, that belonged to the whole name of Campbell'.[21] Nearly 900 Campbells were slaughtered and the Royalist army drove well over 1,000 cattle northward with them.[22] '*S'fada glaodh o Lochow*' no longer rang true.

The Argyllshire raid, the first contact between rival Gaelic forces during the war, revealed an even greater degree of savagery among MacColla's troops than that displayed earlier against the Lowlanders. Generally, when Gael fought Gael, honor and courage were rewarded by a lenient attitude concerning the final kill. If, during a MacDonald-MacLean feud, for example, both sides demonstrated prowess and courage on the battlefield, it was likely that the number of fatalities would be relatively low as each side 'rewarded' the other by sparing as many warriors as possible. Only those who behaved in a cowardly manner would be killed. Thus each clan upheld its honor at minimal cost. When the clans faced the Lowlanders, however, especially those who would not stand and fight manfully, the slaughter that followed resulted from contempt for cowardly behavior. Their attitude toward and relationship with the Campbells was of a different nature entirely. The anti-Campbell clans recognized that their traditional enemies were from the same ethnic and cultural background as they themselves were. They also recalled many brave feats performed by Campbells on the battlefield. But to the Royalists in 1644–1645 Campbell prowess in battle could not overshadow their treason — alliance with the Lowlanders and English. Thus the Argyllshire raid in part was a manifestation of the general opinion that the Campbells had sold their souls to the foreigner for profit, security, and power. Traditional Highland honor would settle for no less than destruction of the ill-gotten gains of MacCailein Mor.

Though the raid into Argyllshire first brought the MacDonalds face to face with the Campbells, their greatest confrontation came at the battle of Inverlochy (2 February 1645) — one of the most spectacular victories in Celtic history. After marching north from MacCailein Mor's ravaged territories, MacColla and Montrose were confronted at either end of the Great Glen by superior forces.[23] MacColla and Montrose chose to advance toward the 3,000 Campbells and Lowlanders, but to preserve the element of surprise they avoided the traditional route down the Great Glen. Instead, they marched south up Glen Tarff, through the snow-covered pass of Glen Turret and over the 'Parallel Roads' into Glen Roy, where they crossed the river Spean and re-entered the Great Glen on the northern shoulder of Ben Nevis near Inverlochy. Such a march would have been difficult enough during the summer when the mountain passes were free of ice and snow, but to traverse thirty miles of trackless wilderness in two days in the dead of winter was quite a feat — even for the hardiest of Highlanders.[24] In addition, they suffered from a shortage of food since they had not had time to make use of their plunder before beginning the trek. 'The most part of them had not tasted a bit of bread these two days, marching high mountains in knee deep snow, and wading brooks and rivers up to their girdle.'[25]

The march to Inverlochy, comparable to Hugh O'Donnell's crossing of the Slievefelim Mountains in 1601, was the Highlanders' severest physical test of the war. It well illustrates the mobility and endurance of the Highland army. They carried with them only what they needed to sustain themselves — weapons, plaids, and oatmeal. Earlier visitors to the Highlands wrote with amazement of their deprivations:

> The Scots are bold, hardy, and much inured to war ... They march from twenty to four-and-twenty leagues without halting, as well by night as day ... They bring no carriages with them on account of the mountains they have to pass ... Neither do they carry with them any provisions of bread or wine ... they will live for a long time on flesh half sodden ... They have, therefore, no occasion for pots or pans; for they dress the flesh of their cattle in the skins, after they have taken them off ... Each man carries a ... little bag of oatmeal ... it is therefore no wonder that they perform a longer day's march than other soldiers.[26]

With the completion of their march down the Great Glen, the Royalist army stood poised on the flank of MacCailein Mor's Campbells. MacColla and Montrose huddled with their men in the cold darkness, having neither food nor fire, and awaited the dawn.[27]

A comparison of the two armies at Inverlochy shows that while the Campbell-Covenanting force outnumbered the Royalists by a two-to-one ratio (3,000 to 1,500), the latter was actually stronger. Both sides possessed little cavalry or artillery and were armed in much the same fashion with sword, musket, target, bow, and axe. The apparent numerical advantage enjoyed by the Campbell-Covenanting army is deceptive; of their 3,000 men about 1,100 were Lowlanders who were unfamiliar with Highland warfare. The remaining 1,900 were Campbells and Campbell allies. If the Lowlanders are discounted, the two armies appear to have been about equal, but the Lowlanders were actually a liability and the Campbells would have fared better without them. The Royalist army, of course, was predominantly Gaelic and was well skilled in carrying out the Highland charge.[28]

At dawn MacColla and Montrose arrayed their troops in battle formation. The Irish were not posted at their customary spot in the middle of the line, but were placed on the flanks to allow them to oppose the Lowlanders on either wing of the main body of Campbells.[29] The Highland clans took the middle of the line so that they could face their traditional enemy, who had brought 'all ... their prime men, ... the greatest strength of the army ... '[30] The men of Clan Campbell stood ' ... stout and gallant ... but were ... worthy of a better chief and a juster cause ... '[31]

The battle began when MacColla's troops charged on the flanks, holding their fire until they were close enough to the enemy to ' ... fire their beards ... '[32] The volley threw the Campbell-Covenanting army into momentary confusion and allowed the Irish to drive the hapless Lowland foot into the hard-fighting Campbells. The Campbell formation was disrupted and their view of the battlefield obstructed.[33] Having to fend off the Irish on both flanks, the Campbell

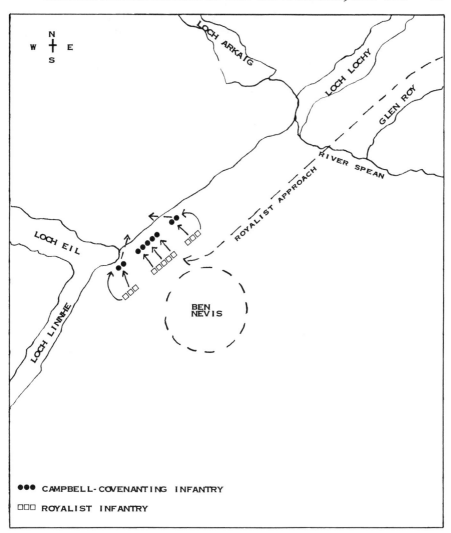

MAP 9.   INVERLOCHY 1 6 4 5

center also faced the onrushing hordes of Clan Donald from the front. When the MacDonalds charged, they caught the Campbell front ranks off balance and drove them back onto their reserves. MacCailein Mor's army fled the battlefield in confusion.[34]

The coordinated attack of MacColla's Irish regiments on the flanks and the MacDonalds in the center of the line was the key to a quick and inexpensive Royalist victory. The Lowland veterans could not stave off MacColla's Irish, and when the battle came to blows, they were no match for the expert Gaelic swordsmen. Their rapid dispersal and retreat toward the center of the line not only blinded the main body of Campbells but also forced them to bunch together in a formation that restricted their mobility, while the charging MacDonalds kept enough distance from one another to allow efficient use of the broadsword and target. Campbell casualties were high — over 1,500. MacColla and Montrose had only four killed and about 200 wounded, a small sacrifice to singe MacCailein Mor's beard and debunk the myth of the Campbells' invincibility in the western Highlands.[35]

The victory at Inverlochy boosted the Highlanders' spirits and brought new recruits to the cause as word spread of MacColla's heroics. The foremost Gaelic poet of the seventeenth century wrote:

> Have you heard of the heroic countermarch made by the army that was at Kilcumin? Far has gone the fame of their play — they drove their enemies before them.
>
> Early on Sunday morning I climbed the brae above the castle of Inverlochy. I saw the army arraying for battle, and victory on the field was with Clan Donald.
>
> . . .
>
> Whoever should climb Tom n h-Aire (would find there) many a freshly hacked paw badly pickled, and the film of death on their lifeless eyes from the slashing they had from sword-blades.
>
> . . .
>
> Alasdair of the sharp cleaving blade, you promised yesterday to destroy them; you directed the rout past the castle, an excellent plan for keeping in touch with them.
>
> . . .
>
> Were you familiar with the Goirtean Odhar? Well was it manured, not by the dung of sheep or goats, but by the blood of Campbells after it had congealed.[36]

> John MacDonald
> 'The Battle of Inverlochy'

In contrast, the mood in the Lowlands was somber: 'This disaster did extremely amaze us. I verily think had Montrose come presently from that battle, he should have had no great opposition . . . scarce till he had come to Edinburgh'.[37] On 11 February both Montrose and MacColla were declared guilty of treason by the Scottish Parliament.[38] The Church of Scotland echoed the sentiment on the following day, denouncing ' . . . the hellish crew under the conduct of the excommunicate and forfaulted Earl of Montrose, and of Alaster Mac-Donald, a

Papist and Outlaw ... '[39] MacColla, Montrose, and the clans cast an ominous shadow upon the Lowlands after Inverlochy and raised the spectre of savage terror. In the winter of 1645 Lowlanders cast frequent nervous glances at the barren, snow-covered Highlands, as if expecting Satan himself to descend. A contemporary observer wrote:

> There is nothing heard now up and down the kingdom but alarms and rumors, rendezvous of clans, every chieftain mustering his men, called weaponshows. Montrose and Mackoll in every man's mouth ... and if a few goats be seen upon the tops of the hills in a twilight it is concluded to be Coll Coll Mackoll (Colonel Alexander MacColl).[40]

MacColla's fierce reputation and rumors of numerous clan risings clouded the Lowlanders' perception of the Highland army's weaknesses. Though the Highland clans were intoxicated by their recent successes against the Campbells, their fighting strength had diminished due to desertion as they moved away from their home territories. As long as they fought at home or in the Campbells' south-western Highlands, they represented an army that could hold its own with any in the British Isles. But as a serious threat below the Highland line, they were hampered by that age-old Celtic inability to keep together an army that could conduct a sustained campaign. In truth the inhabitants of Edinburgh, Perth, Glasgow, and other burghs had little to dread from the Highland army as long as they did not meet the Highlanders on their own terms (irregular warfare) or turf (the wilderness). The solution to the Highland problem was simple: tempt the clans to attack the towns. Nothing except great quantities of plunder could send the Highlanders home faster than a long march with little prospect of a quick and furious attack at its completion. Oddly enough, no commander seriously attempted to frustrate the clans by these means until the campaigns of 1689–1690.

Despite widespread desertion by the clans after the intoxication of Inverlochy had worn off, the Royalist army at Auldearn[41] (May 1645) still contained enough Gaelic troops to give a distinctive Celtic flavor to the battle. MacColla seized the initiative from the advancing Covenanters by personally leading over 400 Irishmen into the enemy's vanguard of 500 Campbells. MacColla initially gave ground under the weight of superior firepower but managed to establish a tenable defensive post behind a series of walls and dikes west of the village. No sooner had he repelled the Campbells' initial assault than he abandoned cover and again led his Irishmen into the fray. His second charge bought Montrose enough time to deploy his infantry flanked on both sides by cavalry.[42] The Irish withstood several determined counterattacks before being driven back to their defenses. The Covenanting cavalry then put pressure on both their flanks and might have annihilated them if Montrose's cavalry had not arrived to rescue MacColla's right wing. The Covenanters were overrun by the main force of Montrose's infantry before they could recover from the shock of the cavalry charge and suffered over 2,000 casualties.[43]

At Auldearn the Gaels demonstrated their traditional unwillingness to remain on the defensive even when they possessed a strong position. Like O'Neill at the

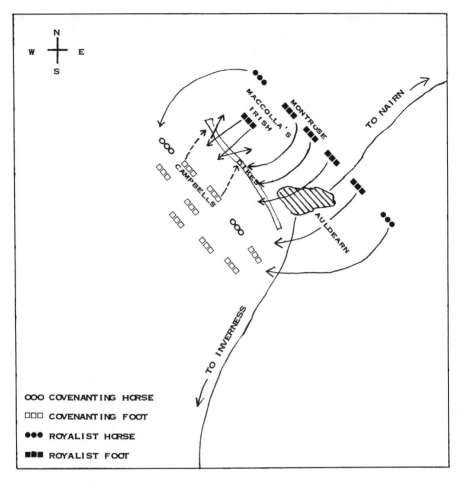

MAP 10. AULDEARN 1645

Moyry Pass, MacColla attacked the attacking army. But whereas O'Neill's men employed natural and manmade obstacles that served to delay the enemy and position them for the well orchestrated volleys, the hardier and heavier-armed Antrim MacDonnells and Highland Scots looked only to possess a piece of ground from which they might sweep down with the Highland charge and hack the enemy ranks to pieces.

Auldearn also illustrated the ever-widening gulf between the battlefield actions of Celtic leaders, on the one hand, and English and Lowland leaders on the other. While the English commanders directed their armies from the rear, MacColla led his troops into battle against the Campbells and provided for his men an example of raw courage and expert swordsmanship. The personal heroics of MacColla and the Gaels were immortalized in verse:

Health and joy to the valiant Alasdair who won the
battle of Auldearn with his army;

With his fine soldiers, who at the outset of their march,
loved to sing his marching song.

You were not a feeble poltroon engaging in the crossing
of swords when you were in the enclosure alone.

Helmeted men with pikes in their hands were attacking
you with all their might until you were relieved by
    Montrose . . . [44]

> John MacDonald
> 'A Song to Alasdair MacColla
> after the battle of Auldearn'

Another bard wrote in a similar vein: 'Many were the warlike feats performed on the battlefield by the MacDonalds and Gordons . . .'[45]

MacColla's and Montrose's success at Kilsyth (August 1645), their last combined victory, resulted from a battlefield scenario that allowed the Gaels to utilize their individual courage and skills to a greater degree than in any previous battle of the war. MacColla's Irish and the Highland infantry occupied the center of the Royalist line, flanked on either wing by cavalry. When the Covenanter cavalry advanced, some of the impatient Gaelic infantry attacked without orders. MacColla then unleashed the remainder of the clans, who vied with each other for the honor of first laying sword to Lowland flesh. Clanranald won the contest and dismounted scores of enemy riders by slashing furiously at their mounts. Montrose had no choice except to order forward the rest of the army. The Irish foot and the cavalry followed hard on the heels of the MacDonalds, MacLeans, and other clans, who fought that day half naked, casting away their plaids to offset the heat. With the Covenanting cavalry routed, the infantry fled from the wild Highlanders. In the ensuing panic over 3,500 of their 7,000 men were killed or wounded.[46]

The Highland element of the Royalist army exhibited several traditionally Celtic military traits that caused control of the battle to slip away from the Royalist generals: an imperviousness to orders from all except their own chiefs; a general lack of discipline; an inability to stand patiently on the defensive; and an all-pervading lust for martial heroics as exemplified by the Clanranald-MacLean contest. But these traits also contributed to the easy and inexpensive victory at Kilsyth. The Gaels' reckless abandon and their reputations as expert swordsmen surrounded them with an aura of savagery that few Lowlanders had nerve enough to face. They routed the last remaining Covenanting army in Scotland and forced most of the leading Covenanters to flee to the safety of England or Ireland.

Kilsyth marked the end of Montrose's ever tenuous control over the Gaels. The country had been at his mercy after Kilsyth, but the Gaels again deserted; as the

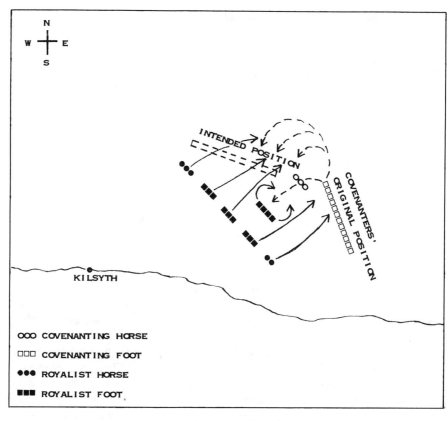

MAP 11 . KILSYTH 1645

Highland clans wandered north into the hills to store away their plunder, Montrose must have sensed the beginning of the end for the Royalist cause. Then MacColla himself left for Argyllshire with 500 Highlanders and 120 of his own troops. Montrose's subsequent defeat at Philiphaugh in September, where he lost the remainder of MacColla's Irishmen, dismissed all hope of subduing the Lowlands.[47] MacColla's and Clan Donald's priorities at no time during the war shone more clearly than when they abandoned the Royalist army and marched into Argyllshire for a second campaign against the Campbells.[48]

MacColla's second campaign in Argyllshire was not a continuation of the war between Royalist and Covenanter, but a resumption of the MacDonald-Campbell civil war. As the Highlanders marched virtually unopposed through the Campbell territories, word spread of MacColla's expedition of plunder. From out of the glens a flood of eager recruits poured forth, especially among the MacDonalds of Clan Ian Mor. Many of the deserters from Montrose's camp after Kilsyth again rose in arms anxious to confront their ancient enemy. About 600 clansmen from Lochaber began ravaging Campbell territories to the north of MacColla's army. In December the two bodies of Highlanders joined, giving MacColla nearly 2,000

Highland fighters who wished to extinguish from the face of the earth the name of Campbell.[49]

Despite the expectations of Clan Donald, the second plundering of Argyllshire turned out to be a pale imitation of the first expedition there in the winter of 1644-1645. It was no more than an uncoordinated campaign of pillage before MacColla's evacuation to Ulster. His troops moved through the rugged south-western Highlands, easily outpacing a stronger Covenanting force in pursuit, and finally reached the Kintyre peninsula. There they remained undisturbed for several months, prepared no defense against a tracking army, and withdrew finally to Islay and then to Ulster, leaving the Scottish branch of Clan Donald to continue the struggle alone.[50]

The successes of the Royalist army stemmed from their tactical superiority over an enemy that had neither the leadership, training, nor nerve to withstand the Highland charge. The Irish and Highland Scots destroyed the Covenanting armies at Tippermuir and Aberdeen with ease, and even when they faced a mixed force of Covenanters and Campbells, the Royalist Gaels prevailed. Their stiffest challenge came when MacColla was temporarily driven back by the Campbells at Auldearn, but the eventual Royalist victory there and at Kilsyth crowned a rapid succession of triumphs that were cheaply won in terms of casualties. Through the campaign the numbers killed and wounded on the Royalist side were minimal. It is difficult to assess the exact casualty figures for the Covenanters, but they were undoubtedly much higher than those of the Gaels. No specific casualty figures are available for the battles of Tippermuir and Aberdeen because both were great slaughters that took place over a wide expanse of ground. Inverlochy produced few Royalist losses, but the Campbells and Covenanters suffered a casualty rate of nearly fifty per cent (1,500 out of 3,000). At Auldearn MacColla's Irish suffered perhaps 100 killed and wounded (out of 400), while the Covenanting army again lost about half of its 4,000 men. A Covenanting army of some 7,000 men was almost totally destroyed at Kilsyth. Such disparate figures provide conclusive evidence of Gaelic tactical superiority.

The military careers of MacColla and O'Neill provide a comparison that points up the Gaelic inability to implement the fundamentals of modern warfare. Both employed a primitive type of offensive warfare based on the fighting skills of individual warriors; neither had the modern nation-state from which to draw the quantities of men and materials necessary to sustain a prolonged series of campaigns. Each was plagued by frequent desertion and a lack of discipline among the troops. Most importantly, neither could win a victory significant enough to destroy the will and power of the enemy. Like many Celtic commanders before and after them, they won most of the battles but lost the war.

MacColla left the Royalist struggle as quickly as he had come, making his contribution to Gaelic warfare, but not fully resolving his initial motivation for joining the fight. The Campbell-MacDonald feud would continue into the next century and complicate the Jacobite cause. Throughout the remainder of the seventeenth century, MacColla's refinement of the charge would be utilized so effectively that the Gaels would have no impulse to develop other tactical and strategic measures. At the same time, the English would revamp their battlefield tactics and improve weapons and training in order to render Gaelic warfare much less effective in the future.[51]

NOTES

1. David Stevenson, *Alasdair MacColla and the Highland Problem in the Seventeenth Century* (Edinburgh: John Donald Publishers, 1980), pp. 82–83. Stevenson, MacColla's latest biographer, writes that the Highland charge was first used by him in Ireland at the battle of Laney in 1642.

2. Great Britain, General Register House, *The Register of the Privy Council of Scotland*, ed. David Masson, vol. 7 (1604–1607), pp. 426–27 (hereafter cited as RPCS); Donald Gregory, *The History of the Western Highlands and Isles of Scotland from A.D. 1493 to A.D. 1625* (Edinburgh: John Donald Publishers, 1881), pp. 311–12; Stevenson, *Alasdair MacColla*, pp. 26–27. For a complete study of the political relations of James VI and I with the Highland clans, see Maurice Lee, Jr., *Government by Pen: Scotland Under James VI and I* (Chicago: University of Illinois Press, 1980).

3. For a description of each of the Statutes of Icolmkill, see *RPCS*, 9 (1610–1613), pp. 25–30.

4. For a thorough discussion of Clan Ian Mor's activities from 1608 to 1614, see Andrew McKerral, *Kintyre in the Seventeenth Century* (Edinburgh: Oliver and Boyd, 1948), pp. 14–31; Gregory, *Western Highlands and Isles*, pp. 317–18; A. and A. MacDonald, *The Clan Donald*, 3 vols. (Inverness: The Northern Counties Publishing Company, 1896), III: 582–92; George Hill, *An Historical Account of the MacDonnells of Antrim: Including Notices of some other Septs, Irish and Scottish* (Belfast: Archer and Sons, 1873), pp. 194–227; Stevenson, *Alasdair MacColla*, pp. 6–31.

5. W. D. Lamont, *The Early History of Islay, 500–1726* (Dundee: Burns and Harris, 1966), pp. 51–59; *RPCS*, 10 (1613–1616), pp. 671–72; Gregory, *Western Highlands and Isles*, pp. 392–97; Stevenson, *Alasdair MacColla*, pp. 47–48.

6. Stevenson, *Alasdair MacColla*, pp. 49–50; Hill, *MacDonnells of Antrim*, pp. 196–97, 231; J. Lowe, 'The earl of Antrim and Irish aid to Montrose in 1644,' *Irish Sword*, 4 (1959–1960): 191–98.

7. C. O'Danachair, 'Montrose's Irish Regiments,' *Irish Sword*, 3 (1959–1960): 61–67; Edinburgh, National Library of Scotland (hereafter cited as NLS), Wodrow MSS, Quarto 29, f. 64v–65; Patrick Gordon, *A Short Abridgement of Britane's Distemper, from the yeare of God 1639 to 1649* (Aberdeen: The Spalding Club, 1844), pp. 65–67; Charles McNeill, ed., *The Tanner Letters, Original Documents and Notices of Irish Affairs in the Sixteenth and Seventeenth Centuries* (Dublin: The Stationery Office, 1943), p. 177; William Forbes Leith, *Memoirs of Scottish Catholics during the XVIIth and XVIIIth Centuries*, 2 vols. (London: Longmans, Green, and Company, 1909), I: 288–89; Alexander MacBain and Rev. John Kennedy, eds., *Reliquiae Celticae, Texts, Papers, and Studies in Gaelic Literature and Philology, left by the late Rev. Alexander Cameron, LL.D.*, 2 vols. (Inverness: The Northern Counties Publishing Company, 1892–1894), II: 179; John Spalding, *Memorialls of the Trubles in Scotland and in England, A.D. 1624–A.D. 1645*, 2 vols. (Aberdeen: The Spalding Club, 1850–1851), II: 386. The dual nature of the war is personified in the characters and backgrounds of the two Royalist leaders. Montrose, whose family lived in the Forth and Earn valleys along the Highland frontier, was the epitome of the young, handsome, articulate cavalier, carrying himself as confidently in the courts of Europe as on the remote battlefields of Scotland. MacColla, on the other hand, was a

product of the tumultuous Gaelic world of the western Highlands and Isles and Ireland. Born supposedly on the remote Hebridean island of Colonsay, the young MacColla was the archetypal Celtic warrior. John Buchan, *Montrose* (London: Thomas Nelson and Sons, 1928; reprint ed., Edinburgh: The Mercat Press, 1979), pp. 34–35; Gordon, *Britane's Distemper*, p. 64; Stevenson, *Alasdair MacColla*, p. 56. For further reference to MacColla's upbringing and character, see Joseph Lloyd, *Alasdair MacColla* (Baile 'Ata Cliat: Clodanna do 'Connrad na Gaeoilge, 1914).

8. J. W. Fortescue, *A History of the British Army*, 13 vols. (London: MacMillan and Company, 1910–1930), I: 179–185; T. N. Dupuy, *The Military Life of Gustavus Adolphus: Father of Modern War* (New York: Franklin-Watts, 1969), pp. 54–67; André Corvisier, *Armies and Societies in Europe, 1494–1789*, trans. Abigail T. Siddall (Bloomington: Indiana University Press, 1979), p. 18.

9. Fortescue, *British Army*, I: 191–96; Peter Young and J. P. Lawford, eds., *History of the British Army* (New York: G. P. Putnam's Sons, 1970; London: Barker, 1970), p. 11–12. For further evidence of the decline in English and Scottish military capabilities between 1603 and 1640, see G. N. Clark, *War and Society in the Seventeenth Century* (Cambridge: Cambridge University Press, 1958); Lawrence Stone, *Social Change and Revolution in England, 1540–1640* (London: Longmans, 1965); Lindsay Boynton, *The Elizabethan Militia, 1558–1638* (London: Routledge and Kegan Paul, 1967).

10. Young and Lawford, eds., *British Army*, pp. 11–12; Fortescue, *British Army*, I: 216–220.

11. Stevenson, *Alasdair MacColla*, pp. 82–83; General Henry Hawley's Description of Highland Warfare, 12 January 1746, quoted in David, Lord Elcho, *A Short Account of the Affairs of Scotland in the Years 1744, 1745, 1746*, ed. Evan Charteris (Edinburgh: David Douglas, 1907; reprint ed., Edinburgh: James Thin, 1973). Hawley's description of the Highland charge, though it was written one hundred years after MacColla's innovations, gives an accurate picture of how the attack unfolded.

12. George Wishart, *The Memoirs of James, Marquis of Montrose, 1639–1650*, ed. A. B. Murdoch and H. F. M. Simpson (London: Longmans, Green, and Company, 1893), pp. 56–60; Gordon, *Britane's Distemper*, pp. 73–74; MacBain and Kennedy, eds., *Reliquiae Celticae*, II: 179; James Fraser, *Chronicles of the Frasers, The Wardlaw Manuscript* (Edinburgh: Scottish History Society, 1905), pp. 286–87; Oxford, Bodleian Library, Carte MSS, 14, f. 36.

13. Wishart, *Memoirs*, pp. 61–62, 66; Gordon, *Britane's Distemper*, pp. 74–75; Fraser, *Wardlaw MS*, p. 287; Carte MSS, 14, f. 36; Stevenson, *Alasdair MacColla*, pp. 88–89.

14. Henry Guthry, *The Memoirs of Henry Guthry, Late Bishop of Dunkeld* (Glasgow: A. Stalker, 1748), pp. 167–78; J. Stuart, ed., *Extracts from the Council Register of the Burgh of Aberdeen, 1643–1747* (Edinburgh: Scottish Burgh Records Society, 1871–1872), pp. 28–29; Thomas Carte, ed., *A Collection of Original Letters and Papers Concerning the Affairs of England from the year 1641 to 1660*, 2 vols. (London: Society for the Encouragement of Learning, 1739), I: 74; Gordon, *Britane's Distemper*, pp. 81–84; Spalding, *Memorialls*, II: 406–07; Wishart, *Memoirs*, pp. 66–68; Carte MSS, 14, f. 36; The Marchioness of Tullibardine, ed., *A Military History of Perthshire, 1660–1902*, 2 vols. (Perth: R. A. and J. Hay, 1908), I: 251–52.

15. Gordon, *Britane's Distemper*, p. 74.

16. Spalding, *Memorialls*, II: 407.

17. Wishart, *Memoirs*, p. 69.

18. MacBain and Kennedy, eds., *Reliquiae Celticae*, II: 179.

19. Wishart, *Memoirs*, pp. 72–73, 79–80; MacBain and Kennedy, eds., *Reliquiae*

Celticae, II: 181; Guthry, *Memoirs*, pp. 168-69, 172; Spalding, *Memorialls*, II: 419; Stevenson, *Alasdair MacColla*, pp. 140-41, 147, 149.

20. Wishart, *Memoirs*, p. 81; MacBain and Kennedy, eds., *Reliquiae Celticae*, II: 183; Spalding, *Memorialls*, II: 442-43; Gordon, *Britane's Distemper*, pp. 97-98; John Willcock, *The Great Marquess, Life and Times of Archibald, 8th Earl, and 1st (and only) Marquess of Argyll, 1607-1661* (Edinburgh: Oliphant, Anderson, and Ferrier, 1903), pp. 171-72.

21. Carte MSS, 14, f. 36.

22. MacBain and Kennedy, eds., *Reliquiae Celticae*, II: 181-83.

23. Edinburgh, Scottish Record Office, GD. 220/3/184 (hereafter cited as SRO). Before marching to meet the enemy, MacColla, Montrose, and the Royalist officers bound themselves together by signing the Kilcumin Bond.

24. Wishart, *Memoirs*, pp. 82-84; MacBain and Kennedy, eds., *Reliquiae Celticae*, II: 183, 185; Gordon, *Britane's Distemper*, pp. 99-100; Carte MSS, 14, f. 36; Guthry, *Memoirs*, pp. 174-75; Leith, *Scottish Catholics*, I: 296-320; Sir Ewen Cameron of Lochiel, *Memoirs of Sir Ewen Cameron of Lochiell, Chief of the Clan Cameron*, ed. John Drummond (Edinburgh: The Abbotsford Club, 1842), p. 70; W. T. Kilgoure, *Lochaber in War and Peace* (Paisley: Alexander Gardner, 1908), pp. 97-98.

25. Gordon, *Britane's Distemper*, p. 100.

26. P. Hume Brown, ed., *Early Travellers in Scotland* (Edinburgh: David Douglas, 1891; reprint ed., Edinburgh: The Mercat Press, 1978), pp. 8-9.

27. Carte MSS, 14, f. 36; Wishart, *Memoirs*, p. 84; Gordon, *Britane's Distemper*, pp. 100-01; MacBain and Kennedy, eds., *Reliquiae Celticae*, II: 185.

28. Gordon, *Britane's Distemper*, p. 101; Spalding, *Memorialls*, II: 444; Stevenson, *Alasdair MacColla*, p. 156.

29. SRO, PA. 11/3, ff. 129v-130, 148v.

30. Gordon, *Britane's Distemper*, p. 101.

31. Wishart, *Memoirs*, p. 84.

32. Gordon, *Britane's Distemper*, p. 101.

33. Spalding, *Memorialls*, II: 444; MacBain and Kennedy, eds., *Reliquiae Celticae*, II: 185; Gordon, *Britane's Distemper*, p. 101; Wishart, *Memoirs*, pp. 84-85.

34. W. Drummond-Norie, 'Inverlochy, 1431-1645,' *Celtic Monthly*, 5 (1896-1897): 84; Gordon, *Britane's Distemper*, pp. 101-02; Spalding, *Memorialls*, II: 444; MacBain and Kennedy, eds., *Reliquiae Celticae*, II: 185.

35. Mark Napier, *Memorials of Montrose and his Times*, 2 vols. (Edinburgh: The Maitland Club, 1848-1850), II: 179; Carte MSS, 14, f. 36; Spalding, *Memorialls*, II: 444-45; Gordon, *Britane's Distemper*, pp. 101-02; Wishart, *Memoirs*, p. 85; MacBain and Kennedy, eds., *Reliquiae Celticae*, II: 185; Guthry, *Memoirs*, p. 179; Willcock, *The Great Marquess*, p. 174.

36. John MacDonald, 'The Battle of Inverlochy,' *Orain Iain Luim, Songs of John MacDonald, Bard of Keppoch*, ed. A. A. MacKenzie (Edinburgh: The Scottish Gaelic Texts Society, 1964), pp. 21-25.

37. Robert Baillie, *Letters and Journals, 1637-1662*, ed. David Laing, 3 vols. (Edinburgh: Bannatyne Club, 1841-1842), II: 263.

38. Great Britain, General Register House, *The Acts of the Parliaments of Scotland*, ed. Cosmo Innes, vol. 6, i (1643-1660), pp. 317-23 (hereafter cited as *APS*).

39. Church of Scotland, General Assembly, *Records of the Kirk of Scotland, containing the acts and proceedings of the General Assembly, from the year 1638 downwards*, ed. Alexander Peterkin (Edinburgh: J. Sutherland, 1838), p. 425.

40. Fraser, *Wardlaw MS*, p. 289.

41. David Stevenson has expertly reconstructed the battle of Auldearn in *Alasdair MacColla*, pp. 166–94. Correcting numerous errors made by H. C. B. Rogers, *Battles and Generals of the Civil Wars, 1642–1651* (London: Seeley Service and Company, 1968), pp. 217–25; S. R. Gardiner, *History of the Great Civil War*, 4 vols, (London: Longman, Green, and Company, 1893–1894), II: 224–55; C. O'Danachair, 'The Battle of Auldearn, 1645,' *Irish Sword*, 1 (1949–1953): 128–32; and others, Stevenson argues that MacColla's attack on the advancing Covenanters saved the day for Montrose, who had yet to deploy his troops into battle formation on the left flank of the Royalist line. MacColla's charge has traditionally been viewed as an impetuous and tactically unsound move that Montrose was hard-pressed to overcome. Earlier historians concluded that Montrose first had to extricate MacColla from danger before turning his full attention to the remainder of the Covenanting army. Stevenson writes that it was MacColla who saved Montrose before Montrose saved MacColla.

42. Gordon, *Britane's Distemper*, pp. 123–24; Wishart, *Memoirs*, p. 99; MacBain and Kennedy, eds., *Reliquiae Celticae*, II: 187–89; Spalding, *Memorialls*, II: 472–74; John MacDonnell, *The Ulster Civil War of 1641 and its Consequences, with the History of the Irish Brigade under Montrose in 1644–46* (Dublin: M. H. Gill and Sons, 1879), pp. 105–06; Fraser, *Wardlaw MS*, p. 295; Stevenson, *Alasdair MacColla*, pp. 181–83.

43. Stevenson, *Alasdair MacColla*, pp. 174, 183; Gordon, *Britane's Distemper*, pp. 124–27; MacBain and Kennedy, eds., *Reliquiae Celticae*, II: 191–93; Spalding, *Memorialls*, II: 473–74; Wishart, *Memoirs*, pp. 100–01; Leith, *Scottish Catholics*, I: 338–39; Fraser, *Wardlaw MS*, pp. 295–96.

44. MacDonald, 'A Song to Alasdair MacColla after the battle of Auldearn,' *Orain Iain Luim*, p. 27.

45. MacBain and Kennedy, eds., *Reliquiae Celticae*, II: 193.

46. Baillie, *Letters and Journals*, II: 422–24; Wishart, *Memoirs*, pp. 124–25; Leith, *Scottish Catholics*, I: 348–49; MacBain and Kennedy, eds., *Reliquiae Celticae*, II: 201; Gordon, *Britane's Distemper*, pp. 140–45.

47. Wishart, *Memoirs*, pp. 137–46; Gordon, *Britane's Distemper*, pp. 153–60; Guthry, *Memoirs*, pp. 199–204; 16 October 1645, SRO, PA. 12/1; Thomas McCrie, ed., *The Life of Mr. Robert Blair, Minister of St. Andrews* (Edinburgh: The Wodrow Society, 1848), pp. 176–77.

48. NLS, MS 1672, f. 13; Guthry, *Memoirs*, p. 204; Wishart, *Memoirs*, pp. 147–48.

49. Sir Norman Lamont, ed., *An Inventory of the Lamont Papers, 1231–1897* (Edinburgh: Scottish Record Society, 1914), pp. 433–34; *APS*, 6, ii (1643–1660), p. 461, 7 (1661–1669), p. 338, SRO, GD. 14/19, Campbell of Stonefield Papers, ff. 113–15, 127, 129–30, 133–34, GD. 112/40/2; Duncan MacTavish, ed., *Minutes of the Synod of Argyll, 1639–1661* (Edinburgh: Scottish History Society, 1943), p. 120.

50. Sir James Turner, *Memoirs of his own Life and Times, 1632–1670* (Edinburgh: The Bannatyne Club, 1829), pp. 45, 237–39; SRO, PA. 11/5. ff. 17–18v. PA. 7/23/2/50; Guthry, *Memoirs*, pp. 242–43; Baillie, *Letters and Journals*, III: 6; McKerral, *Kintyre*, pp. 49–53.

51. For a thorough discussion of the developments within the British military system from the Restoration to the Glorious Revolution, see John Childs, *The Army of Charles II* (London: Routledge and Kegan Paul, 1976); Fortescue, *British Army*, I: 291–341; Young and Lawford, eds., *British Army*, pp. 11–17.

5

Killiecrankie, 1689: Dundee and the Highlanders

The battle of Killiecrankie (27 July 1689) provides both a convenient and illuminating mid-point at which to pause and consider the nature of Celtic warfare as it had evolved from the late sixteenth century. Heretofore, the study of the campaigns of O'Neill, O'Donnell, MacColla, and Montrose has whisked the reader from one battle to another providing him with a fundamental understanding of the strengths, weaknesses, and more importantly, continuity of the Celtic way of war. Killiecrankie, the Highlanders' most spectacular and Pyrrhic victory and the only significant Jacobite-Williamite contest in Scotland during the Glorious Revolution, deserves special attention. It provides a microcosmic view of all that was sound and all that was ineffective in Celtic warfare.

While Inverlochy and Auldearn, in particular, rank alongside Killiecrankie in highlighting the military strength of the Highland clans, the victory at Killiecrankie in 1689 was based on tactical subtleties absent in the two earlier encounters. MacColla and Montrose had presented themselves with opportunities to utilize the full weight of their tactical offensive power; however, they rarely displayed the capacity to arrange a trap the way John Graham, Viscount Dundee, and the clan chiefs did. Dundee's strength lay in his ability to combine the pre-battle movements and psychology of an O'Neill with the primal Celtic charge of a MacColla. The blending of these tactics demanded that Dundee exercise a measure of discipline among the Highland ranks, not so much during the attack as before. MacColla lost control of this aspect of command after Tippermuir and Aberdeen, as O'Neill did at Kinsale. Though Dundee was killed at Killiecrankie and led the clans in that one major battle only, he emerged as a general who, had he lived, might have succeeded where his predecessors had failed.

With the exception of Dundee's pre-battle preparation, the Highlanders' assault at Killiecrankie was of the same basic nature as MacColla's forays a half-century earlier: the clansmen attacked the Lowland army with abandon. The effectiveness of the charge surprised the Highlanders themselves as they surveyed the carnage the following morning:

> Many ... officers and soldiers were cut down through the skull and neck, to the very breasts; others had skulls cut off above the ears ... Some had both their bodies and cross belts cut through at one blow; pikes and small swords were cut like willows; and whoever doubts of this, may consult the eyewitnesses of the tragedy.[1]

Indeed, there were other eyewitnesses who confirmed the terrible slaughter:

> When day returned, the Highlanders went and took a view of the field of battle, where the dreadful effects of their fury appeared in many horrible figures. The

enemy lay in heaps allmost in the order they were posted; but so disfigured with wounds, and so hashed and mangled, that even the victors could not look upon the amazing proofs of their own agility and strength without surprise and horror. Many had their heads divided into two halves by one blow; others had their sculls cutt off above the eares by a back-strock ... [2]

Highland weaponry had not changed much since the days of MacColla and Montrose. The Highland charge was so successful and so perfectly suited to the employment of traditional Celtic weapons that the clans found no need to entertain defensive measures. Indicative of this continued proclivity for the tactical offensive were the clansmen's principal weapons in 1689: the ancient claymore and the newer single-handed broadsword; the light, leather-covered target; the dirk; and the matchlock and the more modern firelock musket (which were still commonly cast away after the first volley). These weapons, for the most

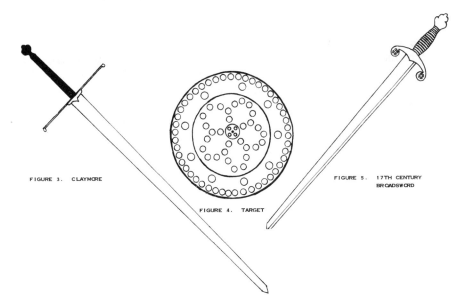

FIGURE 3.   CLAYMORE

FIGURE 4.   TARGET

FIGURE 5.   17TH CENTURY
BROADSWORD

part mainstays in the arsenals of their ancestors, allowed the Highlanders to make use of their quickness and agility against an enemy who increasingly was burdened by the weight of more modern and complex weapons and accoutrements. Major-General Hugh MacKay, commander of the Lowland army at Killiecrankie, was aware of the devastating effect that the Highland charge could have on even the best equipped and trained army when he observed that

> ... the Highlanders are of such a quick motion, that if a battalion keep up his fire till they be near to make sure of them, they are upon it before our men can come to their second defence, which is the bayonet ... When their [the Highlanders'] fire is over, they throw away their firelocks, and everyone drawing a long broad sword, with his targe ... on his left hand, they fall a running toward the enemy ... [3]

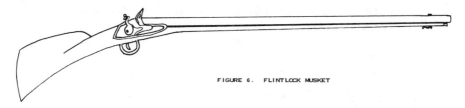

FIGURE 6.   FLINTLOCK MUSKET

MacKay's words accurately describe a Highland warfare based on mobility and facilitated by the use of weapons suited for offensive combat.

Dundee recognized that the strength of the clans lay in their primitive offensive tactics,[4] and he proved wise enough not to tamper with such time-honored and successful methods; therefore, the contributions that he did make to the victory at Killiecrankie came before the Highlanders were unleashed against MacKay's troops. Dundee understood the military culture of the Highlands, with its emphasis on pride and honor, and frequently called upon the clan chiefs for advice and opinion. As Dundee's army neared Blair Castle just before the battle, his Lowland officers suggested that the troops be allowed to rest and await reinforcements. They argued that the castle was secured and that the men could keep their skills sharpened and morale high by engaging in light skirmishes with the enemy's advance guard. To a conventional Lowland general this would have been the proper and accepted course; however, such a timorous path was incomprehensible to the proud Gaels. To be within striking distance of the enemy and refrain from battle was repugnant to the Highland code of honor. Seeing themselves as hardy warriors accustomed to deprivation, they would settle for nothing less than moving on MacKay's army as soon as possible.[5] The chief of the Camerons boasted to Dundee that he would not

> promise upon the event, if we are not the aggressors. But be assured, my Lord, that if once we are fairly engaged, we will either lose our army, or carry a complete victory. Our men love always to be in action ... Employ them in hasty and desperate enterprises, and you will oblige them; and I have still observed, that when I fought under the greatest disadvantages of numbers, I had still the completest victories.[6]

This exhortation, reminiscent of Hugh O'Donnell, moved Dundee to accept the Cameron chief's argument to the delight of the fiery clansmen.[7]

Although Dundee acquiesced, he managed to bridle the impetuosity of the clans long enough to formulate a plan of battle that increased the odds of a Highland victory. Dundee knew of MacKay's intention to advance from Perth toward Blair Atholl, since the castle there was of prime importance to Jacobite movements between the Highlands and Lowlands.[8] When Blair Castle was secured, Dundee and the chiefs faced the decision of where and how to confront MacKay's army. The choice of location by its very nature would determine the manner of confrontation. If the clans met the enemy in the Pass of Killiecrankie,[9] the ruggedness of the terrain would allow only guerrilla tactics. The Highlanders would not be able to attack MacKay's column from the sheer cliffs that flanked the river Garry. If they allowed MacKay to penetrate the pass, however, the clans could then use the Highland charge on the open ground to the north-west. The Highlanders, of course, chose the latter option. The decision to allow MacKay to pass unmolested involved an element of risk that Dundee probably considered but did not intimate to his chiefs. Should the enemy, who held roughly a two-to-one numerical superiority (4,000 to 2,000) as well as a considerable advantage in cavalry,[10] be permitted to deploy in strength and then repulse the initial Gaelic assault, there would be nothing between them and the rest of the Highlands except the disorganized remnants of Dundee's army. An ambush at the pass would have been less risky, but the clansmen would hardly have stood for such passive defensive measures and Dundee knew as much. With a patience and understanding of his men that rivaled O'Neill at Yellow Ford, Dundee then laid the groundwork for victory based on the strength of his army — the Highland charge.

The decision to allow MacKay free access through Killiecrankie Pass was immediately followed by Dundee's next brilliant tactical move: outmaneuvering the enemy and taking him by surprise. Dundee and his advisers determined to seize the high ground that would overlook MacKay's right flank as he emerged from the western mouth of the pass. Dundee knew that the shock value of the Highland charge was greatly enhanced when the Gaels could rush headlong down a slope onto a stationary enemy below; therefore, he avoided the easiest and most obvious route of advance over the old road from Blair Castle to the old Tilt bridge, up Strathgarry beneath the southern shoulder of the Hill of Lude, to the gently rolling fields near which MacKay's troops stood. Expecting MacKay to keep a watchful eye toward Strathgarry, Dundee despatched a small troop of horse that way to divert MacKay's attention from the clans that had already begun the march to secure the high ground.[11]

The route taken by Dundee's army led it to a position that for MacKay made defense difficult and attack impossible. Marching up Glen Fender after crossing the Tilt, the clans skirted the northern edge of the Hill of Lude, descended south down Allt Chluain, and moved south-eastward along a ridge to the lower slopes of Creag Eallaich. This rigorous, roundabout passage put Dundee on the right flank of his adversary at an elevation of 800 to 900 feet, some 300 to 400 feet above MacKay's force.[12] The Williamite army faced westward toward Strathgarry with its left flank anchored on the banks of the Garry and its right extending along a ridge beside Allt Chluain. Dundee's feint down the old Blair road had held MacKay's attention while the clans positioned themselves on his right flank.[13] Though the Highlanders intended to smash the enemy in a pitched battle, their expert use of the terrain and the element of surprise to arrange such a contest was reminiscent of the best tactical ploys of O'Neill and of the ancient Celts.

MacKay noticed Dundee and the clans on the slopes of Creag Eallaich and immediately recognized the danger. MacKay ' . . . made every battalion form . . . to the right upon the ground they stood, and made them march each . . . up the hill, by which means he . . . got a ground fair enough to receive the enemy, but not to attack them . . . '[14] By forcing MacKay's army to wheel to the right, Dundee put their backs to the precipitous defile of the Garry and greatly

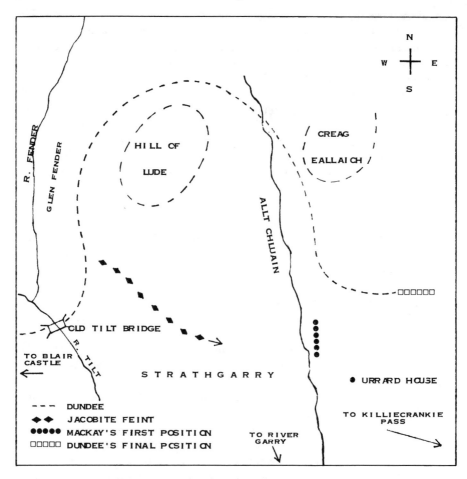

MAP 12.   DUNDEE'S MARCH TO KILLIECRANKIE

diminished the Lowlanders' chances of escape. MacKay's men, who had marched some fifteen miles from Dunkeld to their present position, now suffered not only from fatigue, but from the effects of Dundee's psychological warfare as well. With the clans less than a musket shot away, MacKay's army waited helplessly on the level plain near the low slope of Raon Ruaraidh for the Highlanders to attack.[15]

MacKay extended his divided regiments so as to avoid being outflanked, especially toward the pass. His discontinuous line, standing only three deep, having few reserves, and separated by tracts of marshy ground, presented the clans with an advantage that more than made up for their numerical inferiority.[16]

Most attacking Celtic armies, especially before the advent of rifled firearms and mobile field artillery, possessed a decided edge in that they could choose the point or points in the enemy line where the weight of their assault would fall and then advance toward these targets with impunity until within the enemy's effective musket range.[17] The Highland charge employed the single musket volley at a distance of thirty to fifty yards from the enemy line, not primarily as a destructive force, but as a tactic of psychology and visual obstruction. At this distance a collective volley from either side could cause heavy casualties. If the enemy held their fire until the Highlanders were within effective range and had discharged their customary volley, the powder smoke from the muskets often obscured their vision and made the selection of individual targets difficult; if, on the other hand, the enemy fired before the Highlanders volleyed, the effect of their shot would be diminished by the greater distance, and they would have no time to reload and fire again before the Highlanders were on top of them. At any rate, once both sides had discharged their pieces, the remainder of the battle usually was decided by dint of sword. Since MacKay's thinly spread line held no reserves, they could not expect support once their ranks were pierced. MacKay wrote with a childish sense of frustration that the clans ' . . . never fight against regular forces upon anything of equal terms . . . '[18]

Dundee's positioning of the clan regiments before the battle began was a clever response to MacKay's alignment and thus played a major role in shaping the outcome of the contest. The Highlanders quickly sized up the weaknesses in the enemy's formation. Because they were outnumbered by MacKay's army, Dundee and the chiefs packed their men into tight 'regiments' — each composed of a major clan and its septs — so that certain points along the enemy line would be subjected to the full weight of the Highland charge.[19] Dundee must have hoped that the unengaged enemy battalions would remain stationary and that the attack would be quick enough to render their flanking fire ineffective. The unengaged enemy units would be unable to fire into the mêlée without endangering friend and foe alike. Therefore, the critical phase of the attack would come when the tightly bunched clansmen were within fifty to thirty yards of the line. If the impetus of the charge was not broken, then the remaining Highlanders would probably overpower the enemy shot with broadsword and target. Dundee's decision to forego a line of battle for a quasi-column formation marked a subtle but telling deviation from MacColla's brand of the Highland charge. Had the clans approached MacKay's thinly held line with a similar line formation, the initial volley from the Lowlanders might have devastated them before they could re-form into the tightly packed knots that characterized the earlier Highland charge.

Dundee formed up the clans beginning with the MacLeans, whose 200 men displaced the MacDonalds from their traditional post on the right flank. Next came a 300-man contingent of Irishmen, followed by the Clanranald and Glengarry MacDonalds whose strengths were 600 and 300, respectively. These regiments composed Dundee's right wing — a combined force of some 1,400 men. In the center of the line were the forty-five Jacobite horsemen. To their left were 240 Camerons placed opposite MacKay's own battalion, illustrating Dundee's appreciation of the abilities of the Highland chief, the venerable old Lochiel. Anchoring the left flank was an undetermined number of Sleat MacDonalds and MacLeans, though their total force could not have exceeded 300 men. The strength of the Jacobite left was about 500 men, one-third the number on the right. Though mainly MacLeans and Clanranald, Glengarry and Sleat MacDonalds, the

Highland army contained small elements of MacGregors, Glencoe MacDonalds, Grants, and others.[20]

The Highlanders' right wing contained a much greater number of men than did their left because of the position of MacKay's army. His left contained about 2,250 men, many of whom had had military experience on the continent. His right totaled 2,350 men who were mostly raw recruits recently levied in the Lowlands and England. The right side of MacKay's line extended closer to the Highlanders than did the left, probably to insure that Dundee did not outflank him toward the pass. From their position on the lower slopes of Creag Eallaich, Dundee and his men were able to assess the strengths and weaknesses of the enemy line. Noticing that MacKay's wings were of approximately equal size, Dundee placed the bulk of the Highlanders against the enemy's left, presumably because of the close proximity of MacKay's right. Dundee could have advanced his own right so that it would have stood equidistant with his left from MacKay, but since the Highland left stood between 200 to 300 yards from the enemy, the clans on the right would have had to descend the slope some 200 yards in order to even up their line. Such a move would have made for a more rapid advance, but would have deprived the Highlanders of the high ground that gave the charge its tremendous impact. Despite the limited effective range of the matchlock musket, Dundee's right (which remained between 400 to 500 yards from the enemy) would be subjected to a heavier concentration of fire since the distance between the lines would allow MacKay's troops to get off at least two rounds per man before the Highlanders were upon them. On the Highland left the shorter distance between the armies meant that the clansmen would be exposed to only about half the number of rounds. Dundee probably reasoned that losses would be greater on his right wing and thus placed the better part of his warriors there.[21]

After drawing on the Highlanders' superior mobility to outmaneuver MacKay, Dundee then used the remainder of the afternoon to unnerve his opponent with a traditionally Celtic type of psychological warfare. The mere spectacle of a Highland horde looming menacingly on a hillside was often enough to frighten battle-hardened veterans; continental experience did little to prepare them for the peculiarities of Highland warfare. MacKay himself admitted that his officers and men ' . . . were strangers to the Highland way of fighting and embattling . . . '[22] Indeed, in the late seventeenth century an aura of mystery still clouded the English view of the Highlanders, and the general character traits that were reported exaggerated fears that persisted until Culloden. A contemporary described the clansmen as ' . . . proud, arrogant, vain-glorious boasters, bloody, barbarous, and inhuman butchers . . . '[23] Such an image would not have calmed the pounding breasts of MacKay's anxious soldiers. The Highlander's savage reputation was confirmed by the first glimpse of his warlike countenance. Daniel Defoe wrote that the Highlanders ' . . . made a very uncouth Figure . . . The Oddness and Barbarity of their Garb and Arms seemed to have something in it remarkable'.[24] The psychological effects of occupying strange and inhospitable terrain while waiting for an enemy whose physical appearance equaled the rumors of his character put the foreign soldier at a disadvantage even before the battle began.

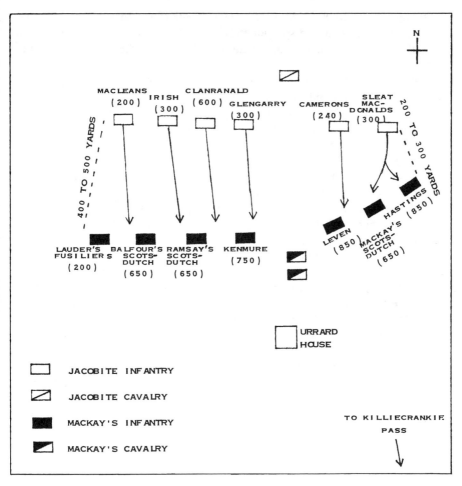

MACLEANS
(200)
IRISH
(300)
CLANRANALD
(600)
GLENGARRY
(300)
CAMERONS
(240)
SLEAT
MAC-
DONALDS
(300)

200 TO 300 YARDS

400 TO 500 YARDS

HASTINGS
(850)

LEVEN
(850)

MACKAY'S
SCOTS-
DUTCH
(650)

LAUDER'S
FUSILIERS
(200)
BALFOUR'S
SCOTS-
DUTCH
(650)
RAMSAY'S
SCOTS-
DUTCH
(650)
KENMURE
(750)

URRARD
HOUSE

JACOBITE INFANTRY

JACOBITE CAVALRY

MACKAY'S INFANTRY

MACKAY'S CAVALRY

TO KILLIECRANKIE
PASS

MAP 13. KILLIECRANKIE 1689

But reputation and physical appearance were not all that the Highland army used to weaken the enemy psychologically. Dundee and the chiefs chose to employ perhaps the most effective pre-battle weapon in the traditional arsenal — the eerie and disconcerting howl. Lochiel, sensing that the enemy was not yet adequately softened up for the slaughter,

> ... commanded his men ... to make a great shout, which ... ran quickly through the whole army ... Locheill cried out, 'Gentlemen, take courage. The day is our own. I am the oldest commander in the army, and have allways observed something ominous and fatall in such a dead, hollow, and feeble noise as the enemy made in their shouting. Ours was brisk, lively, and strong, and shows that we have courage, vigour, and strength. Theirs was low, lifeless, and dead, and prognosticates that they are all doomed to dye by our hands this very night![25]

With the clansmen howling above them, MacKay's troops listened to their commander lecture them dispassionately on the matter of their own safety should they allow ' . . . criminal faint heartedness . . . '[26] to cause them to give way under the Highland onslaught.

The afternoon must have passed with excruciating slowness as the Highlanders kept up their howling and Dundee patiently waited for the glare of the summer sun to fade behind the hills. Amid the turmoil caused by the anticipation of battle, Dundee was practical enough to see that the passage of time was an ally in his cause. Not only would the sun cease to obscure his army's vision, but the longer he forced MacKay's men to maintain their posts, the more fatigued they would be when the assault finally roared down on them. It was Dundee's expert generalship that kept the impatient clansmen from attacking until the moment was right. MacKay's troops periodically attempted to draw the Highlanders to battle by firing into their ranks with musket and cannon, but to no avail.[27]

When the moment came, Dundee had done all that he could to assure that his Highland army possessed every conceivable advantage over the enemy. He had gained the high ground and pinned MacKay's back to the precipitous cliffs of the Garry; he had forced MacKay to string his men out across unfavorable terrain in a long, broken line with few reserves; he had packed his own warriors into tight regiments that were capable of breaking MacKay's line at several strategic points; he had utilized the fierce appearance and reputation of the clansmen to psychologically undermine MacKay's resolve to fight; he had inspired the Highlanders; he had prolonged the wait so that MacKay's men might be worn down physically as well as emotionally; and, finally, he had allowed the sun to disappear so that its glare would not interfere with the attack. The combination of these pre-battle factors and the subsequent Highland charge characterized Celtic warfare at its apogee. Typically, the Celts did not bother to lay elaborate plans, although they did use rugged terrain and their savage appearance and reputation to weaken the enemy. But under Dundee's leadership the impetuous Highlanders enjoyed a battlefield scenario the likes of which had not been constructed since the days of Hugh O'Neill.

Shortly before sunset Dundee ordered his men forward. As they advanced, the Highlanders cast away their ' . . . plads, haversacks, and all other utinsils, and marched resolutely and deliberately in their shirts and doublets, with their fusils, swords, targets, and pistols ready . . . '[28] The MacLeans on the right wing led the attack, since they had the most ground to cover before reaching the enemy. The other clan regiments followed. MacKay's right poured a particularly heavy volley into the onrushing Camerons, Sleat MacDonalds, and MacLeans on Dundee's left almost as soon as they began to advance, and soon all along the line the Highlanders met with a hailstorm of lead. Lochiel noted that it was ' . . . incredible with what intrepidity the Highlanders endured the enemy's fire . . . '[29] The initial phase of the battle belonged to MacKay. The open terrain over which the Gaels advanced gave him a killing ground that he hoped might expose them to a fire destructive enough to break the impetus of the charge. Here the Highlanders were most vulnerable, but the rapidity of the advance did not give MacKay long to capitalize on that vulnerability.

When the Highlanders drew to within one hundred yards of the enemy line, MacKay's shot began to take its deadly effect. Of the approximately 600 to 700 Highland casualties, the majority occurred within this range. Lochiel again observed that though the fire ' ... grew more terrible upon the nearer approach, yet they, with a wonderful resolution, keept up their own, as they were commanded ... '[30] The final volley from MacKay's battalions momentarily staggered the Highlanders, but they leapt forward again and the Lowlanders' opportunity quickly passed. The concentrated firepower of 4,000 men was simply insufficient to check the assault over the last one hundred yards; consequently, the remaining 1,200 Highlanders approached an enemy who no longer had recourse to the musket.

There is no way to determine the number of casualties caused by the Highlanders' single volley. The Highlanders had been instructed to hold their fire until they came to the enemy's ' ... very bosoms ... '[31] This tactic, an integral part of the Highland charge, was designed to confuse the enemy at the last moment. According to Lochiel, Dundee's men carried out the Highland charge with precision, ' ... poureing fire ... in upon them all att once, like one great clap of thounder ... '[32] The Highlanders then flung away their muskets, and their approach over the last few yards, swords in hand, signaled the transition of the battle from gunpowder to the blade.

The fury of the Highland charge was more than MacKay's army could bear. Slashing savagely with broadswords and claymores, the clansmen hewed their way through the hapless enemy soldiers who struggled to thrust their bayonets into the muzzles of their muskets.[33] MacKay's right, which outnumbered the Highlanders among them by more than four to one, initially held their ground, but his left disintegrated almost immediately.[34] The duration of the actual fighting was very short, perhaps less than ten minutes. Lochiel reported that soon after the Highlanders ' ... fell in pell-mell among the thickest of them with their broadswords ... the noise seemed hushed; and the fire ceasing on both sides, nothing was heard ... but the sullen and hollow clashes of broadswords, with the dismall groans and crys of dyeing and wounded men'.[35] Seeing their comrades falling all around them, the remaining men under MacKay's command ' ... in a very short time all did run'.[36]

On the face of it the Jacobite victory at Killiecrankie appeared to be a rousing success that illumined all the strengths of the Highland way of war. Such a judgment is tempting when one considers that the Highlanders inflicted about three times as many casualties (2,000) as they suffered.[37] Indeed, it is difficult at first to find any major faults in the Highland army's performance. After all, it is a well-worn military maxim that one neither questions nor tampers with the recipe of victory. But upon closer inspection, Killiecrankie points up several weaknesses, not exploited by MacKay, that would render traditional Celtic warfare much less effective in the coming century, especially when employed against resolute troops led by commanders who were less than awestruck by the Gaelic military reputation. Several of MacKay's Gael-hunting predecessors had exploited the weaknesses of the Celts, but their insights apparently were lost upon him and continued to elude most of his successors until the last great Gaelic uprisings in the British Isles in 1715 and 1745.

Killiecrankie presents the student of military affairs with a definite, if oftentimes overlooked, contrast between two of the weapons employed in the battle: the sword and the bayonet. Dundee's triumph, based as it was on the use of a weapon on the verge of obsolescence, should not be viewed as an unqualified success to be imitated by future Gaelic armies. In 1689 the time had not yet come when the sword would be superseded by emerging technological developments wrought by the Industrial Revolution. For the last time the Highland clans carried the most renowned weapon of their forebears —the claymore — into a major battle, and on that final day the heroic feats performed with the two-handed monster were remarkable. Though the claymore contributed to the Highlanders' triumph, the new bayonet was the weapon that would come to dominate close-quarter combat in the next century. When the ring bayonet, which could be attached quickly to a musket possessing improved range, accuracy, and rate of fire, replaced the earlier plug type[38] used by MacKay's troops, the Lowlanders and English had a weapon that could greatly diminish the force of the Highland charge. Dundee and the chiefs succeeded at Killiecrankie because the enemy used preponderantly antiquated matchlock muskets and had limited experience in handling the bayonet; however, such an easy victory probably blinded the clansmen to the potential of the improved firelock musket and the ring bayonet and served to reinforce their belief that the old weapons could not be overcome by technology.

The Gaelic view of generalship that was a traditional Celtic strength had become a growing weakness by 1689. The heroics of Dundee, Lochiel, and others who sustained the long-standing Gaelic custom of the warrior-captain who led by example were but a memory to forward-thinking English and Lowland military commanders. In formal battle MacKay and his contemporaries would no more think of wading into the thick of the action than the Highland chiefs would of remaining in the rear while their men covered themselves with martial glory. Of course, there were obvious advantages to both lines of thought. The Lowland and English position helped to safeguard the general, thereby ensuring a central command post from which the battle could be directed; on the other hand, the Highland commanders, forfeiting such direction, inspired their men by example and challenged them to outperform not only one another, but the neighboring clans as well. That is why the initial charge was all important to the Celts; if it failed, the clans then lacked the centralized coordination to regroup and continue the battle. Though Dundee died in the initial charge at Killiecrankie, the Highlanders nonetheless won the day and reinforced yet another element of Celtic warfare that was to become a liability in the new age of warfare. Perhaps Dundee's death should have sobered the chiefs to the reality of the other less spectacular responsibilities of generalship that the enemy had already grasped.

The Highland charge that for nearly half a century had been the foundation of Gaelic tactical doctrine was becoming too predictable by the end of the seventeenth century. Its very simplicity was both a blessing and a curse. Because it lacked sophisticated maneuverings and relied almost solely on physical and psychological shock value, the Highland charge at first presented the enemy with few adequate countermeasures. The only ways to stop the determined Highlanders were either to cut them down with firearms before they reached their objectives or to provide soldiers with sufficient means of combating them hand to hand. Again, MacKay's men lacked sufficient firepower to break the charge, and the plug bayonet was clumsy in the hands of his inexperienced troops. Nonetheless, he did have with him on the battlefield that day two weapons whose day would come in a future conflict. Mobile field artillery[39] and the bayonet, augmented by improved muskets, were the tools of war that were destined to neutralize and finally crush Celtic offensive warfare.

Though MacKay possessed some of the advantages that his successors would use to defeat the Highlanders, he did not have the tactical acumen to win at Killiecrankie. He was unaware of the weakest point in the Celtic armor — their dependence on the wild terrain as a natural ally. By marching through the pass and into the Highlanders' lair, he allowed them to fight on their own terms (i.e., offensively) and on their own terrain. It was not by coincidence that the Gaels' most severe defeats (Kinsale, for example) occurred when they were forced to fight on unfamiliar ground that prevented an effective tactical offensive. To defeat a Celtic army, the English and Lowlanders first had to exploit their desire to attack, even under the most adverse circumstances, or their unwillingness to fight from defensive positions. MacKay did neither. Had he remained on the eastern side of the pass, Dundee would have faced a difficult task in keeping his clans from marching through the defile where they would have met the enemy on much less favorable terrain.[40] If MacKay had been familar with the Gaelic military system, he might have turned the tables and laid his own trap.

Killiecrankie demonstrated the superiority of traditional Celtic offensive tactics when employed against an enemy who had not yet learned to fully exploit his technological and organizational potential and who lacked a thorough understanding of the nature of Celtic warfare. The Highland charge remained a terrifying tactic in the hands of a commander such as Dundee. His skills in arranging the battlefield scenario that enhanced the effects of the attack contrasted with the clansmen's impetuosity and all-consuming love of combat. Together they represented a dynamic combination that outweighed many of the weaknesses of the Celtic military system and drew on its primitive strengths. But in the end the simplicity that had made the Highland charge so difficult to resist proved to be its undoing. When the enemy was properly armed and drilled to stand up to the Highlanders, the latter had no alternatives to their time-honored formula, since they had not bothered to develop any. Killiecrankie was not the last successful Highland charge, but close study reveals a subtle shift in the fortunes of war away from the Gael and toward the disciples of modernity.

That Killiecrankie is remembered as one of the Gaels' most astounding victories can be credited to Dundee's ability to outfox his counterpart by placing his Highland army in a position where its offensive tactics could be carried out with a minimum of risk. But when contrasted with MacColla's accomplishment at Inverlochy where only a handful of Highlanders fell, Dundee's casualty rate of over thirty percent seems extraordinarily high. When one considers the advances made by English and Lowland armies during the interval between these contests, however, it is not surprising that the Highlanders' price of victory rose so dramatically. This increase in casualty rates for the offensively minded Celts, beginning at Killiecrankie and continuing intermittently until reaching a peak with the carnage inflicted on their southern descendants during the American Civil War,[41] marks the dividing line between the era in which their careless heroics dominated the battlefield and the era in which they ultimately bowed to the superior techniques and implements of modern warfare. Killiecrankie, the last truly great Gaelic triumph in the British Isles, not only demonstrated the continuity of Celtic warfare, but more importantly, the divergence of their warfare from that of the traditional enemy.

NOTES

1. Henry Jenner, ed., *Memoirs of the Lord Viscount Dundee, The Highland Clans, and the Massacre of Glenco, and etc.* (London: F. E. Robinson and Company, 1908), p. 20.

2. Sir Ewen Cameron of Lochiel, *Memoirs of Sir Ewen Cameron of Locheill, Chief of the Clan Cameron*, ed. John Drummond (Edinburgh: The Abbotsford Club, 1842), pp. 270–71.

3. Major General Hugh MacKay, *Memoirs of the War Carried on in Scotland and Ireland, 1689–1691* (Edinburgh: The Maitland Club, 1833), pp. 51–52.

4. John Graham of Claverhouse, Viscount Dundee, *Letters of John Grahame of Claverhouse, Viscount Dundee, with Illustrative Documents* (Edinburgh: James Ballantyne and Company, 1826), p. 47; Mowbray Morris, *Claverhouse* (New York: D. Appleton and Company, 1887; London: Longmans, Green and Company, 1888), pp. 202–03; Martin Martin, *A Description of the Western Isles of Scotland*, 2nd ed. (London: A. Bell, 1716; reprint ed., Edinburgh: The Mercat Press, 1981), p. 210; C. S. Terry, *John Graham of Claverhouse, Viscount Dundee, 1648–1689* (London: Archibald Constable and Company, 1905), pp. 335–36.

5. Michael Barrington, *Grahame of Claverhouse, Viscount Dundee* (London: Martin Secker, 1911), pp. 338–39; Lochiel, *Memoirs*, pp. 258–59, 262–64; Mark Napier, *Memorials and Letters Illustrative of the Life and Times of John Graham of Claverhouse, Viscount Dundee*, 3 vols. (Edinburgh: Thomas G. Stevenson, 1862), III: 627–28; Rev. J. S. Clarke, ed., *The Life of James the Second, King of England, collected out of Memoirs writ by his own hand, together with the King's advice to his son and His Majesty's will*, 2 vols. (London: Longman, Hurst, Rees, Orme, and Brown, 1816), II: 350.

6. Lochiel, *Memoirs*, p. 263.

7. *Ibid.*, p. 264.

8. Duke of Hamilton to Lord John Murray, 3 June 1689, Blair Castle, Atholl MSS, Box

29, I (5), 118; John, Duke of Atholl, *Chronicles of the Atholl and Tullibardine Families*, 5 vols. (Edinburgh: By the Author, 1908), I: 294.

9. The ruggedness of Killiecrankie Pass has been described by several authors. Hugh MacKay depicted it as ' ... a strait and difficult pass ... ' two miles below Blair Castle. MacKay *Memoirs*, p. 49. C. S. Terry wrote that 'Some two and a half miles from Pitlochry the valley closes in abruptly. Lofty tree-clad slopes on either side fall sheer to the level of the rock-hewn bed of the yellow stream and its churning sepia pools, seemingly forming a cul-de-sac; Ben Vrackie's blue summit forbidding egress to a venturing host. Soon the dense slopes of the Garry's right bank drop to lesser heights, the roadway winds sharply to the left and the broadening valley opens out toward Blair where Allt Girnaig plashes downward to the Garry at Killiecrankie'. C. S. Terry, *Dundee, 1648-1689*, pp. 333–34. According to Mowbray Morris, Killiecrankie Pass ' ... forms the highest and narrowest part of a magnificent wooded defile in which the waters of the Tummel flowing eastward from Loch Rannoch meet the waters of the Garry as it plunges down from the Grampians ... The only road that then led through this Valley of the Shadow of Death was a rugged path, so narrow that not more than three men could walk abreast, winding along the edge of a precipitous cliff at the foot of which thundered the black waters of the Garry'. Morris, *Claverhouse*, pp. 204–05. Ewen Cameron of Lochiel wrote that only ' ... three men with great difficulty could walk abreast ... ' through the pass. Lochiel, *Memoirs*, p. 258.

10. Lochiel, *Memoirs*, pp. 266–68; Jenner, ed., *Memoirs of Dundee*, p. 19; Captain John Creichton, 'Memoirs of Captain John Creichton, From his own Materials, drawn up and digested by Dr. J. Swift, D. S. P. D.,' in Jonathan Swift, *The Works of Jonathan Swift, Dean of St. Patrick's, Dublin, with notes and a life of the author by Sir Walter Scott*, vol. 12, 2nd ed. (London: Bickers and Son, 1883), pp. 83–84; the Marchioness of Tullibardine, ed., *A Military History of Perthshire*, 2 vols. (Perth: R. A. and J. Hay, 1908), I: 254–55; William Leslie Melville, ed., *Leven and Melville Papers. Letters and State Papers chiefly addressed to George Earl of Melville, Secretary of State for Scotland, 1689-1691* (Edinburgh: The Bannatyne Club, 1843), p. 203; Colin, Earl of Balcarres, *Memoirs touching the Revolution in Scotland, 1688-1690* (Edinburgh: The Bannatyne Club, 1841), p. 44.

11. Tullibardine, ed., *Perthshire*, I: 256; Napier, *Memorials and Letters of Dundee*, III: 628–29; Morris, *Claverhouse*, p. 206.

12. Atholl, *Chronicles*, I: 300; Morris, *Claverhouse*, p. 206; Napier, *Memorials and Letters of Dundee*, III: 629–30; John MacDonald, *Orain Iain Luim, Songs of John MacDonald, Bard of Keppoch*, ed. A. M. MacKenzie (Edinburgh: The Scottish Gaelic Texts Society, 1964), p. 193; MacKay, *Memoirs*, p. 255; Tullibardine, ed., *Perthshire*, I: 256.

13. Barrington, *Viscount Dundee*, pp. 346–47; Napier, *Memorials and Letters of Dundee* III: 630; Tullibardine, ed., *Perthshire*, I: 260.

14. MacKay, *Memoirs*, p. 51.

15. Tullibardine, ed., *Perthshire*, I: 260–61; Barrington, *Viscount Dundee*, p. 346; Lochiel, *Memoirs*, p. 265; Napier, *Memorials and Letters of Dundee*, III: 630; MacKay, *Memoirs*, p. 51.

16. Jenner, ed., *Memoirs of Dundee*, p. 19; Lochiel, *Memoirs*, p. 265; Alexander MacKenzie, *History of the Camerons, with the Genealogies of the Principal Families of the Name* (Inverness: A. and W. MacKenzie, 1884), p. 194; Morris, *Claverhouse*, p. 207; Tullibardine, ed., *Perthshire*, I: 261–62; MacKay, *Memoirs*, p. 52; Balcarres, *Memoirs*, p. 46.

17. Grady McWhiney and Perry D. Jamieson conclude that a mid-nineteenth-century

musket's greatest limitation ' ... was its inaccuracy and short range. Smoothbores had no rifling, and even in the hands of good marksmen they were inaccurate weapons, with an effective range of only a few hundred yards ... Ulysses S. Grant remarked that a man with a musket at a range of a few hundred yards 'might fire at you all day without you finding it out ... ' Tactical theory recognized that individual musket fire was inaccurate and tried to compensate for this by keeping infantrymen in close-ordered lines to concentrate their firepower. Attack tactics were designed to compress men together, keep them well ordered during an advance, and bring them to the opposing line ready for a concentrated volley and bayonet charge'. Grady McWhiney and Perry D. Jamieson, *Attack and Die: Civil War Military Tactics and the Southern Heritage* (University, Alabama: The University of Alabama Press, 1982), pp. 28–31. Between 1689 and 1850 there were considerable improvements in musket firearms, but the preceding observations point up the continuing drawbacks of such weaponry even at the later date. At Killiecrankie, MacKay's men certainly were not as well armed as American soldiers in 1850, nor did they make sound tactical use of the weapons they did possess because of their wide dispersal across the battlefield. The reader shall see, however, that the Highlanders' tactics predated the offensive tactics described above, and indeed were the source of the battlefield tactics employed by their descendants, the American Southerners, in both the Mexican and Civil wars.

18. MacKay, *Memoirs*, p. 51.

19. Lochiel, *Memoirs*, p. 266; Tullibardine, ed., *Perthshire*, I: 262; Balcarres, *Memoirs*, p. 46.

20. Barrington, *Viscount Dundee*, pp. 348, 391–94; Napier, *Memorials and Letters of Dundee*, III: 632–33; Lochiel, *Memoirs*, p. 266; MacKenzie, *Camerons*, pp. 193–94; Morris, *Claverhouse*, p. 207; W. H. Murray, *Rob Roy MacGregor, his life and times* (Glasgow: Richard Drew Publishing, 1982), pp. 94–95; T. B. Johnston and Colonel James A. Robertson, *Historical Geography of the Clans of Scotland*, 3rd ed. (Edinburgh: W. and A. K. Johnston, 1899), p. 82.

21. Lochiel, *Memoirs*, p. 267; Tullibardine, ed., *Perthshire*, I: 261.

22. MacKay, *Memoirs*, p. 52.

23. P. Hume Brown, ed., *Early Travellers in Scotland* (Edinburgh: David Douglas, 1891; reprint ed., Edinburgh: The Mercat Press, 1978), p. 260.

24. Daniel Defoe, *Memoirs of a Cavalier*, ed. James T. Boulton (London: Oxford University Press, 1972), p. 133.

25. Lochiel, *Memoirs*, p. 267.

26. MacKay, *Memoirs*, p. 53.

27. Barrington, *Viscount Dundee*, pp. 349–50; Colonel David Stewart, *Sketches of the Character, Manners, and Present State of the Highlanders of Scotland; with details of the Military Service of the Highland Regiments*, 2 vols. (Edinburgh: Archibald Constable and Company, 1822; reprint ed., Edinburgh: John Donald Publishers, 1977), I: 66; Morris, *Claverhouse*, p. 209.

28. Jenner, ed., *Memoirs of Dundee*, p. 20.

29. Lochiel, *Memoirs*, p. 267.

30. *Ibid.*

31. *Ibid.*

32. *Ibid.*

33. Colonel Clifford Walton, *History of the British Standing Army, A.D. 1660 to 1700* (London: Harrison and Sons, 1894), p. 345; Tullibardine, ed., *Perthshire*, I: 264; Barrington, *Viscount Dundee*, p. 351.

34. MacKay, *Memoirs*, pp. 255, 265.

35. Lochiel, *Memoirs*, pp. 267-68.

36. MacKay, *Memoirs*, p. 255.

37. Tullibardine, ed., *Perthshire*, I: 266; Balcarres, *Memoirs*, p. 47; Jenner, ed., *Memoirs of Dundee*, p. 21.

38. MacKay, *Memoirs*, p. 52; Walton, *British Standing Army*, pp. 340-50.

39. Lochiel, *Memoirs*, p. 265; Barrington, *Viscount Dundee*, p. 349; Tullibardine, ed., *Perthshire*, I: 263; Napier, *Memorials and Letters of Dundee*, III: 633.

40. After Killiecrankie the Highland army's vulnerability was exposed as they attempted to drive an enemy regiment from the town of Dunkeld. Their ineptness at street fighting contrasted with their superb performance in the wild as they helplessly stumbled about through the streets, their swords useless, falling to the enemy's musket fire that issued from the nearby dwellings. Had other Lowland military commanders lured the Highlanders into similar situations, the Highland charge would have been rendered harmless and the clans been much less successful. Lochiel, *Memoirs*, pp. 286-87.

41. McWhiney and Jamieson, *Attack and Die*, pp. 8, 10-11, 19-22.

6

The Jacobite Uprising of 1715: Mar and the Highlanders

The Jacobite uprising of 1715 (the 'Fifteen) continued the reversal of Gaelic military fortunes that had begun at Killiecrankie in 1689. It goes without saying that the Highlanders still based their warfare on the tactics of the Highland charge. The 'Fifteen failed, however, not so much because of this continuity, but because of the attempt by the Jacobite commander, John Erskine, Earl of Mar, to change the Highlanders' strategy. Instead of pursuing an uncomplicated defensive strategy that would have allowed the combined clans to campaign in Scotland, Mar chose to divide his forces and send a significant part of them on a foolhardy offensive into England. If Mar was aware of the catastrophic results of previous Gaelic attempts to implement offensive strategies, he made no effort to correct the mistake. In imposing an offensive strategy upon his altogether unconventional, irregular troops, Mar stressed the organization and discipline that would have better suited a more conventional force. His hesitation and forbearance, which ultimately turned into indecision and impotence, only disillusioned the impetuous Highlanders and caused them to desert in large numbers rather than suffer the boredom of the march and the camp.

What Mar ultimately did was to contradict the success of traditional Highland warfare and play squarely into the hands of the British, who by the early eighteenth century had become a military power of some renown.[1] Unlike Dundee, who set the stage for the attack and then was content to let the clansmen fight in their usual manner, Mar deprived the clansmen of this, the only means of warfare that could have saved them. Under Mar's direction the Highlanders fought in two battles — Preston and Sheriffmuir — and won neither. At Preston they employed defensive tactics and were defeated. At Sheriffmuir they were able to execute the Highland charge on only one side of the battlefield. They won there but lost on the other side because of Mar's indecision and overall poor command and because of the strength of conventional British tactics. By 1715 it became clear that traditional Gaelic warfare might only temporarily stave off the Highlanders' inevitable defeat, while an attempt such as Mar's to transform them into a conventional army would surely speed the process.

To understand the military aspects of the 'Fifteen, it is necessary to look briefly at the Highlanders themselves in the early eighteenth century. The western clansmen who served in the Jacobite ranks were called ' ... 4,000 as good foot as Scotland ever yielded ... '[2] Even as late as 1715 Highland society remained warlike and primitive when measured by the standards of the people to the south. A contemporary Highlander who supported the government and who frequented Edinburgh and London more often than his native hills wrote to George I that

The Highlands of Scotland, being a country very mountainous, and almost inaccessible to any but the inhabitants thereof, whose language and dress are entirely different from those of the low-country, do remain to this day much less civilized than the other parts of Scotland ... The people wear their ancient habit, convenient for their wanderings up and down and peculiar way of living, which inures them to all sorts of fatigue ... they are very ignorant, illiterate, and in constant use of wearing arms ... It would ... be very happy for the government ... that the Highlanders could be governed with the same ease and quiet as the rest of Scotland ... The use of arms in the Highlands will hardly ever be laid aside, till, by degrees, they begin to find they have nothing to do with them[3]

This passage shows that over the preceding century the Highland way of life had changed but little and the government had not changed its attitude toward it. The Highland military reputation was still intact as well; though criticized by those who served with them for lack of discipline, plundering, and frequent desertion, the Gaels won the respect of ally and enemy.[4]

The strategic failure of the 'Fifteen can be attributed partly to the inability of the Jacobite leadership to master the difficulties of commanding an irregular army in the field. Mar, who raised the Jacobite standard as commander-in-chief at Braemar in early September, was largely responsible for the strategic failure.[5] Though an able and thorough administrator, he ' ... was bred up to the pen ... '[6] and lacked the forcefulness and daring of a good field commander. Unlike Dundee and Montrose, he did not have a firm grasp of the nature of Highland warfare and was consequently unable to bolster the clans' strengths and diminish their weaknesses as Dundee had done. Mar's efforts were confined to readying his army for an offensive campaign that he was reluctant to let it fight. The intricate logistical system that he tried to implement was foreign to the Highlanders, and while he fretted over petty administrative details,[7] his men languished without comprehending what their objectives were. A contemporary wrote that Mar ' ... did nothing all this while but write; and ... nobody moved in any one thing ... we followed strictly the rule of the gospel, for we never thought of tomorrow'.[8]

After capturing Perth in late September, Mar was in a position to implement a defensive strategy which, when combined with offensive tactics, would have allowed him to become master of Scotland. By controlling Perth he possessed ' ... all that part of ... Scotland ... north of the River Forth, excepting the remote Counties of Caithness, Strathnaver, and Sutherland, beyond Inverness, And that part of Argileshire which runs Northwest into Lorn and up to Locquhaber ... '[9] The occupation of Perth gave him the option of driving the government forces from either Edinburgh or Stirling. In early October Mar had three separate and active units in the field: his own at Perth (3,500 men); a detachment under the command of William MacIntosh of Borlum that was destined to cross the Firth of Forth and move on Edinburgh (1,500 to 2,000 men); and elements of the western clans raised by General Alexander Gordon of Auchintoul (1,500 men).[10] The main body at Perth alone outnumbered the government army of 3,000 holding Stirling under the vigilant and experienced eye of John Campbell, Duke of Argyll.[11] Mar's auxiliary units in the east and west, therefore, might easily have marched on Edinburgh and Glasgow while Argyll was held at Stirling by the threat of the main Jacobite army at Perth moving southward to attack him. Argyll admitted his precarious position when he wrote that ' ... if the enemy think fit to act with vigour that men of common sense would, in their circumstances, the handful of troops now in Scotland may be beat out of the country ... '[12] But Mar's caution and indecisiveness kept him at Perth while his lieutenants, Borlum and Gordon, were occupied in military sideshows that did nothing to improve the Jacobites' overall strategic position.

By the middle of October Mar was unable to coordinate the movements of his three separate forces whose objectives were not at all clear. He issued only vague instructions to Borlum and made contradictory and nearly impossible demands of Gordon. The first crucial period of the uprising came after Mar sent Borlum across the Firth of Forth, a sound move that forced Argyll to divide his already weak army. Mar hesitated, however, and cast away an opportunity to crush the reduced government army at Stirling. He then excused his own timid performance by blaming the inhospitable terrain and the absence of the western clansmen:

> This is a very poor place, and since you [Gordon] cannot be up with us this week, I have resolved to return too, with most of the army to Perth, and to wait your joining us there, which is now necessary you should with all expedition, as soon as you have dispersed those at Inverary ... so you would make all the haste with it you can, and come with your whole army directly to Perth to join us ... [13]

By the third week in October Mar stood no closer to victory than he had when he first occupied Perth, and his Highlanders were becoming impatient for battle. Meanwhile, Argyll continued to strengthen his position.

As it unfolded, Mar's strategy included a campaign in the south in conjunction with Jacobite supporters along the Borders and in Northumberland. Such a plan might have borne fruit if Mar had given clear instructions concerning his objectives.[14] One of Mar's harshest critics commented that Borlum had ' ... no positive orders, ... for he was never told what his ... orders were ... '[15] Borlum and the Highlanders crossed the Firth of Forth in mid-October and presented enough of a threat to Edinburgh to make Argyll immediately march there from Stirling with about 500 horse and mounted infantry.[16] Had Mar then moved swiftly on the remainder of the government force at Stirling, he might have crushed it before Argyll's return. But Mar's hesitation and Borlum's failure to move decisively against the government forces in the vicinity of the Scottish capital allowed Argyll to secure the city and return to Stirling before any harm was done to the government's cause.

After Borlum failed to drive the enemy from Edinburgh, he moved south toward the Borders, still lacking specific objectives, to link up with the Jacobite supporters from northern England. Mar's southern strategy went awry from the start. Reflecting on the futility of the entire southern campaign, an observer said, ' ... there was a fate attended all their councils, for they could never agree to any one thing that tended to their advantage'.[17] Borlum's Highlanders began to

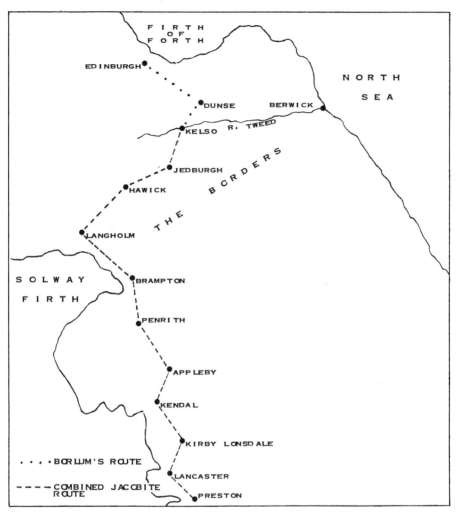

MAP 14. BORLUM'S MARCH INTO ENGLAND

quarrel with their English comrades about the direction the campaign should take. The English Jacobites proposed marching southward into Lancashire to raise the loyal multitudes they believed would join them there; the Scots desired to remain in their own country and perhaps take Glasgow and march in behind Argyll at Stirling. All they could agree to do was to march westward along the Borders until they could determine whether to move north or south.[18]

Mar's failure to give Borlum strict orders to campaign westward meant that the Gaels were being wasted in England when they could have pursued the familiar strategic defensive in Scotland. It also opened the door to disagreement among Borlum's men since only part of the Highlanders would consent to abandon the defense of the homeland for a strategic offensive into enemy territory.[19] Mar's ineptitude is nowhere more evident than in extracts from two letters that he wrote to his chief Jacobite lieutenants in northern England in late October: 'I know so little of the situation of your affairs, that I must leave to yourself what is fit for you to do, ... '[20] and 'I know not what he [Kenmure] is doing, where he is, or what way he intends to dispose of his people ... '[21]

The final decision to move south into Lancashire provoked a violent reaction from Borlum's Highlanders. Some of them simply deserted, but most gathered on a hillside opposite the English and declared that ' ... they would fight if they [their officers] would lead them on to the enemy, but they would not go to England'.[22] As the English Jacobites surrounded the recalcitrant clansmen to force them to march south, the Highlanders ' ... cocked their firelocks and said, if they were to be made a sacrifice, they would choose to have it done in their own country'.[23] Finally and reluctantly, they marched into England.

Borlum's army reached Preston in Lancashire in mid-November, where it went over to the tactical defensive, one of the few occasions during the period under study in which the Gaels found themselves in such a position. Failing to secure the support of a large number of Jacobite supporters on their march south from the Borders, the quarrelsome band of 2,000 men made for the town of Preston, hoping to capture the bridge at Warrington and threaten Liverpool and Manchester.[24] Once within the town on 9-10 November they were confronted by a government force consisting of infantry and dragoons blocking the route to Manchester.[25] The Jacobites faced the choice of whether to attack the British or defend Preston; they chose to defend Preston. Since most of the Jacobite strength rested in Borlum's Highlanders, the decision to defend the town necessarily diminished their chances of success because the Gaels were not adept at fighting in this manner. Despite their being ' ... exceeding good marksmen, ... '[26] they were at their best on the tactical offensive when the musket gave way to the sword and target in close-quarter combat. But because of the way the Jacobite commanders elected to defend the town, the battle of Preston never came to dint of sword.

Although the Highlanders were out of place standing on the tactical defensive, the defense of the town could have been better formulated to provide them with the opportunity of counterattacking in the open. As it was, the Jacobite leaders opted to defend the town itself with a series of hastily constructed barricades. They could have blocked the southern approaches of the British army by positioning themselves opposite the bridge across the river Ribble and along the narrow, sunken lane that led into Preston.[27] Here a strong contingent of Highlanders would have found protection from the British dragoons and could have mounted an attack after disorganizing the enemy horse with musket fire. The natural defenses of the bridge and sunken lane would have afforded them enough cover to have judiciously picked the moment of attack and perhaps kept the British cavalry from ever crossing the bridge.

The Jacobite defense of Preston hinged on the series of four main barricades designed to block British passage of the roads that converged on the town. Borlum reportedly was given the task of preparing the defenses,[28] and in lieu of utilizing his Highlanders' talents with the sword, he placed them with their muskets at vantage points throughout Preston where they could deliver fire on the advancing enemy. The Jacobites also deployed several pieces of artillery taken from Lancaster.[29] The barricades bristled with musket barrels and the artillerymen waited to unleash a barrage into the ranks of the attackers. But the Highlanders were out of their element and did not have the discipline or patience to conduct an effective defense of such cramped quarters, nor did they have the expertise to employ their artillery in deadly fashion.

Early in the afternoon of 12 November the British launched their first attack.[30] Advancing from the north and east, they came within fifty yards of the barricades before the Highlanders' accurate musket fire thinned their ranks and forced them to take cover.[31] Borlum's men attempted to use their artillery, ' ... but the bullets flew upon the houses, so that no execution was done thereby'.[32] After the initial attack had been repulsed, Borlum withdrew his advance elements into Preston to prepare for the enemy's next assault.[33] The Jacobites, because of the Gaels' expert marksmanship, had won the first day of the battle, but their precarious situation was clearly demonstrated by the large number of desertions in the night.[34] Despite heavy British casualties, many of the Highlanders apparently could not stomach another day of hiding behind barricades waiting for the enemy to attack at the time and place of his choosing.

The next morning the British army made its final assault on the town, conducting an unsuccessful attack on one of Borlum's barricades. Though the British were disheartened by the failure of the attack, their morale was bolstered shortly thereafter by news of the arrival of about 2,500 reinforcements, including three regiments of dragoons.[35] By midday the English Jacobites saw the futility of further resistance and began to talk of surrender. The Highlanders, however, had other notions and swore to fight to the death ' ... like men of honour, with their swords in their hands ... '[36] The animosities of the past were thus rekindled between the Scottish and English Jacobites. The Highlanders wished to fight their way out of the town, and when opposition was voiced to that course an observer noted that no ' ... arguments that were used to pacify them [could] quiet them for a great while: Nay, it was astonishing to see the confusion the town was in, threatening, yea killing one another, but for naming a surrender'.[37] Throughout the day the Highlanders turned on their comrades, even going so far as to make an attempt on the life of the English commander.[38] Early the following morning, however, the entire Jacobite force agreed to lay down their arms and surrender Preston to the British.[39] Mar's southern strategy had thus reached its almost inevitable conclusion.

The Highland majority of the Jacobite army were neither trained nor disciplined properly in the use of firearms and artillery to have fought and won with these weapons exclusively, especially from a defensive position such as Preston had afforded them. Even if they had not run short of powder,[40] the Highlanders probably could not have amassed enough concentrated and coordinated firepower to stop a determined British attack once their reinforcements had arrived. Perhaps the Jacobite artillery could have broken the British ranks sufficiently to make the continuation of the battle too costly, but neither the

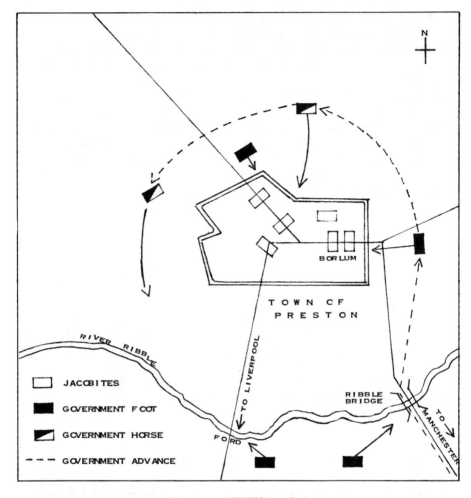

MAP 15. PRESTON 1715

Highlanders nor their English allies were knowledgeable enough to make effective use of their cannon. An observer noted ' ... that a shot aimed at some of the [British] soldiers ... in the street brought down a chimney-top instead'.[41]

From their defensive position at Preston the Highlanders were vulnerable to some of the logistical difficulties that normally plagued regular armies, but they were unable to overcome them under such unfamiliar conditions. Penned up as they were within the town, the clansmen were hampered by a shortage of food and supplies. The Gaels usually kept to the open country where their ability to move about rapidly over difficult terrain enabled them to replenish their rations quite easily. In addition, fighting with the sword and target rather than the musket did away with the need to keep together large stores of powder and shot, and under these conditions the Gaels had little to worry about besides locating a few cattle or bolls of oats to satisfy their hunger.

Perhaps their most important and glaring weakness at Preston was the Highlanders' inability to practice their most devastating tactic — the Highland charge. The cramped quarters of the town were not conducive to the charge, even as a countermeasure, because it initially required an open area on which the troops could be assembled properly for the attack. Furthermore, the charge would not have been effective against forces aligned in the manner of the British at Preston. Ideally, the charge was launched against an opponent who was lined up opposite the Highlanders. The British Army at Preston ringed the town, and even if Borlum had called on his men to counterattack, a concentric assault from the inside out probably would have run out of steam because the farther it advanced, the more the Highland units would fan out from one another and dilute the concentrated shock power of the charge.

While Mar's offensive strategy in the south was falling apart, he attempted to raise the western clans and bring them to action on Argyll's left flank. The real fighting strength of the Jacobite army, these clans had promised their support early in the conflict, but by October only the Glengarry MacDonalds had actually taken the field. Mar agreed to despatch a commander to lead them — Gordon of Auchintoul[42] — whose task it was to rally the clans, but Mar failed to make it clear to Gordon what he should do thereafter. In the beginning merely raising the pro-Jacobite western clans proved difficult enough because of the persistent threat of the Whig clans (Frasers, Munros, Rosses, Sutherlands, and MacKays) north of the Great Glen. By 6 October only about 1,300 to 1,500 men were in arms, mainly Glengarry (500) and Clanranald MacDonalds (550) and MacGregors (250).[43] A few days later the MacLeans brought in 350 warriors and the Campbell Earl of Breadalbane raised a further 200.[44] Expected at any time were the Camerons and Appin Stewarts, whose combined strength of nearly 600 men would give Gordon a total force of about 2,500 warriors.[45]

Once Gordon had gathered the western clans, he led them south toward Argyllshire in mid-October to capture Inveraray Castle and threaten Argyll's position at Stirling from the west. He had received a letter from Mar dated 16 October informing him of the main army's departure from Perth towards Stirling in response to Argyll's move to Edinburgh against Borlum. Mar impressed upon Gordon the absolute necessity ' . . . that [he] march with all expedition to join us as we pass [the] Forth'.[46] About two weeks earlier Mar had issued Gordon emphatic orders as to his proceedings once he reached Inveraray Castle:

> The service you are going about . . . is of great consequence . . . because of the arms Glenderule writes me are lately put into Inveraray; therefore you are to lose no time in going about it with all expedition . . . I will not begin with burning houses, so I hope you will have no occasion of doing that to the house of Inveraray, which, upon resistance, I think you had better do by blockade than storm, you may proceed westward conform to former orders; but by reason of my not marching from hence so soon as I intended, you would not march so far that way . . . [47]

Mar's hurried countermand to Gordon on 16 October was a sensible response to Argyll's march to Edinburgh, but the tone of desperation reveals a mind that was not initiating the action but reacting to it. Before Mar could or would march on Stirling, Argyll returned on 17 October. Gordon could not have marched from the north in time to coordinate an attack with the army from Perth even if Mar had moved as soon as Argyll departed Stirling.[48] Gordon apparently made no attempt to join Mar on the Forth. The clansmen, like their kinsmen under Alasdair MacColla, may have felt compelled to the haunts of their ancient enemy.

Gordon finally marched the western clans to Auchterarder in early November, where he expected to be joined by Mar and the main army from Perth.[49] Though Gordon and his clansmen had given up the siege of Inveraray Castle, coming away ' ... pretty modest and ... not brag[ing] much of their success, ... '[50] they still might have posed a major threat to Argyll's position if Mar had employed them in aiding the main army's passage over the Forth north-west of Stirling. One of Mar's principal officers surmised that the western clans might have departed Argyllshire ' ... to march down the south side of the river, keeping the strong ground, and posted themselves so as to favour our passage of the fords ... '[51] But Mar, though possessed of an overwhelming numerical superiority, was not yet ready to move toward Stirling, and consequently gave Gordon no such orders. The western clans ended up waiting at Auchterarder for their overly cautious commander to venture out to join them. Mar called a council of war on 9 November, knowing that with his numbers he could no longer legitimately postpone an attack on Argyll.[52] His troops had become restless for action; a Jacobite officer complained ' ... of our men's deserting daily, and our spirits lagging, by feeling, more and more every day ... the fallacy of Mar's promises'.[53]

The long-awaited fulfillment of Mar's promises was to be an attack by the main army supported by feints from three smaller detachments. The bulk of the Jacobite force was to pass over the Forth just above Stirling while the smaller detachments moved toward Stirling bridge and to points along the river above and below the town.[54] The plan was ambitious, and if Mar had been more resolute in carrying it out and Argyll less resolute in meeting the challenge, the Jacobite uprising might have taken a more fortunate turn. Argyll's choices were either to meet the diversionary attacks, which would leave Mar's main body free to cross the fords of the Forth unmolested, or to strike at the main army, in which case he might be surrounded by the smaller detachments. Mar's strategy looked good on the drawing board, but execution of the complicated plan depended on coordinating the movements of his own separate forces while he kept an eye on the reaction of the crafty Argyll.

Shortly, both commanders put events into motion that would decide the fate of the uprising. The Jacobite army left Perth early on 10 November and by the end of the day the horse reached Dunning and the infantry marched into Auchterarder.[55] At Auchterarder the western clans joined the army, and on the following day Mar held a review of his troops on a nearby moor. While the Jacobites paused to determine their final order of march, Argyll learned of Mar's position from his spies and quickly concocted a plan of his own.[56] Calling in what reinforcements he could scrape together from Glasgow and the surrounding countryside, he resolved to cross the Forth and occupy Dunblane ahead of Mar. He hoped such a move would preclude a defense of the river, which surely would freeze during the night. If Argyll had stood passively behind the Forth and allowed Mar's plan to unfold, he probably would not have been able to stop the clansmen from crossing the Forth and outflanking him on either side. Argyll decided to do what he could to maximize the efficiency of his cavalry, since the ' ... grounds near Dunblane were much more advantageous for his horse than those at the head of the river ... '[57] While Mar dallied at Auchterarder until 12 November, Argyll anchored his left wing near Dunblane and his right on a desolate elevation known as Sheriffmuir.[58]

Argyll's unexpected occupation of Dunblane upset Mar's original plan of attack and left the Jacobite commander with the choice of giving battle on Argyll's terms or returning once again to Perth. When Mar heard reports of Argyll's position, he scoffed and ordered his army to march on, but late in the afternoon Gordon halted the advance guard near Kinbuck, two miles from Dunblane, to await Mar's arrival. Mar continued to be skeptical of reports of Argyll's presence near Dunblane, however, and ' ... said he'd lay any money that it was not true'.[59] The Jacobite general was indeed in a predicament; for all his planning and patience, he might soon have to do battle on a field of Argyll's choosing. When it became clear to Mar that the government army was in a position to fight, he reportedly

> ... not knowing what hand to turn himself to, and being then conscious of his want of ability for such an undertaking, was stunned, finding there was something more requisite than lies; for it was not with us he was to have to do, it was with the enemy, and blows must decide it.[60]

Both armies spent the cold night preparing for the showdown that would come at dawn.

Mar's decision to give battle on 13 November probably came as no surprise to Argyll: the Jacobite army possessed a tremendous numerical advantage. Mar had exhausted the patience of his men, especially the Highlanders, and could not risk wholesale desertion by electing to return to Perth. The Gaels received the news of the impending battle with a resounding cheer, threw their bonnets into the air, and set about the task for which they had risen.[61] The army was drawn up in two battle lines facing south. The front consisted of eight regiments of Highland foot flanked on either side by three squadrons of horse. The rear consisted of six foot regiments. The entire army totaled about 6,300 foot and 950 horse.[62] Argyll countered with a front rank of six infantry regiments, the total strength of which was about 1,600. On either flank he posted two formations of cavalry and kept two infantry regiments and three cavalry units in the rear. His force totaled about 2,200 infantry and 1,000 cavalry.[63] The two armies advanced toward each other, but neither was able to sustain its formations because of the rough terrain. Both Mar and Argyll therefore lost control of the movements of a significant part of their forces before the battle began.

The march to the battlefield contributed greatly to the unusual nature of the contest that followed. The Jacobites sighted a party of Argyll's cavalry to the south of the heights of Sheriffmuir in the early morning; consequently, Mar transformed his lines into columns. He also ordered his horse and 2,000 Highlanders from the right of his first line to move ahead and take possession of the high ground where Argyll's cavalry had appeared.[64] Argyll now saw that the stretch of marshy terrain which he had intended to cover his right flank had frozen over during the night; he therefore took immediate action to shift the direction of his front to meet the oncoming Jacobites. Argyll moved his army into position and marched it rapidly north-eastward to avoid being outflanked to the right.[65] When he had repositioned his forces, Argyll moved them up the steep slope hoping to gain the heights of Sheriffmuir ahead of Mar. The Duke reached a narrow plain atop the hill and ' ... found the rebels (who had fallen into disorder by breaking their lines ...) forming themselves in battle array ... '[66]

Argyll's attainment of the heights of Sheriffmuir and Mar's attempt to dislodge him before he could establish a tenable defensive position threw the left wings of both armies into confusion. As the government army moved to their right up the slope, the left wing lagged behind attempting to form up for battle. The dragoons were out of position to protect the infantry and Argyll's officers on the left wing did not know that they were being outflanked by Gordon's Highlanders on the Jacobite right. On Mar's left, however, the situation was reversed. The Jacobites crested the hill and saw Argyll's troops arraying for battle about 150 to 200 yards away.[67] Mar's men ' ... arrived in such confusion that it was impossible to form them according to the line of battle projected, every one posted himself as he found ground ... '[68] During the attempt to re-form, most of Mar's horse became concentrated in the center of the field, leaving only a few horse to cover the Jacobite right and none supporting the left.[69]

The battle began when Gordon's regiments on the Jacobite right wing executed the Highland charge against Argyll's disorganized left. The 2,000 Highland foot rushed wildly toward the enemy, firing a few shots, ' ... which drew upon them a general salvo from the enemy ... '[70] The Gaels dropped to the ground to avoid the fire. When the volley ended, they rose, cast away their own muskets, and ' ... drawing their swords, pierced them everywhere with an incredible vigour and rapidity in four minutes time from receiving the order to attack'.[71] The power of the charge was too great for the government infantry, many of whom were veterans of continental war under the command of the Duke of Marlborough. Even with coordinated volleys and ring bayonets, they could not match the broadswords and targets of the Highlanders. They were soon driven into their own cavalry and the entire left side of Argyll's army fled the field in panic.[72]

The clans' success against regular troops surprised observers on both sides. A Jacobite officer said that he ' ... had no great expectation of the Highlandmen's standing the fire of regular troops, and, in all our affairs, it was that which I was most deceived in ... '[73] A government supporter concurred, referring to the Highlanders' performance as ' ... as good, perhaps, as ever came from any disciplined troops'.[74] The effectiveness of the Highland charge at the western end of the battlefield is borne out by the casualty figures. Jacobite losses totaled only about twenty-five dead and a few wounded, while government casualties were estimated at between 200 and 800.[75]

Although the Highland charge broke Argyll's left wing, the Jacobites failed to

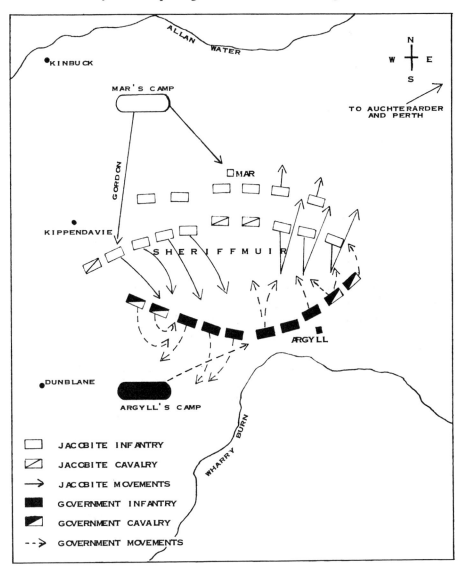

MAP 16.   SHERIFFMUIR   1715

follow up their victory. The government troops were unable to communicate with their right wing and thus feared that it had suffered a similar fate; so they turned and fled toward Dunblane. But instead of vigorously pursuing the enemy infantry, the Jacobite horse allowed a much smaller party of government cavalry to delay them. A witness noted that if

> the cavalry upon the right wing of the rebels [had] fallen in at the same time, the whole left of the royal army had been cut off ... But so it was, that the left of the

king's army having made a ... charge on some of the enemy's squadrons which stood
on their flank ... they [the Jacobite horse] stood all the while looking on to our left,
without attempting to do any thing considerable.[76]

It was about this time that Mar himself rode up to the victorious Jacobite right
wing, ' ... stood a little time, [and] ... rode off, without pretending to give
orders'.[77] It seems as if, at critical moments, Mar could do nothing except hesitate.

Even after the Jacobite right allowed the government left wing to escape, they
still could have moved across the battlefield and aided their comrades on the left;
however, they did not. The battle raged on the eastern end of the field while the
Highlanders and their accompanying horse

> marched up to the top of that part of the hill, called the Stoney Hill of Kippendavie,
> where they stood without attempting anything, with their swords drawn, for near
> four hours space, to the great surprise of our left, who were ... so near to them that
> had they but tumbled down stones or fired pistols, they could have not missed the
> killing of several.[78]

Mar had over 2,000 Highlanders and a good part of his horse perfectly positioned
to sweep down on either the government's retreating left wing or the flank of
Argyll's three infantry regiments (1,000 men) and five cavalry squadrons (about
450 men) who were hotly engaged with the Jacobite left wing.[79] Incredibly, Mar
did not move.

The action on Mar's left flank had begun at about the same time that Gordon's
Highlanders struck on the opposite side of the field. The Jacobites made the initial
charge here as well, though lacking protection from the cavalry. Argyll's horse
soon took them in the left flank, a move that ' ... gave an immediate turn to the
dispute ... '[80] Argyll's assumption of personal command of his right wing[81] and
his experience in the combined use of infantry and cavalry halted the Highland
charge in its tracks.[82] The Gaels were steadily driven back, even though they
managed to rally several times during the three-hour contest.[83] The marshy area
on Mar's left flank, which he had thought would provide a natural protective
barrier, had frozen over during the night and now allowed the passage of Argyll's
cavalry.[84] The Duke, therefore, was able to break the Highlanders' line with a
well-orchestrated push by his combined forces. By the middle of the afternoon the
Highlanders on Mar's left stood with their backs against the Allan Water where
many were slaughtered or drowned attempting to escape.[85]

Argyll allowed himself to get caught up in the excitement at the eastern end of
the battlefield and forgot about his own left wing. As his cavalry drove the
Highlanders to the Allan Water, he learned of the severe reverse on his left and
immediately called together his troops to march back toward Mar's right wing. By
now the odds favored the Jacobites even more than at the outset of the battle; Mar
had over 4,000 men still assembled for battle, while Argyll had slightly over 1,000.
He posted them all behind some mud and turf enclosures at the foot of the hill of
Kippendavie, fully expecting the Jacobites to attack.[86]

Though Mar had consistently thrown away opportunities for victory, he now had one final chance to redeem himself. Possessed of the higher ground and a tremendous numerical advantage, Mar and the rested Highlanders could not have avoided victory if they had pressed home a determined attack. Near four o'clock in the afternoon it appeared that Mar had decided to settle the issue. His army advanced slowly to within 400 or 500 yards of the enemy but for unknown reasons did not attack; instead, they drew away and dispersed.[87] Mar had once again thrown away a chance to win the battle. A Jacobite officer sharply rebuked Mar years later for having ' . . . no mind to risk himself, . . . ' therefore missing ' . . . the favourablest [opportunity] that [was] ever offered of getting out of the danger he had plunged [his army] in . . . '[88] With Mar's unexpected retreat the battle of Sheriffmuir ended and along with it the hopes for a successful uprising. Jacobite casualties totaled about 230 killed, wounded, and captured, while the government lost between 600 and 700 men.[89] Each side claimed victory, but the most important effect of the battle was that the Jacobites lost the initiative. Argyll marched safely back to Stirling and Mar returned to Perth with little hope of bringing another army into the field.

Unlike Dundee at Killiecrankie, Mar did not lay a solid foundation for victory, partly because he failed to recognize the strengths and weaknesses of the clansmen. That is not to say that Mar was unaware of their military reputation and capabilities, but he did not understand the nature of the Highlanders and their methods of warfare. Mar's failure to understand and thus to prepare for the Highland way of war is evidenced by his failure to do any of the following: gain suitable ground from which the Highland charge could be staged effectively, keep Argyll from determining the field of battle and positioning his forces so that they offset his numerical inferiority, insure that his own regiments were properly organized before attacking, provide for the inspiration of his own men while psychologically undermining the enemy's position, and control the timing of the attack so that his effort was well coordinated and directed.[90] Mar's lack of preparation neutralized an overwhelming numerical advantage, while Dundee's attention to detail had allowed a much smaller force to destroy an army twice its size. It should come as no surprise, then, that during a critical phase of the battle of Sheriffmuir a Highlander wistfully cried out, 'Oh! For one hour of Dundee'.[91]

At Sheriffmuir Mar's pre-battle movements kept the Highlanders from employing their tactical strengths earlier and more advantageously than they did, and when the Gaels finally were able to execute their attack, they did so under less than ideal conditions. Mar's formation of the lines into marching columns in order to attain the heights of Sheriffmuir ahead of Argyll's main force demonstrated that he overestimated the level of discipline among the Highlanders. The march up the hill disrupted the clans' formation, as well as Argyll's better-trained regiments, and only by sheer chance did Mar's right wing emerge to find an enemy on the other side of the battlefield that was even more disorganized than itself. The near-disaster on Mar's left occurred because the clan regiments there faced an enemy that was well positioned, well led, and highly disciplined. If Mar had possessed the foresight to allow his clansmen to advance in line of battle formation to the heights, they would have been ready to take on the enemy at a moment's notice and probably would have put Argyll's entire army to flight.

It would be convenient to attribute the course of events at opposite ends of the battlefield to a disparity in strength between the two armies, though both the Jacobites and the government contingents proved to be stronger on their respective right wings. But while it is true that the clansmen on Mar's right enjoyed the support of most of the Jacobite horse, they were by no means superior fighters when compared to those clansmen employed on the left. On the front of the Jacobite right stood some 2,500 MacLeans, Clanranald, Glengarry, and Sleat MacDonalds, and Breadalbane Campbells, while on the left there were about half that number of Glencoe MacDonalds, Appin Stewarts, and Camerons. When the reserves in the second line are counted, the Jacobites on both wings enjoyed such a superiority that had they struck simultaneously and in good order, they would have carried the day. But because of Mar's error in marching them to the battlefield, they were forced to depend on good fortune rather than judicious planning.

Despite Mar's lack of military skill in arranging and directing the battle, the Highlanders acquitted themselves well. A contemporary government supporter wrote that they fought skillfully and displayed a ' . . . merciless and most savage nature . . . '[92] The Gaels were thought to be ' . . . unfitted to contend singly against the modern combination of infantry, cavalry, and artillery, . . . '[93] but they proved themselves capable of standing up to cavalry and infantry attack against Argyll's right wing. The ultimate defeat there had more to do with how they arrived on the battlefield than with their ability to contend with the government's combined forces. Argyll did not underestimate the Highlanders' strength against his tandem of cavalry and infantry. Had he done so, he probably would have attacked first; instead, he held back his troops on the right wing even though the Gaels were clearly disordered. Argyll thus stood his ground until the Highlanders forced the action. A Jacobite participant who was unabashedly critical of his Highland allies reportedly referred to their performance against Argyll as ' . . . the most favourable of all testimonies in support of Highland tactics and prowess'.[94] It was unfortunate for the Jacobites that their strategy was not as praiseworthy.

NOTES

1. For a thorough study of the British army in the early eighteenth century, see Charles Dalton, *George the First's Army, 1714–1727*, 2 vols. (London: Eyre and Spottiswoode, 1910–1912).

2. Spottiswoode Society, *The Spottiswoode Miscellany: A Collection of Original Papers and Tracts, Illustrative Chiefly of the Civil and Ecclesiastical History of Scotland*, ed. James Maidment, 2 vols. (Edinburgh: The Spottiswoode Society, 1845), II: 452–53.

3. Captain Edward Burt, *Letters from a Gentleman in the North of Scotland to his Friend in London*, 2 vols. (London: Ogle and Duncan, 1822), II: 254–59.

4. John, Master of Sinclair, *Memoirs of the Insurrection in Scotland in 1715*, ed. James

MacKnight (Edinburgh: The Abbotsford Club, 1858), pp. 26, 86, 181–82; Robert Patten, *The History of the Late Rebellion, with Original Papers and the Characters of the Principal Noblemen and Gentlemen Concern'd in it*, 2nd ed., 2 vols. (London: J. Warner, 1717), II: 116; Peter Rae, *The History of the Rebellion, Rais'd against his Majesty King George I by the Friends of the Popish Pretender* (London: A. Millar, 1746), p. 305.

5. Alister N. Tayler and Henrietta Tayler, *1715: The Story of the Rising* (London: Thomas Nelson and Sons, 1936), p. 41.

6. James Keith, *A Fragment of a Memoir of Field-Marshal James Keith written by himself, 1714–1734* (Edinburgh: The Bannatyne Club, 1843), p. 3.

7. For examples of Mar's concern over his supply situation, see Mar to General Gordon of Auchintoul, 4 October 1715, Mar to Earl of Breadalbane, 14 October 1715, Mar to Magistrates of Montrose, 14 October 1715, quoted in Rae, *History of the Rebellion*, pp. 431, 441–44.

8. Sinclair, *Memoirs*, pp. 92–93.

9. *Ibid.*, p. 235.

10. J. C. M. Baynes, *The Jacobite Rising of 1715* (London: Cassell, 1970), pp. 56, 71; List of the Clans supporting the government and in rebellion, 1715, Edinburgh, Edinburgh University Library, Laing MSS, I. 347; Tayler, *1715: The Story of the Rising*, pp. 109, 114, 231–35.

11. John, Duke of Argyll to William Stewart, undated, London, British Library, Additional Manuscripts, 35838, f. 390 (hereafter cited as Add. MSS); Argyll to Lord Stanhope, 21 September 1715, London, Public Record Office, State Papers, Scotland, S.P. 54/8/80.

12. Argyll to Stewart, Add. MSS, 35838, f. 390.

13. Mar to Gordon, 19 October 1715, quoted in Rae, *History of the Rebellion*, pp. 450–51.

14. Baynes, *Jacobite Rising*, pp. 72–73; Patten, *History of the Late Rebellion*, II: 115.

15. Sinclair, *Memoirs*, pp. 129, 142.

16. Argyll to Stewart, Add. MSS, 35838, f. 390; Mar to Gordon, 19 October 1715, quoted in Rae, *History of the Rebellion*, pp. 450–51.

17. Patten, *History of the Late Rebellion*, I: 66.

18. Patten, *History of the Late Rebellion*, I: 66–68; Rae, *History of the Rebellion*, pp. 269–71.

19. About 500 of Borlum's total force of 1,500 Highlanders left the army and marched north toward Glasgow where many of them were captured by government forces. Helen Armet, ed., *Extracts from the Records of the Burgh of Edinburgh, 1701–1718* (Edinburgh: Oliver and Boyd, 1967), p. 368.

20. Mar to Viscount Kenmure, 21 October 1715, quoted in Sinclair, *Memoirs*, p. 145.

21. Mar to General Forster, 21 October 1715, *ibid.*, p. 148.

22. Patten, *History of the Late Rebellion*, I: 68.

23. Rae, *History of the Rebellion*, p. 271.

24. R. E. Hutchinson, *The Jacobite Rising of 1715* (Edinburgh: Board of Trustees of the National Galleries of Scotland, 1965), pp. 23–24; Tayler, *1715: The Story of the Rising*, pp. 82–83; Rae, *History of the Rebellion*, pp. 316–17.

25. Sir Walter Scott, *Tales of a Grandfather, being the history of Scotland from the earliest period to the close of the rebellion, 1745–46*, 2 vols. (London: Adam and Charles Black, 1898), II: 923.

26. Patten, *History of the Late Rebellion*, I: 88.

27. Scott, *Tales of a Grandfather*, II: 923.

28. Baynes, *Jacobite Rising*, p. 117; Ralph Arnold, *Northern Lights: The Story of Lord Derwentwater* (London: Constable, 1959), p. 113.

29. Henry Paton, ed., *Papers About the Rebellions of 1715 and 1745* (Edinburgh: Scottish History Society, 1893), p. 520; Rae, *History of the Rebellion*, p. 316.

30. Baynes, *Jacobite Rising*, p. 119; Paton, ed., *Papers About the Rebellions*, p. 521; Rae, *History of the Rebellion*, pp. 318–19.

31. Paton, ed., *Papers About the Rebellions*, p. 521; Rae, *History of the Rebellion*, pp. 319–20; Patten, *History of the Late Rebellion*, I: 113.

32. Paton, ed., *Papers About the Rebellions*, p. 521.

33. Patten, *History of the Late Rebellion*, I: 108.

34. Baynes, *Jacobite Rising*, p. 122.

35. Arnold, *Northern Lights*, p. 118; Rae, *History of the Rebellion*, p. 320.

36. Patten, *History of the Late Rebellion*, I: 118.

37. Rae, *History of the Rebellion*, p. 322.

38. Patten, *History of the Late Rebellion*, I: 124.

39. D. Murray Rose, *Historical Notes or Essays on the '15 and '45* (Edinburgh: William Brown, 1897), pp. 83–84.

40. Rae, *History of the Rebellion*, p. 321.

41. Patten, *History of the Late Rebellion*, I: 116.

42. General Alexander Gordon of Auchintoul served with both the French and Russian armies, and upon his return to Scotland in 1711 he took over the family estate. In 1715 he dedicated himself to the Jacobite cause. After commanding the Jacobite army following its retreat from Perth in early 1716, he fled to France. He returned to take part in the abortive rising of 1719, and again took ship for France. He returned to Scotland in 1727 and died unheralded at Auchintoul in 1751. Tayler, *1715: The Story of the Rising*, pp. 231–35.

43. List of the Clans supporting the government and in rebellion, 1715, Laing MSS, I. 347; Baynes, *Jacobite Rising*, p. 56. The intentions and actual whereabouts of the MacGregors and Rob Roy are somewhat difficult to determine. Rob Roy's latest biographer, W. H. Murray, writes that the MacGregors were employed in an operation against Dumbarton Castle before joining the western clans at Strathfillan and again moving south to threaten the Lowlands. Rob Roy and his clansmen apparently participated·in the operations at Inveraray before joining Mar's main army at Sheriffmuir. W. H. Murray, *Rob Roy MacGregor, his life and times* (Glasgow: Richard Drew Publishing, 1982), pp. 172–81.

44. Campbell loyalties were divided during the 'Fifteen. Iain Glas, first Earl of Breadalbane, who was reportedly able to raise 1,000 men, cast his lot with the Jacobites. Those supporting George I included Argyll himself and his brother, the Earl of Islay, under whose influence a large number of Campbell lairds signed a bond of loyalty to the king at Inveraray in mid-September. Tayler, *1715: The Story of the Rising*, pp. 109, 114; Baynes, *Jacobite Rising*, p. 59; L. D. to Laird of Cartsburn, 27 September 1715, Laing MSS, II. 480, 1.

45. The Keppoch MacDonalds were expected to provide 250 men to the Jacobite cause, but they never joined Gordon. Baynes, *Jacobite Rising*, p. 59.

46. Mar to Gordon, 16 October 1715, quoted in Rae, *History of the Rebellion*, pp. 446–47.

47. Mar to Gordon, 4 October 1715, *ibid.*, p. 430.

48. Argyll to Stewart, Add. MSS, 35838, f. 390; Mar to Gordon, 19 October 1715, quoted in Rae, *History of the Rebellion*, pp. 450–51. The main Jacobite army got as far as Auchterarder and Dunblane before Mar cautiously withdrew it when he heard of Argyll's

return to Stirling. Letter addressed to Mr. Charles Mackie at Leyden, 29 October 1715, Laing MSS, II. 90.

49. Letter from William, Marquis of Annandale, 2 November 1715, Laing MSS, II. 502.

50. Sinclair, *Memoirs*, p. 187.

51. *Ibid.*, p. 157.

52. Rae, *History of the Rebellion*, p. 299; Tayler, *1715: The Story of the Rising*, p. 95. The strength of the Jacobite army is difficult to assess, though it was surely at least twice as large as Argyll's 3,000 to 4,000-man force. Of contemporary authors, Rae's estimate of 12,000 is one of the higher figures, while Keith's total of 6,000 infantry and 800 cavalry is one of the lower estimates. The Master of Sinclair gave a figure of about 8,000. Of the more modern writers, Baynes agrees with Keith's estimate that Mar took south nearly 7,000 actives to meet Argyll. The Marchioness of Tullibardine concurs. Rae, *History of the Rebellion*, p. 299; Keith, *Fragment of a Memoir*, p. 16; Sinclair, *Memoirs*, p. 208; Baynes, *Jacobite Rising*, pp. 133–34; Marchioness of Tullibardine, ed., *A Military History of Perthshire, 1660–1902*, 2 vols. (Perth: R. A. and J. Hay, 1908), I: 276n.

53. Sinclair, *Memoirs*, p. 158.

54. Rae states that the three diversionary attacks were to be carried out by separate 1,000-man forces. Rae, *History of the Rebellion*, p. 299.

55. Sinclair, *Memoirs*, p. 203. Mar carried with him eleven pieces of artillery, but it proved useless because of a shortage of ammunition. Tullibardine, ed., *Perthsire*, I: 274n.

56. Tullibardine, ed., *Perthshire*, I: 277; Rae, *History of the Rebellion*, pp. 299–300.

57. A. F. Steuart, ed., *News Letters of 1715–16* (Edinburgh: W. and R. Chambers, 1910), p. 72.

58. Tullibardine, ed., *Perthshire*, I: 277; Steuart, ed., *News Letters*, p. 73; Rae, *History of the Rebellion*, p. 301.

59. Sinclair, *Memoirs*, p. 207.

60. *Ibid.*, p. 209.

61. *Ibid.*, pp. 210, 213–14.

62. The Jacobite front line, from left to right, was as follows: Appin Stewarts (260 men), Camerons (300), Glencoe MacDonalds (300), MacLeans (350), Clanranald MacDonalds (565), Breadalbane Campbells and smaller dependent clans (400), Glengarry MacDonalds (460), and Sleat MacDonalds (700). These Highland foot regiments totaled some 3,300 men. They were flanked on the right by the Perth (70), Fife (90), and Angus (100) horse squadrons, and on the left by Keith's (180), Stirlingshire (80), and Gordon's (400) horse squadrons. The horse totaled nearly 950. The second line consisted, from left to right, of the Struan Robertsons (200), Athollmen (300), Panmure's regiment (420), Drummonds (500), Gordons (800), and Seaforth MacKenzies (700), plus a few ill-mounted and ill-equipped MacKenzie horsemen. The strength of the second line totaled nearly 3,000 men. Baynes, *Jacobite Rising*, pp. 140–41; Tayler, *1715: The Story of the Rising*, p. 98; Tullibardine, ed., *Perthshire*, I: 279.

63. Argyll intended that his army should be drawn up, from left to right, as follows: Carpenter's dragoons (180 men), Kerr's dragoons (180), Clayton's infantry (240), Montagu's infantry (240), Morrison's infantry (240), Shannon's infantry (340), Wightman's infantry (250), Forfar's infantry (320), Evan's dragoons (180), and Portmore's dragoons (180). These units made up the front line of the government army. The rear was formed, left to right, as follows: Stair's dragoons (90), Orrery's infantry (320), Egerton's infantry (250), another detachment of Stair's dragoons (90), and the Gentlemen Volunteers (60). Baynes, *Jacobite Rising*, pp. 140–41; Tullibardine, ed., *Perthshire*, I: 280n.

64. Sinclair, *Memoirs*, p. 214.

65. Rae, *History of the Rebellion*, pp. 303–04.

66. *Ibid.*, p. 304.

67. Keith, *Fragment of a Memoir*, pp. 17–18.

68. *Ibid.*, p. 18.

69. Patten, *History of the Late Rebellion*, II: 56; Tullibardine, ed., *Perthshire*, I: 281–82; Sinclair, *Memoirs*, p. 215; Baynes, *Jacobite Rising*, pp. 142–43; John Shearer, *The Battle of Sheriffmuir. Related from Original Sources* (Stirling: Eneas MacKay, 1898), pp. 29–30.

70. Sinclair, *Memoirs*, p. 217.

71. *Ibid.*

72. Rae, *History of the Rebellion*, p. 305.

73. Sinclair, *Memoirs*, p. 211.

74. Rae, *History of the Rebellion*, p. 305.

75. Sinclair, *Memoirs*, p. 228. Such great disparity in Sinclair's estimates is difficult to explain. The lower figure seems more nearly correct, for the government army's casualties over the entire battlefield were slightly less than 500 killed and wounded and 130 captured. Since most of their losses came on the left wing, it is not unrealistic to estimate their losses there as between 300 and 400 men. Tullibardine, ed., *Perthshire*, I: 286; Baynes, *Jacobite Uprising*, p. 152; Rae, *History of the Rebellion*, p. 310; Patten, *History of the Late Rebellion*, II: 39–45.

76. Rae, *History of the Rebellion*, p. 306

77. Sinclair, *Memoirs*, p. 219.

78. Rae, *History of the Rebellion*, pp. 306–07.

79. Tullibardine, ed., *Perthshire*, I: 285; Sinclair, *Memoirs*, pp. 222–23; Tayler, *1715: The Story of the Rising*, pp. 101–02.

80. Rae, *History of the Rebellion*, p. 305.

81. Robert Campbell, *The Life of the Most Illustrious Prince John, Duke of Argyle and Greenwich* (London: Charles Corbett, 1745), p. 189.

82. Having served under the Duke of Marlborough on the continent during the War of the Spanish Succession, Argyll learned first hand the revolutionary cavalry tactics practised by that great military leader. Dalton, *George the First's Army*, I: 2–3.

83. Sinclair, *Memoirs*, p. 225; J. S. Keltie, *History of the Scottish Highlands, Highland Clans and Highland Regiments*, 2 vols. (Edinburgh: Thomas Jack, 1887), I: 463–64.

84. Scott, *Tales of a Grandfather*, II: 913.

85. Sinclair, *Memoirs*, pp. 225–26; Tullibardine, ed., *Perthshire*, I: 282; Spottiswoode Society, *Miscellany*, II: 428; Rae, *History of the Rebellion*, pp. 307–08.

86. Tullibardine, ed., *Perthshire*, I: 285–86; Rae, *History of the Rebellion*, pp. 307–08; Baynes, *Jacobite Rising*, pp. 150–51.

87. Tullibardine, ed., *Perthshire*, I: 285–86; Baynes, *Jacobite Rising*, pp. 150–51; Rae, *History of the Rebellion*, pp. 307–09; Shearer, *Sheriffmuir*, p. 34; Hutchison, *Jacobite Rising*, p. 27; T. C. F. Brotchie, *The Battlefields of Scotland, Their Legend and Story* (Edinburgh: T. C. and E. C. Jack, 1913), p. 207.

88. Sinclair, *Memoirs*, pp. 222–23.

89. Sinclair, *Memoirs*, p. 228; Campbell, *Life of Argyle*, p. 204; Baynes, *Jacobite Rising*, p. 152; Keith, *Fragment of a Memoir*, p. 20; Patten, *History of the Late Rebellion*, II: 39–45, 51–52, 59; Rae, *History of the Rebellion*, p. 310; Tullibardine, ed., *Perthshire*, I: 286; Hutchison, *Jacobite Rising*, p. 28; Spottiswoode Society, *Miscellany*, II: 441.

90. For Dundee's pre-battle actions at Killiecrankie see Chapter 5 above.

91. Sinclair, *Memoirs*, p. 223; Scott, *Tales of a Grandfather*, II: 912.

92. Richard Henderson to Madam Lockhart, 16 November 1715, Laing MSS, III. 375.

93. Sinclair, *Memoirs*, p. xxvii. This observation comes not from Sinclair himself, but from James MacKnight, editor of the Jacobite officer's memoirs.

94. *Ibid.*, pp. xxviii–xxix.

7

The 'Forty-Five: Jacobite Strategy

Times passes wearily in Elphin to-night; last
night I thought it passed wearily too; and
though wearily I find to-day go by, yesterday
lacked nothing in its weary length.

Wearisome to me is each succeeding day; it was
not so we used to be, with no fighting, no
raiding, no learning of athletic feats.

With no love for courting or hunting, the two
crafts my mind was bent on; no going in battle-
ranks or combat. Alas it is the end for me.

No catching of hind or stag, — not thus was my
desire; no mention of prowess or of hound. —
Time passes wearily in Elphin to-night.[1]

Oisean
'Elphin'

These verses might well have served as an epitaph for the Gaelic world after its
death blow on lonely, windswept Drummossie Moor in the spring of 1746. The
battle of Culloden ended the 'Forty-five, the last Jacobite attempt to return the
Stuarts to the throne of Great Britain. In the next half-century the Scottish
Highlands became sheep pasture, the clansmen became outlaws, British soldiers,
or emigrants, and the once-proud clan chiefs became absentee landlords with
luxurious dwellings in Edinburgh, Glasgow, and London.[2] The subjugation of the
Celtic fringe was a small step in the development of Anglo-Saxon commercialism,
but to the Gaels in the British Isles it meant the end of their traditional way of life.

Often when critical analysis strips away fable and legend from a desperate
enterprise such as the 'Forty-five, an even more captivating story is revealed. For
eight months during 1745 and 1746 the Scottish Gaels, poorly led and equipped,
held at bay the armed might of Great Britain in a tragic, yet inspirational and
heroic, struggle. They risked all and lost all, and the strategy with which they
carried through that dangerous gamble in itself is as worthy of study as are the
romantic escapades of Prince Charles Edward Stuart, the man whose cause they
elected to champion.

Though the Highland army fell in part because of a strategy that was poorly
suited to their manner of warfare, it was during those dark days after Culloden that
the clansmen demonstrated their resolve and character by refusing to accept their

100

setback as final. Weary and worn by long, unproductive marches and a lack of food, they waited to avenge Culloden, despite the disheartening observation from Lord George Murray, their ablest commander, that ' . . . there was neither money nor provisions to give: so no hopes were left'.[3] The Highlanders' wish to continue the fight after the bankruptcy of Jacobite strategy was reflected in the verse of their bards, one of whom wrote:

> O remnant that remains of us
> Let us close up our ranks,
> With courage and with firm resolve
> To make our last attempt;
> Determined ne'er again to turn
> Our backs upon our foes
> O, let us rise for the crown's true heir,
> Now is his only hour!
> O Scotland! Art thou not ashamed
> At the poor part thou'st played
> Leaving a handful of the Gaels
> To face the foeman's blade?
> Come, summon up your mighty strength,
> O warlike Scota's sons,
> Let us revenge on George's folk
> The royal blood of the clans . . . [4]

> Alexander MacDonald
> 'A Fragment'

But Charles had departed to wander in the Hebrides, leaving those who had stood beside him with nowhere to turn for direction or support, and thus to their miserable fate.

Highland warfare had not changed since the 1715 uprising. After receiving training and developing the habits of warriors within their individual clans at an early age, the Highlanders would ' . . . be commanded by none but their own chiefs, who will not serve under one another, [thus] there must be as many regiments as clans in a Highland army'.[5] The close-knit social structure of the clans and their rivalries with one another precluded any sort of military organization that might have led to efficiency and discipline on the battlefield. The haphazard melange of clan regiments that characterized the Highlanders' military organization mirrored a neglect of the rudiments of regular warfare. An officer in Prince Charles's army wrote that ' . . . it is hard to make Highlanders do . . . regular duty . . . they are not so much masters of that sedate valour that is necessary to maintain a post . . . '[6] Charles nevertheless ignored their irregular organization and attempted to use them as a conventional force. Consequently, he faced low morale and widespread desertion.[7]

Between 1715 and 1745 the British enacted a number of changes designed to improve their chances of success against the Highland clans. Most British soldiers, having no first-hand knowledge of their adversaries' way of war, entertained ' . . . such a terrible impression of the Highlanders, that they thought they had no chance unless they were greatly superior in numbers ... '8 Nonetheless, the British steeled themselves to the task at hand, and in the three decades between Sheriffmuir and Culloden they refined their strategy, organization, weapons, and policy to suit the particular rigors of Highland warfare. The reorganization of the British army's artillery arm between 1715 and 1745 played a major role in defeating the Highlanders. In 1715 the government was unable to outfit a permanent artillery train, but between 1716 and 1727 four permanent artillery companies were formed that eventually were merged into the Royal Regiment of Artillery.[9] Another concurrent improvement, the introduction of lighter, mobile horse artillery, allowed the British to traverse the rugged countryside with less difficulty than before. Of the three major battles of the 'Forty-five — Prestonpans, Falkirk, and Culloden — the English horse artillery was a deciding factor only in the last. Its ineffectiveness or absence at Prestonpans and Falkirk may have prompted a Jacobite officer to comment that artillery was ' ... greatly over-rated; [but] I do not doubt ... that, in the course of time, an army will think itself lost, if it has not these enormous masses to drag after it, the cause of so much embarrassment ... '[10] At Culloden, however, this line of thought was disproved by the performance of the British horse artillery arm, where it was perhaps not so much overrated by the British as it was underestimated by the Jacobites, at least by Prince Charles.

British Highland policy between the 'Fifteen and the 'Forty-five turned partly on the Disarming Act of 1725.[11] In that year Field Marshal George Wade went to the Highlands to enforce Parliament's legislation. Most of the disaffected clans relinquished a few rusty swords and muskets, but the loyal Whig clans generally complied with the act's demands. The result, of course, was that the Jacobite clans remained armed and ready for action while the Whig clans were virtually disarmed. An English traveler in the Highlands, perhaps basing his reflections on the intent and not the actual outcome of the Disarming Act, predicted that the ravages of war would no more plague Scotland.[12] Those closer to the government, however, understood the weaknesses of the policy:

> This act has been found by experience to work the quite contrary effect from what was intended by it; and, in reality, it proves a measure for more effectually disturbing the peace of the Highlands, and of the rest of the kingdom. For ... all the dutiful and well-affected clans truly submitted to the act ... and gave up their arms, so that they are now completely disarmed; but the disaffected clans either concealed their arms at first, or have provided themselves since with other arms.[13]

That the Disarming Act failed to pacify the Highlands or to strengthen the government's position there becomes evident when one notes that most of the Campbells were without weapons when Prince Charles landed in Scotland.[14]

Despite the failure of the British to enforce the Disarming Act, they did derive some direct benefits from the formation of four Highland companies that initially were intended to help carry out the policy. Officers were drawn from the Whig clans — notably the Campbells and their allies — but the rank and file came from all corners of the Highlands. Service in arms for the government already was popular among the Campbells, and by 1739 sufficient other clansmen had joined to form a permanent Highland regiment about 800 strong. These pro-government Highlanders proved valuable throughout the 'Forty-five, serving as scouts, spies, guides, and pickets, as well as regular troops.[15]

The intent of British military policy was to force the Highlanders to fight conventionally as a regular army so that the British could bring into play their superior firepower, discipline, and numbers. Most of the British troops had gained their combat experience in Flanders, where they fought on level plains interrupted occasionally by gently flowing rivers. As a consequence, they were unprepared to deal with the difficulties of fighting in the harsh Highland environment. Also, a more civilized sort of war was fought on the continent, replete with elaborate rules and formalities. The Gaels, of course, conformed to none of these niceties simply because to them 'rules of warfare' was a contradiction in terms. Until Culloden Charles and his lieutenants frustrated British designs by keeping to the tenets of traditional Celtic warfare: utilization of the clans' mobility and endurance and the Highland charge. Throughout most of the campaign the Jacobite officers allowed their troops ' . . . to adhere to their ancient and simple manoeuvre, [rather] than to teach them imperfectly, the more complicated movements . . . '[16] The observations of their officers reflected the Highlanders' distate for the implements of modern warfare, without which they could hardly be tempted to fight the British in formal battle. One officer noted that ' . . . all kinds of firearms are directly at variance with the natural disposition of the Highlanders . . . The sword is the weapon which suits them best'.[17] Another observed that it was ' . . . cannon and cavalry . . . [that] the Highlanders seemed most to dread . . . '[18] At Culloden the clans finally met the British under conditions in which the latter were able to bring their superior conventional strength into effect.

In the opening phase of the 'Forty-five uprising Britain's strategic superiority was not readily apparent. Two weeks after Prince Charles raised his standard at Glenfinnan in mid-August, he was at the head of about 2,000 hastily assembled clansmen and a small troop of Lowland cavalry.[19] Sir John Cope, commander-in-chief of the royal forces in Scotland, had been charged with marching north to crush the rising before it got under way. Conflicting reports as to the size and strength of the Jacobite army may have clouded the government's judgment concerning the proper course of action.[20] Amid the confusion Cope marshaled his 1,400-man army of inexperienced levies near Stirling on 20 August with orders to proceed against Charles.[21] Due to the poor state of his army Cope feared marching any farther north than Crieff, and rightly so.[22] Besides being outnumbered, his soldiers were unprepared to face the confident Highlanders, who ' . . . wished with uncommon ardour to come to an engagement'.[23] Once past Crieff Cope wisely chose to avoid the Highland army at the rugged Corryarrack Pass. Instead he marched away toward Inverness, leaving the Lowlands open to attack.[24]

Prince Charles decided to move rapidly south from the Highlands. First, however, he had to harness the impetuous clansmen who desired to follow Cope to Inverness.[25] That accomplished and the only government field army in Scotland on the run, he forged ahead toward the unprotected Lowlands. It was argued that

Cope might have remained at Stirling, as Argyll had contemplated doing in 1715, to contest the Highlanders' passage of the Forth or to strengthen his army by additional recruitment before taking on the Jacobites.[26] But the Forth was fordable at several points and Cope could not possibly have remained at Stirling and brought the Jacobites to action before they slipped by into the Lowlands.[27] Lending credence to this opinion, Lord George Murray, who had joined the Jacobite army in Perth in early September,[28] wrote of the clansmen that there ' ... never were any troops that have made such vast marches, out so early, always dark before encamping, ... scrimpt for provisions, and yet [in] high spirits'.[29] So Charles was wise to proceed southward with this highly mobile army regardless of the action Cope chose to take. By avoiding the royal army, the Jacobites were all but assured of arriving in the Lowlands at full strength. Establishing themselves south of the Forth was of greater value to them than was destroying Cope's band of raw recruits.

Prince Charles entered Edinburgh in mid-September with a rag-tag army of 2,000 Highland foot, ' ... the half completely armed, the others [armed] with pitch forks, scythes, a sword or a pistol, or some only with a staff or stick — a troop of 36 horse ... and one ... piece of cannon'.[30] What a humiliation it must have been for the government to see Edinburgh fall to this motley group with hardly a shot fired in its defense! Neither Montrose and MacColla, Dundee, nor Mar had come near taking the ancient Scottish capital. Now Charles was but a victory away from bringing the Lowlands, except for a few isolated castles, notably Edinburgh and Stirling, under his control. Cope obliged the Jacobites by transporting his army by sea to Dunbar, east of Edinburgh, where it landed on the very day Charles entered the city. Four days later the Highlanders routed Cope's army.[31]

The Highlanders' occupation of Edinburgh and their subsequent victory over Cope at Prestonpans (the tactical elements of which will be discussed in detail in the following chapter) marked the culmination of an effective Jacobite strategy. Charles and his officers had overpowered a weaker army by employing their own in such a way as to emphasize the strengths of the Highlanders. The march from Lochaber to Perth and on across the Forth utilized the Highland army's exceptional speed and mobility. With this advantage they could bring Cope to battle under favorable circumstances at almost any time. By occupying Edinburgh Charles had forced Cope to risk his army against a Jacobite force of comparable size that was inspired by its sweep across the Lowlands. Cope's army suffered such a crushing blow at Prestonpans that the Jacobites doubted if it could ever recover.[32] Indeed, the victory ' ... made the Prince the entire master of Scotland ... '[33] What remained to be seen was whether he could take full advantage of that mastery.

Jacobite strategy throughout the initial phase of the uprising had been to drive out the government army and gain control of Scotland. By late September this was accomplished. But after Prestonpans Charles wrote to his father, acknowledging that the victory had clouded his immediate strategic objectives: ''Tis said my victory should put me under new difficulties which I did not see before, and ... this is the case'.[34] In the immediate aftermath of Prestonpans, however, his

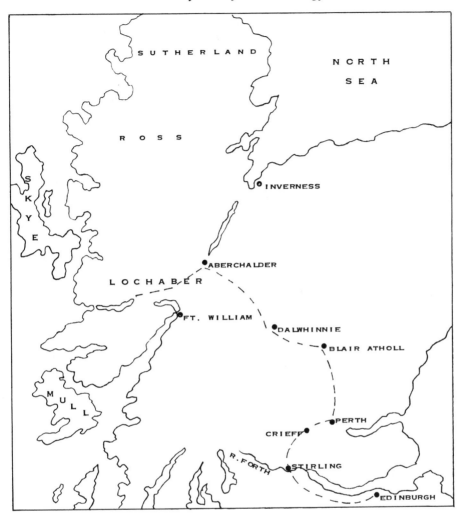

MAP 17. JACOBITE MARCH FROM LOCHABER TO EDINBURGH

situation did not appear so troubled. When the Jacobites returned to Edinburgh, their forces nearly doubled to between 5,000 and 6,000 men.[35] Shortly thereafter Charles received a shipment of arms and ammunition from France; when combined with several pieces of artillery taken at Prestonpans, his army gained a substantial arsenal.[36] Prince Charles now had two options: he could remain in Scotland and consolidate his position, or he could embark on a strategic offensive and march into England.

As the campaign shifted into its second phase, Charles faced a dilemma that had plagued Mar in 1715: the Highlanders were becoming restless because of inactivity in Edinburgh, but most of the chiefs opposed a march into England. Now that there was no royal army in the field in Scotland, Charles could bring his men to action only if he sought out the enemy farther south. The prospect of leaving Scotland to pursue the strategic offensive, however, threatened to bring on widespread desertion, especially since the chiefs were not enthusiastic about the plan.[37] Charles clearly wished to risk an invasion of England, however, and he waited in Edinburgh ' ... with the greatest impatience ... '[38] On 30 October he called a council of war to determine which direction the campaign would take.

The debate over strategy between Charles and his officers at the October council began a fatal rift in the Jacobite ranks that continued to widen until their defeat at Culloden.[39] A faction headed by Lord George Murray opposed the march into England for several reasons: first, there had been no genuine show of support from France; second, the English Jacobites had given no indications that they would rise for Prince Charles; third, there undoubtedly would be numerous desertions among the Highlanders both before and during the march; fourth, the opportunity for a successful campaign had already passed while the army remained inactive in Edinburgh; and fifth, the Jacobite army would be greatly outnumbered.[40] Charles parried with his opinion that once he was among Jacobite sympathizers in England they would rally to his cause. He argued further that the Jacobites had to demonstrate to France their credibility as a fighting force before aid would be forthcoming. Murray reluctantly agreed to support Charles's plan. Although he doubted the validity of the Prince's arguments concerning support from England and France, he apparently feared that continued inactivity in Scotland would result in the dissipation of the army. The officers finally decided by a single vote to proceed with the fateful march.[41]

With a lack of unanimity and poorly defined objectives the Jacobites set out for England at the beginning of November,[42] much as O'Neill and O'Donnell had departed Ulster a century and a half earlier. Gaelic armies had seldom operated effectively when pursuing a strategic offensive; the year 1745 was to be no exception. Though their speed and endurance allowed the Highlanders to penetrate far into England without encountering any real danger, they had little chance of striking a fatal blow against the Hanoverian dynasty. With a small army of between 5,000 and 6,000 men, less than 4,000 of whom were Highlanders,[43] the Jacobites reached Derby in early December. There, about 130 miles (or less than a week's march) from London, they halted and took stock of the situation. What transpired between Charles and his officers at Derby deepened the distrust and animosity that had begun in Edinburgh and signaled the start of a long retreat.

Relations between Charles and his council, particularly Murray, had worsened on the march south.[44] At the crucial council of war at Derby the Scottish officers, for the most part shunned by Charles in favor of his Irish aides, stood their ground and refused to be swayed by their master's desire to press on. Charles argued that the march to London must be made lest the morale of the army be broken. Though faced with the prospect of encountering two field armies — Wade's and Cumberland's — that greatly outnumbered his own, Charles knew his men could not be diverted before they reached the English capital. The rapid and elusive march of the Highlanders had maneuvered the two government forces out of position and, as a result, they could not hope to outrace the Jacobites to London.

Charles and his officers received news, however, that a third army was gathering on the outskirts of the city. The Jacobites were now outnumbered five or six to one. The officers who were opposed to the attack did not believe that the Highlanders could triumph against such odds.[45] The crux of their argument was captured in the memoirs of one officer:

> The enterprise was bold, nay rash, and unexampled. What man in his senses could think of encountering the English armies, and attempting the conquest of England, with four thousand five hundred Highlanders? It is true they were brave, resolute, and determined to fight to the very last, selling their lives as dearly as possible, and having no alternative but victory or death; but still the disproportion between this handful of men and the whole force of England was so great as to preclude the slightest hope of success.[46]

When the Highland army reached Derby, the clan rank and file, who had so vehemently opposed the campaign at first, sided with Charles, their ' . . . heroic ardour . . . animated, on that occasion, to the highest pitch of enthusiasm, and [they] breathing nothing but a desire for . . . combat'.[47] Many of the chiefs also believed that the attack should be made simply because they felt they had come too far to turn back. They predicted that whatever course was taken the Jacobite army would face a difficult task.[48] Murray thought that the Highlanders had served Charles well by marching into England, but ' . . . that certainly 4,500 Scots had never thought of putting a king upon the English throne by themselves'.[49] The Highlanders at Derby reacted to their situation much as O'Neill's Irish troops had done on the eve of Kinsale: they had been averse to leaving home to pursue a strategic offensive but balked at jeopardizing their honor by turning away from the enemy without doing battle. At Kinsale O'Neill had been unable to overcome his warriors' will to fight; at Derby, however, because of the influence of Murray and other factors, the Highlanders were restrained from charging headlong into what probably would have been a crippling defeat.

A potentially disastrous split between the Highlanders and most of the Jacobite officers was averted when news reached the camp of Lord John Drummond's arrival in Scotland with a French expeditionary force. Several Highland clans had also risen and were gathering near Perth. The size of Drummond's force was greatly exaggerated and in reality numbered only about 800 men,[50] but Murray immediately confronted Charles and argued that it would be madness not to join those forces in Scotland since it was now evident that there would be no French landing in England. Most of the Highland chiefs sided with Murray.[51] Though they were willing to retreat to Scotland, the chiefs proposed that they bring the enemy to action en route. Wade's army lay within striking distance of the route of retreat, and many of the chiefs believed they might pounce on it and ' . . . retire gloriously from England with arms in our hands, which would console the Highlanders, whose hopes would be disappointed by their retreat'.[52]

Faced with continued opposition from Murray and the chiefs and the prospect of joining with Drummond's army in Scotland, Charles reluctantly sanctioned a

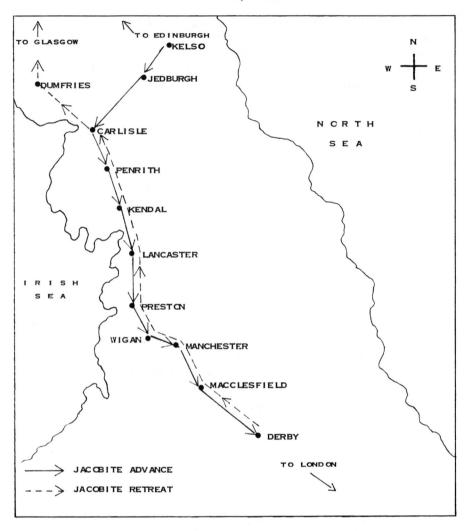

MAP 18.   JACOBITE MARCH TO AND FROM ENGLAND

retreat.[53] But opinion within the Jacobite ranks remained divided. Reflecting on the fateful decision at Derby, one of Murray's supporters wrote that

> The case was he [Charles] knew nothing about the country nor had not the smallest idea of the force that was against him, nor where they were situated. His Irish favourites ... had always represented the whole nation as his friends, had diminished much all the force that was against him, and he himself believed firmly that the soldiers of the regulars would never fight against him, as he was their true Prince.[54]

Another observer, on the other hand, said that

> How far this [the retreat] was the properest course has been much canvassed; some thinking the intelligence from Scotland of the great numbers convened in arms or

landed from France was an imposition and that the Prince with great unwillingness consented to a retreat. One thing is certain, never was our Highlanders in higher spirits notwithstanding their long and fatiguing march ... so that we judged and were able to fight double our numbers ... and would to God we had pushed on though we had been all cut to pieces, when we were in a condition for fighting and doing honour to our noble Prince ... rather than to have survived and seen that fatal day of Culloden ... [55]

With such arguments and counter-arguments circulating throughout their ranks, the Jacobites marched away from a showdown on English soil.

The retreat began before the first shafts of sunlight pierced the gray, misty morning of 6 December, a day that came to be known in the annals of Jacobite history as 'Black Friday'.[56] The retreat indeed marked a strategic turning point in the campaign; on that day the Jacobite leadership all but admitted the inevitability of defeat. Many of the officers never recovered from the disappointing attempt to take the war into the heartland of the enemy, and the tenuous unity of the Jacobite leadership was strained beyond reconciliation. Thereafter they almost continually argued over whether to advance or retreat, attack or defend, until the superior weight of British arms brought about their downfall the following April.

But for the indomitable fighting spirit of the clan rank and file, the retreat itself could have caused the collapse of the rising. But morale among the Highlanders remained high even as the retreat began because they thought they were advancing on London. When, however, they ' ... began to know by day-light, from the marks they had taken of the road, that they were going back, there was an universal lamentation amongst them'.[57] But their disappointment faded as they neared their homeland. They had marched the 170 miles from Derby to Carlisle in only two weeks in the dead of winter![58] An officer wrote regarding the remarkable progress of Charles's troops that

> At no time was the gallant spirit of the Highland army displayed to greater advantage than on the return to Scotland. Daily confronted with the disheartening spectacle of retreat, marching through a hostile country in midwinter, and opposed to an enemy from whom no mercy was to be expected, they effected an orderly retirement and crossed the Border with a total loss of less than 100 men.[59]

Though it produced no positive results for the Jacobite cause, the campaign into England was a remarkable achievement. More than anything else, it demonstrated the resilience of the Highlanders, who, under adverse weather conditions, had negotiated terrible roads and had come within 130 miles of the enemy capital while evading the regular armies of both Wade and Cumberland. The campaign was by no means distinguished by its orderliness or discipline, but the Highlanders had managed to return to Scotland without any significant losses in manpower.

Once back in Scotland the Jacobites found their position much less secure than when they had begun their march into England, and Charles now faced a choice between again clearing the Lowlands of the enemy or of falling back into the Highlands where he might replenish his army during the winter months and enlist further recruits from among the clans. In numerical terms the Jacobites could not hope to match the British, who in time were sure to move into the Lowlands in pursuit of them. Even after Charles returned and joined with Drummond and the other clan regiments, his strength did not exceed 8,000 to 9,000 men.[60] By January 1746 General Henry Hawley already had amassed about 10,000 infantry and three regiments of dragoons near Edinburgh.[61] But Charles chose to remain in the Lowlands and the result was the battle of Falkirk (17 January).[62] Falkirk demonstrated that the Highlanders were more than a match for some of the government's best regular troops. Even so, the British were capable of bringing forward still more armies of comparable size that in the long run would certainly overpower the Highlanders.

Charles's decision to give battle at Falkirk was sound strategy, but in the aftermath of the victory the Jacobites were unable to grasp the fundamental strategic elements that would allow them to conduct a successful campaign against the British. First and foremost, they marched away from the Lowlands, leaving a nucleus of men around whom the enemy would build an even stronger force. This demoralized the Highlanders and also jeopardized any chances the Jacobites had of regrouping undisturbed in the Highlands. The Jacobites' tactical success at Falkirk was thus not translated into a strategic advantage. Instead, Charles insisted on returning to the fruitless siege of Stirling Castle where he frittered away his strength and widened the rift among his officers, while the British recuperated in Edinburgh.[63] A Jacobite officer bitterly criticized Charles's decision, lamenting that the army ' ... ought to have pursued the English with the rapidity of a torrent, in order to prevent them from recovering from their fright: we should have kept continually at their heels, and never relaxed, till they were no longer in a condition to rally ... '[64] The Jacobite debacle after Falkirk indeed showed ' ... how little ... they ... knew of war, except the mere fighting part of it'.[65]

As the Jacobite army lay inactive in the Lowlands, its strength and morale slowly seeped away. Many of the clansmen succumbed to the temptation to return home and deposit their plunder. Toward the end of January Murray and the chiefs petitioned Charles to sanction a further retreat into the Highlands. Their reasons for such an action were twofold: first, heavy desertion due to prolonged inactivity; and second, the inability of the army to carry on with the siege of Stirling Castle. The Gaels, of course, did not possess the patience or the discipline of regular troops, nor were they trained in the use of artillery. They were, therefore, unfit for conducting the type of campaign that Charles envisioned. The best course might have been to put themselves in a position similar to the one they were in immediately following Prestonpans the previous September when they had banished the royal army from Scotland. But Charles hesitated until the army was too weak and disorganized to pursue any other course except retreat.[66]

Despite the poor condition of the army at the end of January, Charles fervently opposed a further withdrawal into the Highlands. He perhaps now realized the mistake he had made by not following up Falkirk by crushing the remainder of Hawley's army and thus sought to stay on in the Lowlands to try and regain that lost opportunity. Charles raised some valid questions concerning a flight to the

Highlands: ' ... how much more will that raise the spirits of our enemys and sink those of our own people? Can we imagine, that where we go the enemy will not follow, and at last oblige us to a battle which we now decline?'[67] Charles went on to express his disgust over his growing powerlessness in the face of his principal officers: 'I have an army that I cannot command any further than the chief officers please, and therefore if you are all resolved upon it I must yield ... but with greatest reluctance ... and ... I wash my hands of the fatal consequences which I foresee but cannot help'.[68] Though Murray favored a retreat, he admitted that ' ... it will be very unpleasant ... '[69]

The 150-mile retreat from Stirling to Inverness allowed the Jacobites to catch their breath and attempt to devise some sort of plan to deal with their desperate situation. Along the way relations between Charles and his Scottish officers worsened considerably, especially when the Prince found that the rate of desertion had been greatly exaggerated by Murray and the chiefs.[70] But once at Inverness the army began sorting out some of its problems. A major concern involved further recruitment as well as reorganization of existing clan regiments that had become disordered on the march north. An officer observed that the ' ... clans are flocking in so fast that already they are like the locusts of Egypt covering the face of the earth, so our spirits are now higher than ever they were low'.[71] Another concern was the presence of the Earl of Loudoun's regiment across the Moray Firth in Ross-shire, but the Jacobites quickly dispersed that force after reaching Inverness.[72] In the area of logistics Charles's army sought to secure its position by laying aside a store of provisions. Consequently, small bands were despatched to collect supplies and food from the surrounding countryside.[73] But the haul was meager and the Jacobites continued to be plagued by a dearth of rations until the end of the campaign.[74]

While the Jacobites attempted to consolidate their position in the Inverness area, the Duke of Cumberland, the new government commander in Scotland, devised plans to put an end to the uprising. Cumberland arrived in Edinburgh and realized that he could not overtake the Highlanders who had just begun their retreat north. He then made his leisurely way to Aberdeen and reached the city on 25 February. With him Cumberland brought fifteen regiments of infantry (some of which had recently fled from the Jacobites at Falkirk), two regiments of cavalry, and a body of Campbells and associated septs from Argyllshire and the north-east. Cumberland's army totaled between 9,000 and 10,000 men. While they waited at Aberdeen for the weather to clear, a fleet of supply ships sailed along the coast to provision them.[75] Cumberland's methodical preparations revealed a military mind of no particular genius. Much as Union General Ulysses S. Grant would do against Robert E. Lee's inferior Confederate Army of Northern Virginia in the American Civil War, Cumberland determined to finish off his enemy with a sledgehammer blow using his superior numbers and equipment. He apparently never considered any other approach in dealing with the Jacobites, and had they not obliged him by giving battle on an open field, Cumberland's strategy would have been exposed as the unimaginative planning that it was.

Cumberland's march from Aberdeen toward Culloden began on 8 April and

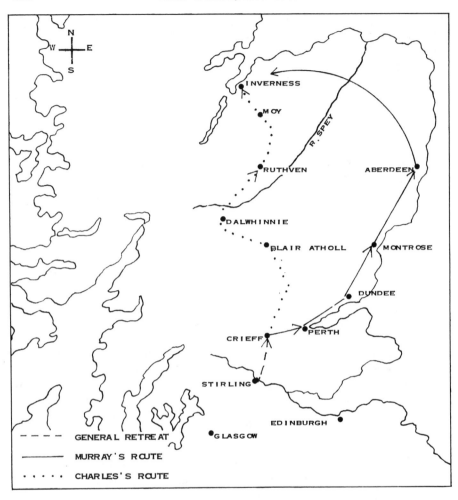

MAP 19. JACOBITE MARCH FROM STIRLING TO INVERNESS

presented Charles with what he considered to be a favorable opportunity to strike at the British as they attempted the crossing of the river Spey. The lower stretch of the river winds its way down from Strathspey and empties into the Moray Firth about halfway between Cullen and Elgin. In April 1746 the Spey was fordable at several places, and when unguarded was no trouble to cross. But Charles decided to make the river a first line of defense. Accordingly, he despatched Lord John Drummond with 2,000 Highlanders and Irish piquets to contest Cumberland's passage. With such a small force Drummond could not have stopped the enemy, but Charles apparently believed that he could delay them sufficiently to allow the widely dispersed Jacobite army to reassemble in the Inverness area. Charles failed to consider that the Gaels did not establish and maintain defensive positions well, and their attempt to do so on the Spey proved to be a waste of time and effort.

Cumberland's army approached on the morning of 12 April, and Drummond hurriedly withdrew from the banks of the river and marched off toward Elgin.[76] A rider despatched from the camp at Culloden witnessed the retreat:

> As we came near Elgin we found the guard on the Spey in full march back to Elgin, who gave out that they were neither able to guard the river nor fight the enemy after they had passed ... This guard was under the command of Lord John Drummond ... it was thought more advisable to retreat till we should be joined by the rest of our army ... [77]

Charles's latest strategic miscalculation put the Jacobites in a situation where only the most imaginative and daring strategy could save them.[78] In their present position the Jacobites suffered from an acute shortage of food and other essential provisions. Much of their strength had been sapped by attempts to reduce several government garrisons in the Highlands, and with the enemy in possession of Blair Castle all communications with the Lowlands were cut. To complicate matters, Charles was weakened from a bout of pneumonia and his officers continued in their bickerings and disagreements. As news of Cumberland's advance reached the army, a wave of fear mixed with enthusiasm spread through the ranks. Half-crazed from hunger and a desperate desire for combat, the Highlanders made their way toward the open parks of Culloden.[79]

The Jacobites' final effort to agree upon and implement a strategy turned on three questions that were hotly debated by Charles and his subordinates and later by historians: first, should they defend Inverness by awaiting Cumberland on the plain ground of Culloden (or Drummossie) Moor; second, should they abandon the town and move to the rugged ground south of the river Nairn; or third, should they attack Cumberland before he reached Culloden? Many of the Jacobite officers knew that the answers to these questions would decide the fate of the uprising; but when they turned to Prince Charles, they found him unable to see the gravity of the situation. One of the officers wrote that Charles

> ... was in a sanguine and exalted frame of mind, and said that he had no doubts as to the issue of the approaching conflict with ... Cumberland; he believed that the English soldiers would with difficulty be got to attack him. He refused to listen to any suggestion ... and when a rendezvous in the event of defeat was spoken of, he replied that only those who were afraid could doubt his coming victory ... As he had consulted only with his favourites everything was in the greatest disorder. The persons capable of serving him were suspected or neglected, and those in whom he had placed his trust had not the ability to be useful to him.[80]

The first issue that had to be resolved was whether the open moor of Culloden provided an advantageous position on which to meet Cumberland's army. As Charles would hear no talk of retreat, it fell to his officers to persuade him that their present location was inappropriate to the Highlanders' way of war. Murray vehemently opposed standing on the moor. The flat stretch of ground would provide Cumberland with the perfect opportunity to employ his superiority in cavalry and artillery against which the Jacobites would have little chance of victory. Murray was familiar enough with Highland warfare to know that the offensively minded Gaels would not defend even a strong position, much less one that offered no protection from the enemy's guns. And if they would not defend, only one option remained — an attack across the level ground into a hailstorm of British musket, grapeshot, and cannister. Until now the Jacobites had avoided meeting the enemy under conventional circumstances, and Murray had played no small role in the making of such decisions. On the eve of Culloden he pleaded once more with Charles and his fellow officers for a strategy that avoided fighting the British on their own terms.[81]

Murray's opposition to standing on Culloden Moor led to the second important question of whether to attempt to move south of the river Nairn. On 15 April Murray despatched two officers to reconnoitre the rising ground across the river. It was discovered to be rugged and boggy, and would be unsuitable for the enemy's cavalry and artillery. The terrain, furthermore, would provide the Highlanders with a high stand of ground from which to launch their traditional charge. Murray argued that even if Cumberland pursued and proved too strong to fight, the Duke then could be drawn further into the mountains where his lines of communication would be vulnerable and his army weakened from crossing the inhospitable territory. In effect, Murray's plan called for avoiding the stronger enemy army until a battlefield scenario could be arranged that would utilize the Highlanders' abilities and negate some of the enemy's advantages.[82] Charles and his Irish favorites countered Murray's argument by saying that they stood to lose Inverness if they abandoned their present position. Also, Charles seemed determined to put the entire issue to a test of arms as quickly as possible; he saw Murray's strategy as dilatory and thus demoralizing to the army. While Charles sought to be done with the battle as rapidly and as heroically as possible, his principal officers struggled to hammer out a viable strategy for the army's survival.[83]

When both factions within the Jacobite ranks had presented their arguments, Murray in a fit of desperation raised a third option — a night attack on Cumberland's camp near the village of Nairn. Now that his plan to retire south of the Nairn water had been blocked, Murray seemed determined to do whatever he could to keep the army together and to avoid meeting the enemy on Culloden Moor. With desertion increasing daily and the troops starving, Murray knew that desperate measures were necessary. At about the same time that Murray's officers were viewing the ground across the river, another party was riding to reconnoitre Cumberland's camp. When Charles received the news that Cumberland's army apparently had no intention of moving that day, he called a council of war.[84] The officers and chiefs gathered and

> Murray made a speech, wherein he enlarged upon the advantages Highlanders have by surprising their enemy, and rather attacking in the night than in daylight, for as regular troops depend entirely upon their discipline, and on the contrary the Highlanders having none, the night was the time to put them most upon an equality, and he concluded that his opinion was that they should march at dusk of the evening ... [85]

Murray reasoned that the night attack would neutralize Cumberland's numerical superiority, discipline, and cavalry and artillery and also give the Highlanders the opportunity to employ their swords in close combat.

Though Murray advocated the night attack on Nairn, he did have several reservations, the most important of which concerned timing and the consequences of a repulse. He believed that the Jacobites must reach the camp no later than one or two o'clock in the morning lest the early April sunrise reveal them to the enemy. Because of the late sunset at that time of year, however, the army could not begin their march before about eight o'clock. They would have at most six hours to traverse the twelve miles to Nairn. To further complicate matters, the army could not keep to the roads between Culloden and Nairn for fear of detection by enemy patrols. The Highlanders were inured to long, fatiguing marches, but other elements in Prince Charles's army were not as hardy and experienced. They would have to average about two miles per hour across boggy ground in the dark of night. When other officers questioned the ability of the army to accomplish such a feat, Murray agreed to accept personal responsibility for the outcome. Further queries arose about the course of action in the event of a repulse or outright defeat. Murray proposed that the army then return by the main road to regroup on the strong ground around Kilravock Castle and from there retire south of the Nairn. That Murray believed Culloden Moor altogether unsuitable for doing battle is evidenced not only by his support for a night attack, but also by his unwillingness to give up the idea of moving across the Nairn.[86]

Charles blindly accepted Murray's plan for the night attack, giving little thought to its potential drawbacks. Charles believed that his army, even without several key clan regiments that were operating away from the main camp, was strong enough to defeat Cumberland. Rationalizing a clearly emotional decision, Charles said that his men were in such dire need of provisions that an attack was necessary to procure food and supplies from the enemy. Just as Lee's Confederate army would later march to Gettysburg for shoes, Charles's men would hasten to Nairn for victuals! The Prince's misunderstanding of the situation on the afternoon of 15 April revealed a military mind as unimaginative as that of his royal opponent. Where Cumberland was pedestrian, Charles was impetuous. Unlike his predecessors, especially Montrose and Dundee, Charles had not the patience and sagacity to temper his zeal and successfully lead a Highland army. If Charles (or admittedly, Murray) had remembered the difficulty of moving during the night to attack at Prestonpans, he might not have exuded so much confidence. He accepted the night march because it promised quick results —positive or negative — and did not require him to make careful plans.[87]

The march failed because it was a desperate attempt undertaken without adequate preparation by an army that was severely hampered by a lack of food and other provisions. It began around eight o'clock in the evening with Murray and most of the Highland regiments (about one-third of the army) in the van, followed by the remainder of the clans, the Lowlanders, and the Irish piquets in the rear. The smaller and more mobile van was to cross the river Nairn as it neared Cumberland's camp and then attack from the south-east. The larger rearguard

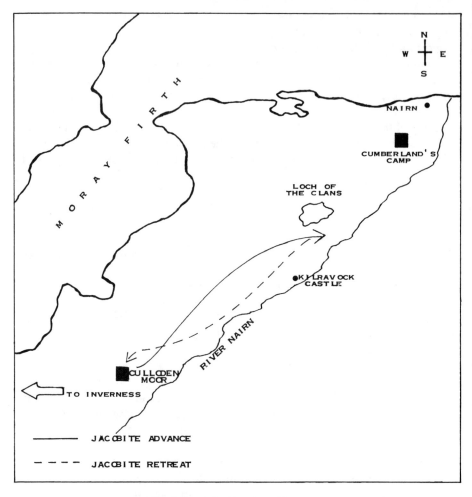

MAP 20 .   NIGHT MARCH TO NAIRN

was to march straight toward the sea and attack from the north-west. Such a manoeuvre in the dead of night required a great deal more strength and coordination than the Jacobites possessed. The troops had received only a single biscuit apiece the night before, spent under arms on the open moor, and on the day of the march. To make matters worse, there had been no plans laid for coordinating the movements of the van and rear. Besides vague instructions concerning the two-pronged attack, the men had been told only to avoid the use of firearms during the assault. The 4,000 Jacobites toiled through ankle-deep bogs, the rear echelons all the while lagging farther and farther behind. Murray consequently slowed his pace until he finally received word to halt between one and two o'clock in the morning about four miles from the enemy camp.[88]

Murray's halt of the van signaled the end of the enterprise and the beginning of another disagreement between him and Charles and also revealed a great deal about Murray's concept of generalship. By two o'clock the first faint rays of sunlight had begun to pierce the horizon, and Murray reasoned that the remaining distance could not be covered before daylight. The numerous reports of the participants give a muddled picture of what transpired in the quarter of an hour between the halt of the march and the retreat to Culloden.[89] Whether Murray ordered the retreat based on his own judgment, against specific orders to the contrary, or at Charles's command can never be known for certain. What is certain is that whoever ordered the retreat acted wisely. Several years after the event Murray composed a defense against those who had attempted to blacken his name:

> Whatever may be the rules in a regular army, (and it is not to be supposed I was ignorant of them), our practice had all along been, at critical junctures, that the commanding officers did everything to their knowledge for the best ... I own I disobeyed orders; but what I did was the only safe and honourable measures I could take.[90]

Murray admitted that he had at some time disobeyed orders but did not specify that he had at Nairn; his statement was meant to convey the idea of general independent initiative that he and other Jacobite officers had exercised throughout the campaign. More than the others Murray realized that a Highland army was most effective when allowed the latitude to adapt to rapidly changing circumstances. The rigidly defined chain of command that characterized conventional armies of the day simply could not be instituted within the Highland regiments because the Gaels were led most effectively by a commander at the front. Murray knew at two o'clock on 15 April that the outnumbered and exhausted clansmen could not survive an attack on an alert and heavily armed British army. And since Charles still would not sanction a retreat south of the Nairn, he thought it best to return to Culloden Moor where the men could recharge and make ready to meet the enemy under what he hoped would be more favorable conditions.

The abortive night march so fatigued the Jacobite army that it was in no shape to fight once it returned to Culloden Moor. The first troops staggered into the park enclosures between five and six o'clock on the cold, dreary morning of 16 April, many drifting off to seek food or rest.[91] A follower of Charles thought that Cumberland ' ... must have been blind in the extreme to have delayed attacking us, in the deplorable situation in which we were, worn out with hunger and fatigue ... '[92] The army numbered no more than 5,000 to 6,000 men and clearly could not have defended the open moor against almost twice as many fresh British troops. For the first time Charles seemed to sense his desperate situation but still would hear no talk of a retreat from the moor. Though no council of war was held before the battle, Murray again pleaded his case for a move south of the Nairn. A large body of MacPhersons were reportedly approaching from that direction, and Murray desired to link up with them and then rest the men before giving battle. Charles had one last chance to reconsider his strategy and save the army, but, backed by several of his Irish officers, he decided to stand his ground.[93] Murray wrote sarcastically that the cause was betrayed by those

... who were determined against a hill campaign, as they called it. What I can aver is, that myself and most of the clans ... were for this operation [the river crossing] ... It is true Sir Thomas Sheridan, and etc. could not have undergone it: so we were obliged to be undone for their ease.[94]

Charles held fast to ' ... an overweening estimate of the irresistable prowess of the Highlanders, whom he had on all previous occasions seen victorious ... '[95] But as one of his chief officers soberly reviewed the state of the Highlanders, he concluded that they ' ... were not possessed of supernatural strength'.[96] As the prospect of imminent battle loomed nearer, other officers implored Charles to change his mind and listen to reason:

There is no doubt the Highlanders could have avoided fighting till they had found their advantage in so doing ... they could have marched by ways that no regular troops could have followed them ... the Highlanders had neither money nor magazines ... [but] they could not have starved in that season of the year, as long as there were sheep or cattle to be had ... Perhaps such succours might have come from France, as would have enabled the Highlanders to have made an offensive instead of a defensive war ... But any proposition to postpone fighting was ill received [by Charles] and was called discouraging [to] the army.[97]

Charles was stubbornly intent on fighting, and Murray and the others could only cast anxious glances to the west and hope that the dispersed regiments would arrive before the enemy.[98]

When the Highlanders heard of Cumberland's advance about mid-morning on 16 April, they somehow forgot about their hunger and fatigue and for a few hours seemed as if they would justify Charles's confidence in their superhuman strength and prowess. As Charles, Murray, and the other officers mounted their horses, beat of drum and skirl of pipe revived the spirits of the clansmen: ' ... this little army was in the highest spirits imaginable; one would not have thought them the same that but a week ago were grumbling and finding fault with everything'.[99] Murray had managed to draft a set of orders to coordinate the army,[100] and not long after the Jacobites had drawn up on the flat and boggy moor the enemy column approached.

From the march into England the previous winter to the defeat on Culloden Moor, Prince Charles had implemented an unsound strategy that was both over-ambitious and highly unsuited to the Highlanders' manner of warfare. It is unfair to condemn Charles for his courage in invading England at the head of a victorious, and seemingly invincible, army; he must, however, be blamed for ignoring the recommendations of the clan chiefs and officers who advised him against the march. Cameron of Lochiel, MacDonald of Keppoch, and Lord George Murray, among others, knew that as the Highlanders moved farther from their homeland their willingness to conduct a campaign, except under the most desperate circumstances, evaporated. The Jacobites need not have stood idly by after Prestonpans, however, even though there was no government army left in Scotland. Charles might have despatched the Highlanders on a mission that many of them undoubtedly would have relished — the destruction of Campbell hegemony in Argyllshire and the south-western Highlands. While the clansmen ravaged Argyll, Charles and the Lowland elements of the army could have consolidated their position in the south and east.

The 400-mile march into England committed Prince Charles to an offensive strategy that his Highland army was unable to see through to a successful conclusion. When the bedraggled army returned to Scotland in January 1746, they found the situation differed dramatically from what it had been before their departure. The battle of Falkirk was a rousing tactical victory, but it failed to clear the Lowlands of the enemy as Prestonpans had done. Charles consequently had to choose between remaining in hostile territory or marching another 150 miles into the Highlands. At the time of the retreat to Inverness, Charles should have realized that his only chance of success lay in wearing down the enemy through a series of protracted guerrilla campaigns until aid might come from France; the Highlanders were adept at irregular warfare. Charles, however, opted for conventional battle on the open plain at Culloden. Several years after the uprising an historian of the Jacobite period proposed what perhaps would have been an ideal solution to the army's strategic woes: 'Had . . . Charles slept during the whole . . . expedition, and allowed Lord George Murray to act for him, according to his own judgment, there is every reason for supposing he would have found the crown of Great Britain on his head, when he awoke'.[101]

NOTES

1. Neil Ross, ed., *Heroic Poetry From the Book of the Dean of Lismore* (Edinburgh: Scottish Gaelic Texts Society, 1939), p. 9.

2. For a penetrating study of the depopulation of the Highlands during the latter half of the eighteenth century, see John Prebble, *The Highland Clearances* (London: Martin Secker and Warburg, 1963; Harmondsworth: Penguin Books, 1969).

3. Lord George Murray, 'Marches of the Highland Army,' in *Jacobite Memoirs of the Rebellion of 1745*, ed. Robert Chambers (Edinburgh: William and Robert Chambers, 1834), p. 124.

4. Alexander MacDonald, 'A Fragment,' in *Highland Songs of the Forty-Five*, ed. John Lorne Campbell (Edinburgh: John Grant, 1933; reprint ed., Edinburgh: Scottish Gaelic Texts Society, 1984), p. 119.

5. James Maxwell of Kirkconnell, *Narrative of Charles Prince of Wales' Expedition to Scotland in the Year 1745* (Edinburgh: The Maitland Club, 1841), p. 60.

6. *Ibid.*, pp. 133–34.

7. References to Highland desertion are numerous in the writings of those who fought with the clans. One such revealing passage cautioned that 'Every man that knows the Highlanders might lay his accounts with their marching home after a scuffle, and therefore I am surprised that none of you ever insisted upon taking all manner of precautions for keeping the army together, without which, making an appearance may be compared to a flash of powder, that vanishes in an instant, and scarce leaves a vestige behind it.' Robertson of Drumachine to James Robertson of Blairfetty, 12 January 1746, in *Jacobite Correspondence of the Atholl Family during the Rebellion, MDCCXLV-MDCCXLVI*, ed. J. H. Burton (Edinburgh: The Abbotsford Club, 1845), pp. 138–39.

8. Maxwell, *Narrative*, pp. 52–53.

9. J. W. Fortescue, *A History of the British Army*, 13 vols. (London: MacMillan and Company, 1910–1930), II: 48–49.

10. The Chevalier de Johnstone, *Memoirs of the Rebellion in 1745 and 1746*, 2nd ed. (London: Longman, Hurst, Rees, Orme and Brown, 1821), pp. 11–12.

11. George Lockhart, *The Lockhart Papers Containing Memoirs and Commentaries upon the Affairs of Scotland from 1702 to 1715, by George Lockhart, Esq. of Carnwath, His Secret Correspondence with the Son of King James the Second from 1718 to 1728, and his other Political Writings; Also, Journals and Memoirs of the Young Pretender's Expedition in 1745, by Highland Officers in his Army*, 2 vols. (London: William Anderson, 1817), II: 159–61; J. B. Salmond, *Wade in Scotland* (Edinburgh: The Moray Press, 1934), pp. 38–39.

12. Daniel Defoe, *A Tour through the Whole Island of Great Britain* (Harmondsworth: Penguin Books, 1971), p. 637.

13. Lord Milton to Marquis of Tweeddale, 16 September 1745, quoted in John Home, *The History of the Rebellion in the Year 1745* (London: T. Cadell, 1802), p. 303.

14. Sir James Fergusson, *Argyll in the Forty-Five* (London: Faber and Faber, 1951), p. 34; Johnstone, *Memoirs*, p. 21n.

15. Fortescue, *British Army*, II: 49–50; Charles Fraser-MacKintosh, ed., *Letters of Two Centuries Chiefly Connected with Inverness and the Highlands, from 1616 to 1815* (Inverness: A. and W. MacKenzie, 1890), pp. 222–23.

16. Johnstone, *Memoirs*, p. 120.

17. *Ibid.*, p. 113.

18. David, Lord Elcho, *A Short Account of the Affairs of Scotland in the Years 1744, 1745, 1746*, ed. Evan Charteris (Edinburgh: David Douglas, 1907; reprint ed., Edinburgh: James Thin, 1973), p. 266.

19. Walter B. Blaikie, ed., *Itinerary of Prince Charles Edward Stuart from his landing in Scotland July 1745 to his departure in September 1746* (Edinburgh: Scottish History Society, 1897), p. 10; Elcho, *Affairs of Scotland*, p. 253; Robert Chambers, *History of the Rebellion of 1745–1746* (Edinburgh: W. R. Chambers, 1869), p. 47.

20. Some government officials believed that Charles's army was little more than an undisciplined rabble that could be quickly dispersed, but rumor had it that some 9,000 French troops had landed in Lochaber to join the clans. Marquis of Tweeddale to Craigie, 17 August 1745, Edinburgh, National Library of Scotland, MS 3060, p. 60; James Dewar of Lassodie to Professor Charles Mackie, 4 September 1745, Edinburgh, Edinburgh University Library, Laing MSS, II. 90.

21. General John Cope to Marquis of Tweeddale, 9 August 1745, S.P. 54/25/54, Cope to Tweeddale, 10 August 1745, S.P. 54/25/58, Cope to Tweeddale, 13 August 1745, S.P. 54/25/66, London, Public Record Office, State Papers, Scotland, Series ii (hereafter cited as S.P. 54); Johnstone, *Memoirs*, pp. 10–11; Sir Robert Cadell, *Sir John Cope and the Rebellion of 1745* (Edinburgh: William Blackwood and Son, 1898), p. 44.

22. Cope to General Joshua Guest, 27 August 1745, S.P. 54/25/101.

23. Edinburgh, National Library of Scotland, Blaikie Collection, MS 298, ff. 87, 89 (hereafter cited as NLS, MS 298).

24. Cope's Council of War, 27 August 1745, S.P. 54/25/106; Johnstone, *Memoirs*, p. 11; Cadell, *Cope and the Rebellion of 1745*, p. 55.

25. NLS, MS 298, ff. 89–90; Lockhart, *Lockhart Papers*, II: 485.

26. Chambers, *History of the Rebellion*, p. 53; Home, *History of the Rebellion*, p. 306.

27. Johnstone, *Memoirs*, pp. 18–19n.

28. John Murray of Broughton, *Memorials of John Murray of Broughton Sometime Secretary to Prince Charles Edward, 1740-1745*, ed. R. F. Bell (Edinburgh: Scottish History Society, 1898), pp. 187-88; Maxwell, *Narrative*, p. 31; Blaikie, ed., *Itinerary*, p. 10; Sir John Gordon, *The Correspondence of Sir John Gordon, Bart. of Invergordon* (Edinburgh: n.p., 1835), p. 7; John O'Sullivan, 'O'Sullivan's Narrative,' in Alister Tayler and Henrietta Tayler, *1745 and After* (London: Thomas Nelson and Sons, 1938), p. 67.

29. Lord George Murray to Duke of Atholl, 15 September 1745, in *Atholl Correspondence*, ed. Burton, pp. 15-16. Murray had taken to arms for the Jacobite cause in 1715 and 1719 and during the 'Forty-five served as Charles's Lieutenant-General. Between 1719 and 1745 he had gained a great deal of military experience as a mercenary in the service of Sardinia. Both criticized and praised for his role in the campaign of 1745-46, Murray was without doubt the ablest of the Jacobite officers.

30. Elcho, *Affairs of Scotland*, p. 253.

31. Blaikie, ed., *Itinerary*, pp. 15-16; Gordon, *Correspondence*, pp. 13, 22.

32. Chambers, *History of the Rebellion*, pp. 129-30; Duke of Atholl to Sir Alexander MacDonald MacLeod, 25 September 1745, Lord George Murray to Duke of Atholl, 24 September 1745, in *Atholl Correspondence*, ed. Burton, pp. 24-25, 27-28; Samuel Boyse, *An impartial history of the late rebellion in 1745. From authentic memoirs, particularly, the journal of a general officer, and other original papers, yet unpublished. With the characters of the persons principally concerned. To which is prefixed, by way of introduction, a compendious account of the royal house of Stuart, from its original to the present time.* (Reading: D. Henry, 1748), p. 82.

33. Johnstone, *Memoirs*, p. 45.

34. Prince Charles Stuart to his father, 21 September 1745, in Spottiswoode Society, *The The Spottiswoode Miscellany: A Collection of Original Papers and Tracts, Illustrative Chiefly of the Civil and Ecclesiastical History of Scotland*, ed. James Maidment, 2 vols. (Edinburgh: The Spottiswoode Society, 1845), II: 492.

35. The strength of the Jacobite army near the beginning of October 1745 was as follows: Highland regiments (13) — 2,960 men; Lowland regiments (5) — 2,850 men; horse squadrons (3) — 260 men. Chambers, *History of the Rebellion*, p. 172. The Chevalier de Johnstone estimated that the Jacobite army was somewhat smaller: between 4,000 and 5,000 men. Johnstone, *Memoirs*, p. 52.

36. Chambers, *History of the Rebellion*, pp. 165-66; Elcho, *Affairs of Scotland*, pp. 274-76; John Stuart, ed., *The Miscellany of the Spalding Club*, 2 vols. (Aberdeen: The Spalding Club, 1841), I: 350-51; O'Sullivan, 'O'Sullivan's Narrative,' pp. 89-90.

37. Johnstone, *Memoirs*, pp. 52-53; Elcho, *Affairs of Scotland*, p. 304.

38. Secretary Murray to Duke of Atholl, 2 October 1745, in *Atholl Correspondence*, ed. Burton, pp. 49-50.

39. James Maxwell of Kirkconnell, a follower of Charles, noted that the dissensions that began at the council of 30 October ' . . . continued ever after, and their fatal influence was not always confined to the council: by degrees it reached the army . . . ' Maxwell, *Narrative*, p. 55.

40. F. J. McLynn, *The Jacobite Army in England 1745: The Final Campaign* (Edinburgh: John Donald Publishers, 1983), pp. 8-10; Maxwell, *Narrative*, p. 54; Elcho, *Affairs of Scotland*, pp. 304-05.

41. Katherine Tomasson, *The Jacobite General* (Edinburgh: William Blackwood and Sons, 1958), pp. 68-69; F. J. McLynn, *France and the Jacobite Rising of 1745* (Edinburgh: Edinburgh University Press, 1981), p. 89.

42. For a thorough and expertly written account of the Jacobite march into and out of England in late 1745, see McLynn, *The Jacobite Army in England 1745.*

43. Home, *History of the Rebellion*, p. 137; O'Sullivan, 'O'Sullivan's Narrative,' pp. 87–88.

44. The first indications of an open break between Charles and Lord George Murray occurred at Carlisle on the march south. There Murray threatened to resign his commission, but was persuaded to remain Charles's second in command. Winifred Duke, *Lord George Murray and the Forty-Five* (Aberdeen: Milne and Hutchison, 1927), p. 111.

45. Blaikie, ed., *Itinerary*, pp. 29–30, 89; Duke, *Murray and the Forty-Five*, pp. 122–23; John C. O'Callaghan, *History of the Irish Brigades in the Service of France* (Glasgow: Cameron and Ferguson, 1870; reprint ed., Shannon: Irish University Press, 1968), pp. 376–77; Lord George Murray, 'Marches,' p. 54; C. S. Terry, *The Rising of 1745 with a Bibliography of Jacobite History 1689-1788* (London: David Nutt, 1900), pp. 97–98; O'Sullivan, 'O'Sullivan's Narrative,' p. 100.

46. Johnstone, *Memoirs*, p. 54.

47. *Ibid.*, p. 67.

48. *Ibid.*, pp. 70–71.

49. Elcho, *Affairs of Scotland*, p. 339.

50. On 22 November Lord John Drummond landed on the east coast of Scotland accompanied by his own regiment of Royal Scots and some 300 Irish piquets under the command of Brigadier Walter Stapleton. Meanwhile, the Frasers, MacKenzies, Farquharsons, and MacKintoshes, among other clans, had risen and placed themselves under Lord Strathallan at Perth. These combined clans numbered about 3,000 and when joined with Drummond's contingent represented an army nearly as large as the one at Derby. Katherine Tomasson and Francis Buist, *Battles of the '45* (London: B. T. Batsford, 1962; reprint ed., London: Book Club Associates, 1978), p. 88; O'Callaghan, *Irish Brigades*, pp. 396–97; Blaikie, ed., *Itinerary*, p. 27; Johnstone, *Memoirs*, pp. 68–70; Lockhart, *Lockhart Papers*, II: 495.

51. Of all the chiefs, only Ranald MacDonald of Clanranald favored a continuation of the march. Among Murray's most ardent supporters were Donald Cameron of Lochiel and Alexander MacDonald of Keppoch, both of whom saw advantages in a retreat to Scotland. McLynn, *The Jacobite Army in England 1745*, pp. 126–27; Duke, *Murray and the Forty-Five*, pp. 122–23; Tomasson, *The Jacobite General*, pp. 111–12; Murray, 'Marches,' p. 57; O'Sullivan, 'O'Sullivan's Narrative,' p. 102.

52. Johnstone, *Memoirs*, pp. 72–73.

53. Queries sent to Charles in Rome, quoted in Home, *History of the Rebellion*, p. 340; Johnstone, *Memoirs*, p. 83.

54. Elcho, *Affairs of Scotland*, p. 340.

55. Lockhart, *Lockhart Papers*, II: 495.

56. Blaikie, ed., *Itinerary*, p. 30; Johnstone, *Memoirs*, p. 73; Maxwell, *Narrative*, p. 79.

57. John Hay, 'John Hay's Account,' quoted in Home, *History of the Rebellion*, p. 338.

58. Johnstone, *Memoirs*, p. 98n.

59. Elcho, *Affairs of Scotland*, pp. 87–88.

60. Johnstone, *Memoirs*, pp. 110–11; Elcho, *Affairs of Scotland*, p. 371.

61. Andrew Lumisden, 'A Short Account of the Battles of Preston, Falkirk, and Culloden,' in *Origins of the 'Forty-Five and other Papers Relating to that Rising*, ed. Walter B. Blaikie (Edinburgh: Scottish History Society, 1916), p. 409.

62. The tactical aspects of Falkirk will be discussed in detail in Chapter 8.

63. John Daniel, 'A True Account of Mr. John Daniel's Progress with Prince Charles

Edward in the Years 1745 and 1746, written by himself,' in *Origins of the 'Forty-Five*, ed. Blaikie, p. 199; Elcho, *Affairs of Scotland*, p. 381; O'Sullivan, 'O'Sullivan's Narrative,' p. 114.

64. Johnstone, *Memoirs*, p. 135.

65. Major-General Alexander B. Tulloch, *The '45 From the Raising of Prince Charlie's Standard at Glenfinnan to the Battle of Culloden*, 3rd ed. (Stirling: Eneas MacKay, 1908), pp. 52–53.

66. Address from the chiefs to Charles, 29 January 1746, quoted in Home, *History of the Rebellion*, pp. 352–54; Johnstone, *Memoirs*, p. 140; Daniel, 'Progress,' p. 201; Elcho, *Affairs of Scotland*, pp. 382–84; Maxwell, *Narrative*, pp. 133–34; Robertson of Drumachine to Duke of Atholl, 11 January 1746, Lord George Murray to Duke of Atholl, 5 February 1746, in *Atholl Correspondence*, ed. Burton, pp. 135–37, 186.

67. The Prince to the Highland Chiefs, 30 January 1746, in *Itinerary*, ed. Blaikie, p. 76.

68. The Prince to the Highland Chiefs, n.d., *ibid.*, p. 78.

69. Murray to the Prince, 29 January 1746, *ibid.*, p. 75.

70. Maxwell, *Narrative*, pp. 115–16; Duke, *Murray and the Forty-Five*, p. 157; 'John Hay's Account,' quoted in Home, *History of the Rebellion*, pp. 355–56.

71. David, Lord Ogilvie to Lady Ogilvie, 20 February 1746, Laing MSS, II. 502.

72. Johnstone, *Memoirs*, p. 161; Loudoun to Cumberland, 22 February 1745, S.P. 54/29/3.

73. Order from Colonel John Roy Stewart, 14 March 1746, Francis Gordon to Mr. Harry Milne, 24 March 1746, Lord John Drummond to the Commander of the MacKintosh battalion, 26 March 1746, Mr. Bagot to Officers of Botriphnie Parish, 6 April 1746, NLS, MS 298, ff. 5, 7–7v, 11.

74. A few weeks before Culloden several of Charles's officers proposed that shipments of meal and other provisions be sent to the Highlands in the event of the British attempting to take Inverness or march on the Great Glen. They hoped that such a store would allow the Jacobite army to avoid being forced to give battle under unfavorable circumstances. The plan, however, was ' . . . reckoned a timorous advice and rejected as such . . . ' Lockhart, *Lockhart Papers*, II: 534–35.

75. Lockhart, *Lockhart Papers*, II: 517–18; Chambers, *History of the Rebellion*, pp. 275–76; Blaikie, ed., *Itinerary*, p. 38; Colonel James Allardyce, ed., *Historical Papers Relating to the Jacobite Period 1699–1750*, 2 vols. (Aberdeen: New Spalding Club, 1895), I: 299–300.

76. David, Lord Ogilvie to Lady Ogilvie, March 1746, Laing MSS, II. 502; Blaikie, ed., *Origins of the 'Forty-Five*, pp. 159–60; Johnstone, *Memoirs*, pp. 168–69; Elcho, *Affairs of Scotland*, p. 420.

77. Lockhart, *Lockhart Papers*, II: 507.

78. Daniel, 'Progress,' p. 210; David, Lord Ogilvie to Lady Ogilvie, March 1746, Report from camp at Nairn, 15 April 1746, Laing MSS, II. 502, 349.

79. Sir Robert Strange, *Memoirs of Sir Robert Strange and Andrew Lumisden*, ed. James Dennistoun, 2 vols. (London: Longman, Brown, Green, and Longmans, 1855), I: 55; Duke, *Murray and the Forty-Five*, p. 177; Johnstone, *Memoirs*, pp. 170–72.

80. Elcho, *Affairs of Scotland*, pp. 89–90.

81. Murray's reasons for opposing the position on Culloden Moor are documented in Murray, 'Marches,' p. 121; Murray to William Hamilton, 5 August 1749, quoted in Home, *History of the Rebellion*, pp. 361–63; Lockhart, *Lockhart Papers*, II: 526–29; Johnstone, *Memoirs*, p. 180n.

82. Murray, 'Marches,' p. 121; Johnstone, *Memoirs*, p. 180n; Lockhart, *Lockhart Papers*, II: 526; Murray to Hamilton, 5 August 1749, quoted in Home, *History of the Rebellion*, pp. 361–63.

83. Lockhart, *Lockhart Papers*, II: 526; Johnstone, *Memoirs*, p. 180n; Murray to Hamilton, 5 August 1749, quoted in Home, *History of the Rebellion*, pp. 361–63.

84. Elcho, *Affairs of Scotland*, p. 90.

85. *Ibid.*, p. 426.

86. Lockhart, *Lockhart Papers*, II: 518–19, 525; Elcho, *Affairs of Scotland*, p. 427; Murray to Hamilton, 5 August 1749, quoted in Home, *History of the Rebellion*, pp. 361, 363–64; Johnstone, *Memoirs*, p. 104.

87. Murray to Hamilton, 5 August 1749, quoted in Home, *History of the Rebellion*, pp. 361, 363–64; Lockhart, *Lockhart Papers*, II: 524–25; Tulloch, *The '45*, pp. 53–54.

88. Lumisden, 'Preston, Falkirk, and Culloden,' pp. 414–16; Lockhart, *Lockhart Papers*, II: 508–09, 518–19, 527–28; Strange, *Memoirs*, I: 57; Daniel, 'Progress,' p. 211; Johnstone, *Memoirs*, pp. 172–74; Elcho, *Affairs of Scotland*, pp. 427–28.

89. The controversy over who to blame (or credit) for the retreat was perhaps the most passionately debated issue in the accounts of contemporary writers. Murray himself wrote afterwards that ' ... if the line had all marched at an equal pace, I still believe we might have been at Nairn by two in the morning ... I am positive that I was stopped ... fifty times before I had marched six miles ... now it was two o'clock ... By this time most of the officers of distinction were come to the van, and there was a halt ... and this was the first full halt the van had made; for when I had information that the lines were not joined, I always chose to march slow; for a halt in the van always occasions a much greater one in the rear, when the march begins again ... It was at this halt ... that ... it was found to be two o'clock in the morning. Several of the officers that came from the rear assured us, that many of the men had left the ranks, and had laid down ... This must have been occasioned by faintness for want of food ... the van ... were four full miles from Nairn at two in the morning. At this halt, all the principal officers, who were come to the van, agreed that the thing was now impossible ... Mr. O'Sullivan also came up to the front, and said His Royal Highness would be very glad to have the attack made; but as ... Murray was in the van, he could best judge whether it could be done in time or not. Perhaps ... O'Sullivan may choose to forget this, but others are still alive who heard him ... there was not one officer present that thought it possible to make an attack, when they could not have hopes of surprising the enemy. To get back to Culloden, so as the men could have some hours of refreshment, was what they all agreed in ... it was agreed to march back with as much expedition as possible, which I ordered accordingly ... ' Murray to Hamilton, 5 August 1749, quoted in Home, *History of the Rebellion*, pp. 364–67.

A Highland officer supported Murray's account, writing that O'Sullivan indeed came forward and said that ' ... the Prince ... was very desirous the attack should be made, but as ... Murray had the van and could judge the time, he left it to him whether to do it or not.' But further on in his account the officer wrote that ' ... it was the Prince's positive orders that the attack should be made ... ' Murray's decision to retire was then ' ... contrary to the Prince's inclination'. Lockhart, *Lockhart Papers*, II: 508–09, 519, 528.

Andrew Lumisden reported that after halting, the officers at the front ' ... determined that by the time they advanced two more miles it would be daylight. Thus, the attack was judged as impractical ... Murray himself ordered the retreat, as the Prince was too far in the rear to be consulted'. Lumisden, 'Preston, Falkirk, and Culloden,' p. 416. The Chevalier de Johnstone, who served both Charles and Murray as an aide-de-camp, was more critical of Murray. He wrote that Charles despatched a rider to the front ' ... with orders to fall upon the camp ... As soon as [Murray] received the answer of the Prince, he instantly retrograded by a road to the left ... He observed ... that it was too late; that the day would begin to appear before they could arrive at the camp ... ' According to Johnstone, Murray thus began the retreat without orders from the Prince and without full approval from the other officers and chiefs in the van. He ' ... had never, in critical conjunctures, waited for orders from the Prince to determine in what manner he should act'. Johnstone, *Memoirs*, pp. 173–74, 182n.

David, Lord Elcho remembered that Cameron of Lochiel ' ... came from the front to the Prince ... and told him that now as it was daylight the project ... had failed, and that it was better to march back than go and attack ... [Lochiel] insisted strongly upon going back, and said all the officers in the front were for going back. The Prince was not for going back, and said it was much better to march forward and attack, then march back and be attacked afterwards ... ' Elcho, *Affairs of Scotland*, pp. 427–28.

John William O'Sullivan, one of Charles's Irish favorites, was much more critical of Murray's actions and blamed the retreat solely on Lord George's disobedience of Charles's order to attack: 'Being within a mile of the Camp, he [Murray] sends Locheil to the Prince to let him know yt he did not think proper to continu his march, because he cou'd never be strong enough for them, & besides it would be day. The Prince sends Locheil back to tel 'em obsolutely to go on, yt he'l answer, yt he'l be stronger than he was, when he quitted the field of battle, yt he cou'd not imagine what a quantity came in since, & yt he'd answer for all. Locheil came back to the Prince to tell him, yt the men declined attacking ... ' O'Sullivan, 'O'Sullivan's Narrative,' p. 156. One of Charles's more inept administrators, John Hay, also attributed the retreat to Murray's independent action. Hay wrote that he rode up during the last halt and ' ... heard ... Murray arguing against going on, particularly with Hepburn of Keith. He [Hay] immediately rode back to Charles, who was in the rear of the first column, and told him, that if he did not come to the front of the army, and order ... Murray to go on, there would be nothing done. Charles, who was on horseback, set out immediately, and riding pretty fast met the Highlanders marching back. He was extremely incensed, and said ... Murray had betrayed him'. 'John Hay's Account,' quoted in Home, *History of the Rebellion*, p. 371.

The testimony of John Daniel was even more damning of Murray's conduct. He wrote that ' ... when we were supposing to surround them ... Murray began to be missing ... In that situation did we remain a considerable time, till, by day breaking fast in upon us, we heard that ... Murray was gone off with most of the clans ... ' Daniel, 'Progress,' p. 211. The Prince's own recollections several years later absolved Murray of the responsibility for ordering the retreat; however, they do not agree with reports made by other Jacobite officers. Charles wrote from Rome that ' ... Murray led the van ... in the night march, and M. le Comte [i.e. Charles] marched in the rear. Upon the army's halting, M. le Comte rode up to the front to enquire the occasion of the halt. Upon his arrival ... Murray convinced M. le Comte of the unavoidable necessity of retreating'. 'Answer by Charles at Rome,' quoted in Home, *History of the Rebellion*, p. 372. Such conflicting evidence indeed makes difficult the task of determining the course of events during the halt of the night march.

90. Murray to Hamilton, 5 August 1749, quoted in Home, *History of the Rebellion*, pp. 369–70.

91. Lumisden, 'Preston, Falkirk, and Culloden,' p. 417; Elcho, *Affairs of Scotland*, pp. 429–30.

92. Johnstone, *Memoirs*, p. 185.

93. Elcho, *Affairs of Scotland*, pp. 429–30; Lockhart, *Lockhart Papers*, II: 509, 530; Murray to Hamilton, 5 August 1749, quoted in Home, *History of the Rebellion*, pp.

367–68; Maxwell, *Narrative*, pp. 147–48; Murray, 'Marches,' p. 123; Johnstone, *Memoirs*, p. 187.

94. Murray to Hamilton, 5 August 1749, quoted in Home, *History of the Rebellion*, pp. 367–68.

95. Peter Anderson, *Culloden Moor and Story of the Battle, with description of the Stone Circles and Cairns at Clava* (Stirling: Eneas MacKay, 1920), p. 68.

96. Johnstone, *Memoirs*, p. 186.

97. Lockhart, *Lockhart Papers*, II: 535–36.

98. Large detachments of the Camerons and MacDonalds under Lochiel and Keppoch, respectively, were marching rapidly from Fort William to join the army. Lord Cromarty with some 700 men was also away, as were the MacKinnons and MacGregors. Cluny MacPherson was still in Badenoch but was expected to arrive at any time. 'The absence of so many men was perfectly well known in the army, and it seemed very strange that Charles should make a movement which brought him nearer his enemies ... ' Home, *History of the Rebellion*, pp. 218–19.

99. Maxwell, *Narrative*, p. 140.

100. Murray's order, supposedly containing a 'no quarter' clause, was the subject of a great deal of controversy after the battle. Cumberland used the alleged clause as an excuse to unmercifully persecute the Jacobites after the battle. As will be seen below in Lord Elcho's memoirs in which the order is contained, no such clause existed. 'It is His Royal Highness' positive orders that every person attach themselves to some corps of the army and to remain with that corps night and day till the battle ... be finally over; this regards the foot as well as the horse. The order of the battle is to be given to every general officer and every commander of regiments or squadrons. It is required and expected that each individual in the army as well officer as soldier keeps their post that shall be allotted to them, and if any man turns his back to run away the next behind such man is to shoot him. Nobody on pain of death to strip the slain or plunder till the battle be over. The Highlanders all to be in kilts, and nobody to throw away their guns ... ' Elcho, *Affairs of Scotland*, p. 461.

101. This comment is from the editor of Johnstone, *Memoirs*, p. 186n.

8

The 'Forty-Five: Jacobite Tactics

Despite the poorly conceived and implemented strategy of the Jacobites in the 'Forty-five uprising, their tactics under irregular battlefield conditions were extremely effective. The old Highland charge continued to be the centerpiece of Jacobite tactical doctrine and it succeeded remarkably well against regular British troops in the early stages of the uprising. Although between 1715 and 1745 the British had concentrated on diminishing the shock value of the charge, they were unable to stand up to the Highlanders in the first two major battles of the campaign. In January 1746 General Henry Hawley, a grizzled old veteran familiar with Gaelic warfare, instructed his men as to the proper way to defend against the Highland charge. He told them to fire by ranks, three deep, when the clansmen were ten or twelve paces away. Hawley went on to caution his soldiers that if they fired too soon, they probably would miss their target and have no chance to reload before the Highlanders were upon them.[1] By 1745 both sides realized that if the clansmen were allowed to make effective use of their traditional weapons, the broadsword and target, the British regulars could not defeat them even with the new flintlock musket, enhanced as it was by the iron ramrod and socket bayonet, and the platoon firing system.[2] A key to breaking the Highland charge was defense in depth. At both Killiecrankie and Sheriffmuir the Highlanders had smashed the enemy's single line. The three-deep formation proposed by Hawley was little more than a single line reinforced for more platoon firepower, but the refined concept ultimately rendered the Highland charge ineffective. The British at Culloden drew up in a true two- or three-line defense in depth and, consequently, found it much easier to absorb the shock of Gaelic offensive tactics.

Prestonpans and Falkirk were Highland victories because the Gaels initially outmaneuvered the British and then outfought them at close quarters. The clansmen defeated a government army at Prestonpans that was short on combat experience by marching around its flank during the night and attacking through an early morning fog. At Falkirk the Highlanders beat a more experienced British army by first surprising it and then drawing it to fight on rugged terrain where its improved tactics and weaponry could not be effectively utilized. On both occasions the clansmen used the natural surroundings and the elements to offset their inferiority in weapons, organization, and discipline.

The Gaels met their match, however, on the broad, level moor of Culloden, where the British took advantage of a killing ground that was ideal for their musketry, artillery, cavalry, system of supportive firepower, and hand-to-hand bayonet skills. For the first time since Alasdair MacColla had unveiled the Highland charge in the 1640s, the British utilized their own strengths to counter

Gaelic offensive tactics. What traditionally had been the Gaels' greatest tactical asset became their greatest liability.

The Jacobites at the battle of Prestonpans (21 September 1745) faced an enemy in possession of an extremely strong defensive position. The day before the battle General Sir John Cope's army was drawn up just to the east of the town. Its back was to the sea; its front was protected by a flat, marshy stretch fronted by ditches and walls; its left was fronted by a morass; and its right was protected by high garden walls.[3] The Jacobite leaders recognized the strength of the enemy's position and dared not attack it from their encampment due south near the village of Tranent. The two armies each numbered about 2,500 men, but Cope had some 600 dragoons and six pieces of artillery.[4] Despite the almost impregnable nature of Cope's defenses and the cold, misty rain that fell throughout the night of 20 September, the Highlanders were in high spirits and eager to give battle; however, Prince Charles and his officers would not risk a heavy casualty toll by attacking across the wide stretch of open ground between their camp and the enemy's front line.[5] One of Charles's officers summed up the Jacobite's situation when he wrote: ' . . . we saw no possibility of attacking . . . without exposing ourselves to be cut to pieces in a disgraceful manner.'[6] Charles therefore plotted a move, reminiscent of Dundee's strategems in 1689, that would allow them to attack Cope the next morning under more favorable circumstances.

To neutralize Cope's strong defensive position, Charles decided to march before sunrise around Tranent and to the eastern flank of the enemy. Enlisting the aid of a local guide, the Highlanders set out and crossed the marsh to the south-east of Cope's position. The first column traversed the narrow track across the bog undetected, but Cope's sentries spotted the second column and the general wheeled his army to the left. Their sudden move disorganized the government troops. As the clansmen passed from the marsh and turned sharply to the left near Seton House, they disappeared silently about 800 yards from Cope's army into a thick morning mist. Cope had underestimated the Highlanders' ability to cross the bog between Tranent and Seton House and, consequently, had not posted a guard in that vicinity. Even though the march was detected and the Jacobites had some

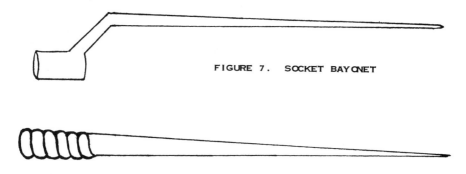

FIGURE 7.   SOCKET BAYONET

FIGURE 8.   PLUG BAYONET

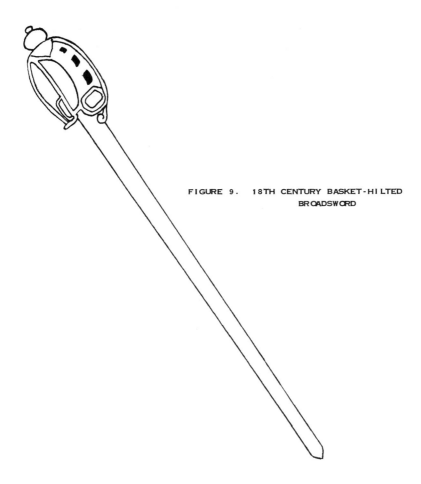

FIGURE 9.   18TH CENTURY BASKET-HILTED
BROADSWORD

difficulty in forming their battle lines, it was a brilliant and daring move that allowed the clans to stage their traditional charge against an enemy who was in no position to defend against it.[7]

With the Jacobite army now hidden amid the fog and mist on the open field to the east, Cope tried to rearrange his inexperienced troops. He knew that the Highlanders were now to his left but how far away they were he could only guess. Cope placed 2,000 infantry in the center of the new line almost parallel to the old road from Cockenzie to Tranent. Unlike his former position facing south, which was covered by a broad marsh and a series of enclosures and ditches, Cope's new front afforded him almost no protection. On the flanks he placed most of his dragoons, and the remainder he left in the rear as a reserve. The small arsenal of artillery anchored the right flank of his line and was protected by a guard of 100 foot. An observer had suggested that Cope attack the Jacobites before they attacked him, but that opportunity, if it had ever existed, was past. All he could do now was wait for the Highlanders to make their move.[8]

While Cope was struggling to put his army in proper fighting order, the Highlanders had assembled into battle formation and were slowly closing the distance between their lines and the enemy by creeping ahead under a protective cover of fog. To conceal their movements further, the first line of clansmen fell to their knees and crawled toward the enemy. By the time the morning sun began to burn off the mist, the Jacobite front line was within 200 yards of Cope's. Charles's front ranks consisted of about 1,900 to 2,000 of his best armed and trained clansmen. The right wing (under the Duke of Perth) was composed of the MacDonalds of Clanranald (250–300 men), Glengarry (300–500), Keppoch (300–330), and Glencoe (120); the left (under Lord George Murray) was composed of the Perth regiment (200), the Appin Stewarts (200–250), and the Camerons (500). Within these main clan regiments were small groups of MacGregors, Glenmoriston Grants, and others. The Jacobite reserve contained 500 to 600 poorly armed men and a small detachment of horse. The left wing had inadvertently advanced before the right, making the entire line somewhat oblique, and the enemy therefore spotted the fierce Camerons first.[9]

The Highlanders emerged from the mist less than 200 yards from Cope's front line, their war cries piercing the morning silence. The clansmen broke into a trot, muskets in hand, and formed up into the tightly packed wedges that gave the Highland charge its tremendous impact. A government officer described the horde that would in a moment smash the ranks of his hapless regiment:

> ... most of them seemed to be strong, active, and hardy men; ... and if clothed like Lowcountry men, would appear inferior to the King's troops; but the Highland garb favoured them much, as it showed their naked limbs, which were strong and muscular; ... their stern countenances, and bushy uncombed hair, gave them a fierce, barbarous, and imposing aspect ... [10]

The execution of the Highland charge over the final 100 yards was marred by just one potentially disastrous error. Murray had ordered the Camerons on the extreme left of the Jacobite front line to fan out farther to the left to avoid being outflanked by Cope's dragoons. As Lochiel's men drew off in that direction, they left a wide gap in the center of the Jacobite line. The gap between the two Highland wings might have allowed the center of a better army than Cope's to set up a coordinated crossfire that surely would have taken a heavy toll of the attackers. Before the opportunity became readily apparent to the government army, however, Charles's second line came forward to fill the gap. Now that the Highlanders had reordered their ranks as they advanced (a most unusual accomplishment for an irregular army), they bore down with characteristic swiftness upon Cope's flanks amid harmless musket volleys fired too soon by the impatient government infantry. The clansmen responded with a volley of their own and then flung away their muskets in favor of the broadsword and target. Murray had personally led the Camerons across the last few yards that separated the lines and saw the enemy dragoons and infantry struggle in vain to reload before the Highlanders reached them.[11]

Despite the overwhelming preponderance of firepower contained within the artillery, infantry, and dragoons, the government army learned (as had MacKay at

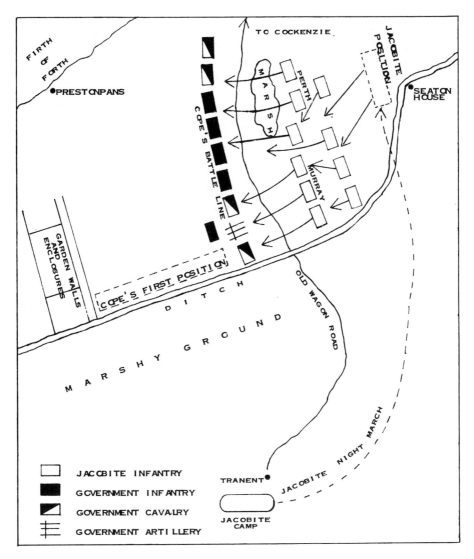

MAP 21.   PRESTONPANS   1745

Killiecrankie) that modern firearms alone were not capable of stopping the Highland charge. Cope's six pieces of artillery on the right wing might have caused a great execution of the attackers, but they were poorly serviced and managed to fire only once before being overrun by Murray's men.[12] The performance of the government infantry, too, was inept, reflecting their unfamiliarity with the Highland charge. Though some of them were veterans of continental war, they were unable to execute their much-heralded system of platoon firepower against a rapidly advancing enemy. Few men in Cope's front line fired more than one round before the Highlanders were upon them. Curiously, they did not have their bayonets fixed and had no time to attach them after expending their first load.[13] When the Highlanders hit, the government infantry buckled and broke instantly, threw down their muskets, and fled from the battlefield. An observer noted that ' . . . none of the soldiers attempted to load their pieces again, and not one bayonet was stained with blood . . . '[14] In the pursuit that followed, many of Cope's men ran into the enclosure that had served as their camp the night before and were cut down by the clansmen. Others gave themselves up at once.

The destruction of Cope's army cannot be blamed solely on the lack of firepower from the infantrymen, since the dragoons failed to protect the infantry's flanks. The dragoons put up an effective fire at the outset of the battle, and consequently drew the attention of the clansmen. Seeing confusion among the attacking Jacobites, the government horse advanced, firearms blazing, into the ranks of the Highlanders. Before they got well under way, however, the clansmen greeted them with a counter-volley. The dragoons turned to flee, and the Highlanders charged into their midst, slashing at the horses' heads and legs.[15] On both flanks the Jacobites drove the dragoons from the battlefield, leaving Cope's infantry unprotected: ' . . . the two Regiments of Dragoons who should have supported the Infantry . . . shamefully deserted their Commanders, and fled without once looking behind them'.[16] With the dispersal of the dragoons Cope's hope of victory vanished.

Prestonpans illustrated the Gaels' tactical superiority over an opponent not sufficiently trained or led and unfamiliar with the Highland way of war. The battle lasted no longer than fifteen minutes,[17] and the performance of his troops so impressed Charles that thereafter he ' . . . entertained a mighty notion of the Highlanders, and . . . imagined they would beat four times their number of regular troops'.[18] Charles, however, deceived himself in equating Cope's rabble with the best regular troops in the British army. The government dragoons were poorly disciplined, many of the infantrymen were fit only for guarding baggage, and the artillery arm was inadequately staffed with sailors. As it was, Cope's bedraggled outfit was routed by about 1,900 to 2,000 of Charles's front-line troops, who were unsupported by artillery or horse. The Highlanders did their job so quickly and thoroughly that the Jacobite second line had no reason to join the fray.[19] A Jacobite officer described the effect of the Gaelic offensive: 'The field of battle presented a spectacle of horror, being covered with heads, legs, and arms, and mutilated bodies; for the killed all fell by the sword'.[20] Cope's losses confirmed the superiority of Highland arms: 300 to 400 killed, including five or six officers; 400 to 500 wounded, including sixty to seventy officers; and 1,400 to 1,600 captured, including seventy to eighty officers.[21]

Charles's easy victory at Prestonpans obscured several fundamental drawbacks in Highland tactics. Flushed with success, Charles did not pause to consider what might have happened had the impetus of his undisciplined attack been blunted by an effective fire from the enemy's artillery and musketry. At no time during the battle were the Jacobites able to coordinate the movements of their two wings; therefore, if they had suffered a setback on either flank it is unlikely that they could have made the necessary adjustments to regroup and stage a further attack. In addition, the principal Jacobite officers and chiefs led the assault. If they had fallen in a withering fire, their regiments would have been left without direction. Though the clansmen executed a nearly perfect Highland charge, their victory was not based on tactical acumen. Charles certainly had some idea of Cope's deficiencies before the battle, but he could not have been sure how the Highlanders would perform against a regular British army, and the cheap victory definitely left him over-confident and gave him unrealistic expectations of their capabilities.

The battle of Falkirk (17 January 1746) demanded of the Highlanders a stronger tactical effort than Prestonpans. When the Jacobites returned from England and undertook the siege of Stirling Castle, they soon found their position threatened by a relief force of 8,000 to 10,000 foot and three regiments of horse under General Henry Hawley. Hawley's 6,000 regulars were not raw recruits; rather they were veterans who had distinguished themselves on the continent at Dettingen and Fontenoy. In addition, Hawley commanded some 1,000 to 1,200 Argyllshire Highlanders and about 900 dragoons who had some measure of combat experience. Hawley's artillery train consisted of ten pieces ranging from one to six pounds and several mortars that were useless except in siege operations. Well armed, heavily accoutred, and impressively attired in stiff uniforms, the government army must have appeared formidable to the ragged Highlanders.[22]

Charles's Highlanders could not expect to break Hawley's army without employing their skills with sword and target — a situation that was dependent, of course, upon their reaching the enemy with sufficient numbers and impact all across the line. To accomplish this required that they be not only swift and determined, but also possessed of a certain degree of discipline. When operating within separate clan regiments, the Highlanders were able to perform a simple maneuver to bring them from column to line of battle,[23] and each attacking regiment was capable of carrying out the movements required to effect the Highland charge. When the independent clan units were advancing furiously toward the enemy, however, they were no more than that — separate, uncoordinated units without centralized control. Combined attacks by unco-ordinated units had won important victories for O'Neill, MacColla and Montrose, and Dundee, but those victories were due less to tactical coordination among the clan regiments than to enemy weakness, imaginative pre-battle movements and alignments, and a combination of emotion, individual skill, and luck. Prestonpans had been a victory determined by similar factors. At Falkirk, however, the Gaelic military system faced its most formidable enemy to date. Defeating Hawley's well-armed regular force of superior numbers and discipline would require more than emotionalism and dexterity with the broadsword and target. It would require sagacious planning, favorable terrain, and a degree of cooperation between the clan regiments that had so far eluded the Jacobites. No one realized more than Lord George Murray the difficulty of this task. He wrote that if the enemy were to put up a stiff resistance, ' . . . it would not be possible to make [the Highlanders] keep their ranks, or rally soon enough upon any sudden emergency . . . '[24]

When the Jacobites learned of Hawley's approach toward Falkirk, Charles and the chiefs and officers began formulating a plan that would give their troops the tactical advantage. The Jacobite army totaled between 7,000 and 8,000 men and they were encamped near the historic field of Bannockburn.[25] The Jacobite officers understood that surprise could be a crucial ally in offsetting their numerical inferiority and lack of cavalry and artillery. This task was made easier because Hawley held them in such contempt that he had neglected to provide adequate security measures. He did not post the customary screen of skirmishers to intercept the enemy and was so confident that the Highlanders would not dare attack him that he accepted an invitation to breakfast with Lady Kilmarnock on the day of the battle.[26] While Hawley breakfasted, Charles despatched a small force to reconnoitre the ground of Falkirk Moor near Hawley's camp. When Charles received news of the enemy's location, he marched off to engage Hawley. Leaving about 1,000 men to continue the siege, the Jacobites moved forward in two columns intending to occupy the high ground one mile south of Falkirk. Around noon on 17 January the Jacobite columns headed north-east toward the Torwood to deceive Hawley as to their real destination. They proceeded along this route and then wheeled sharply to the south-east, crossed the Carron water, and scrambled up the hill overlooking Hawley's camp. The rapidity of the Jacobite advance caught the enemy by surprise and drew them out to fight on terrain that was perfectly suited for the Highlanders' brand of warfare.[27]

The Highlanders' attainment of the summit of Falkirk Moor not only surprised Hawley and misled him as to Charles's real intentions, but also gave the Jacobites a decisive advantage in terms of the weather and terrain. Hawley believed that Charles intended to hold the government army near Falkirk by taking the hill and then quickly marching back into England. Accordingly, the government general left his breakfast and despatched his dragoons to take possession of Falkirk Moor and, if possible, engage the Highlanders before they slipped away. Hawley hoped that the clansmen could be enticed to give battle to his cavalry and thus permit his infantry and artillery to reach the field before Charles's men departed. As Hawley's troops took up arms and moved forward, a severe storm of rain and wind blew hard into their faces. They had fallen into the Jacobites' trap by marching up the hillside toward the broad ridge at the top. The dragoons found the rugged heath unsuitable for mounting an effective charge, the infantry regiments had to march cautiously while trying to keep their powder and pieces dry, and the artillery train became stuck at the foot of the hill. Charles enjoyed almost every conceivable advantage at the outset of the contest. Now he could only hope that his Highlanders would translate their superior position into a rousing victory.[28]

The Jacobites' position atop Falkirk Moor gave them the option of rushing down the slope onto the struggling government troops or of waiting for the enemy to charge and then launching a strong counter-attack. When Charles saw the dragoons riding up the hillside, he ordered forward Murray on the right wing with 1,500 to 2,000 clansmen to defend the main body of the Jacobite army against a flank attack. Murray advanced with three MacDonald regiments until his right was protected by a small morass that restricted the movements of Hawley's cavalry. Murray's move anchored the right of Charles's line at the eastern end of the battlefield and permitted the remainder of the army to align itself farther westward facing north. From his vantage point on the ridge Murray could see the enemy infantry moving slowly toward him. Off to his left a broad ravine divided the higher ground where the Jacobite center and left stood from the lower ground over which the enemy would soon pass. While the ravine would prevent Hawley from employing his cavalry on that side of the field, Murray reasoned that it also might hamper efforts to execute the Highland charge. As the two armies drew closer, however, the advantage clearly lay with the Highlanders. They held a position similar to Dundee's at Killiecrankie: they could attack at the moment of their choosing. Hawley's army, on the other hand, would find any sort of offensive action extremely difficult because of the ruggedly rising ground that lay before them.[29]

Hawley formed up his army in two lines in an attempt to provide some manner of defense in depth against the Highland charge, and Charles drew up his lines two deep as well, placing his best clan regiments along the front. Hawley's infantry regiments lay just north of the ravine, and were protected, he hoped, from the full weight of a Highland assault. His dragoons were stationed slightly ahead of the infantry on the left wing beside the morass where they had stood while the foot advanced up the hill.[30] The Highlanders were outflanked on the left by Hawley's foot, but on the right they outdistanced the British dragoons. The ravine did not extend as far as the three MacDonald regiments under Murray on the extreme right, but the other seven clan regiments stood along the depression and were greatly outnumbered by Hawley's entire body of infantry directly in front of them. Charles had not made it clear who was in command of the left side of the front line, and the Jacobite second line was somewhat shorter on the left than the first line.[31] As the armies arrayed for battle, it was evident that each was stronger on its right flank, a situation reminiscent of Sheriffmuir in 1715.

The first action occurred on the Jacobites' right wing opposite Hawley's dragoons. The enemy cavalry, which had stood within two hundred yards of Charles' front line for a full quarter of an hour, made several feints. Murray, on foot with broadsword and target, moved through the MacDonald ranks and instructed them not to advance or fire until he gave the order. Hawley apparently believed that the Highlanders could not resist giving battle to his cavalry and thus would be prevented from marching away unscathed into England as he suspected was their intention. Hawley probably also believed that the Highlanders were unable to withstand a determined cavalry attack. He had been on Argyll's right wing at Sheriffmuir and had witnessed the devastating effects of the government horse on Mar's clansmen. Whatever his reasons were for despatching 900 dragoons to oppose some 1,500 to 2,000 MacDonald infantry, his delusions concerning the Highlanders' prowesss were soon evidenced.[32] As the enemy cavalry poured forth a round of fire and broke into a full trot toward Murray's regiments, a Jacobite volunteer ' . . . doubted not but that they would have ridden over us without opposition . . . and bear us down without difficulty . . . but I soon found myself mistaken . . . '[33] Seeing that the dragoons fully intended to drive home their charge, Murray ordered his clansmen to present arms.[34] The battle of Falkirk had been joined.

The MacDonald regiments on the Jacobite right wing broke the charge of Hawley's dragoons by combining superb marksmanship with dexterity with the broadsword. The cavalry advanced and Murray, sword drawn, led his men slowly toward the enemy. Round after round whizzed past the grim-faced Highlanders, but they held their fire as ordered. The dragoons carried out their assault with the utmost gallantry, outnumbered as they were by the fierce MacDonalds. When the two lines were within ten to fifteen yards of one another, Murray ordered his troops to fire, which they did with telling efficiency. In less than half a minute the ranks of Hawley's horse had become so disordered that they were unable to continue their attack. Murray had managed to keep the MacDonalds in good order until they fired, but after their volley the clansmen threw down their pieces and charged into the beleaguered cavalry despite Murray's orders to the contrary. The remainder of the three dragoon regiments attempted to retreat but found the way blocked by their own infantry; therefore, the only route of escape was to their right across neutral ground. As they galloped away, they confused the first line of Hawley's foot and allowed the other clan regiments to attack across the ravine.[35]

The MacDonalds' performance against Hawley's dragoons exemplified the positive and negative aspects of Gaelic warfare. When led by a resolute commander of Murray's caliber, the Highlanders showed that they were capable of a certain measure of order and discipline. By holding their fire until they had established a strong defensive position on the right flank of the Jacobite front line, Murray's men presented the enemy horsemen with the task of initiating contact with three of the best clan regiments. In the past Gaelic armies had preferred to absorb cavalry attacks and then to launch their own assault with a musket volley followed by the charge with sword and target. Much as their forebears had done under MacColla and Montrose at Tippermuir, Aberdeen, and Kilsyth, the MacDonalds waited on strong ground for the cavalry to attack and then broke the enemy formation with an accurate musket barrage. At that moment, when Hawley's cavalry regiments were disordered and on the verge of disintegration, the Highlanders might have crushed the government army. It was then, however, that the MacDonalds broke ranks and rushed after the fleeing dragoons, disordering their own formation. The pursuit was short-lived and the enemy horse rode quickly from the field, but by then Murray's regiments were so scattered that he could not reorganize them. Hundreds of the clansmen moved on to attack the enemy militia that stood behind the dragoons, while others simply wandered aimlessly around the battlefield. In a matter of minutes the Highlanders had forfeited their advantage with a wild, undisciplined attack that could not properly be termed a Highland charge. Had they stood their ground, they might have swept down upon the exposed flank of Hawley's foot and cut off its retreat while the other clan regiments along the front cut down the fleeing dragoon regiments.

Murray, the architect of the Highlanders' repulse of the enemy cavalry, was severely (and unjustly) criticized for the disorder that ultimately resulted on the Jacobite right wing. A fellow officer blamed him for holding back the

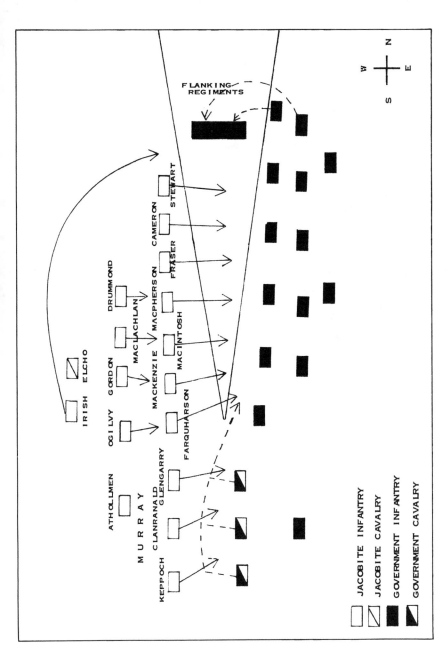

MAP 22. FALKIRK 1746

JACOBITE INFANTRY

JACOBITE CAVALRY

GOVERNMENT INFANTRY

GOVERNMENT CAVALRY

MacDonalds: ' ... we let an opportunity slip out of our hands, which never afterwards presented itself again. This piece of conduct belonged chiefly to Lord George Murray, who would not permit the army to pursue any farther'.[36] Murray, however, had vainly tried to stop his men, realizing that the clansmen were more useful to the army holding their formation and then mounting the Highland charge against the enemy foot. Murray knew the strengths and weaknesses of Highland warfare; he consequently did all that was in his power to keep the Gaels from throwing away the tactical advantage on his side of the field. He failed, and the uncontrollable fury of the clansmen eventually deprived Charles's army of a complete victory.

The flight of the dragoons gave the Jacobite left an opportunity to attack the enemy without facing the full weight of the enemy firepower. There the government infantry outflanked Charles's regiments and was protected to some degree by the ravine. Hawley's foot also enjoyed a decided superiority in numbers and firepower. The retreat of the dragoons, however, broke the ranks of the infantry and shielded the clan regiments from the British muskets long enough for the Highlanders to have mounted an attack. Most of Hawley's infantry units on that side of the field never regained their composure once the cavalry rode through their lines.[37] The Highlanders on the left were thus presented with a perfect opportunity to stage the charge.

The Jacobite left wing threw away the chance to execute an effective attack because its commander[38] did not possess the military skills that Murray had exhibited at the outset of the battle on the right side of the line. As the dragoons passed before them, the anxious clansmen discharged a volley into the enemy formation. If they had been adequately led, they would have withheld fire until the enemy cavalry had left the field and then executed the Highland charge. But they expended their fire and the Camerons, Stewarts, and others found that in the blowing rain they could not reload. The enemy foot lay directly in front of them. Without the customary musket volley at short range, the clansmen could not hope to carry out an effective attack; nonetheless, the Highlanders drew their swords and crossed the ravine toward an enemy struggling in vain to reorder his ranks.[39]

If the Jacobite officers had coordinated the movements of their various units on the left side of the battlefield, the clansmen might have destroyed the bulk of Hawley's infantry there. As it was, the Highlanders crashed into the enemy foot regiments opposite them but were outflanked by three of Hawley's units and were unable to bring to battle the entire enemy front. On Hawley's extreme right wing the three regiments that were not engaged wheeled sharply to the left to bring to bear on the advancing Highlanders a heavy flanking fire. This move apparently went unnoticed by the Jacobite commanders on the left, for they continued to press home the attack against the disintegrating enemy regiments directly ahead of them. Had Charles or one of his lieutenants moved decisively at that moment and called forward the Drummonds and MacLachlans from the left of the second line, they might have routed Hawley's infantry that stood on the flanks of the attacking infantry. Before such a move could be made, however, many of the second-line troops had already rushed ahead on the heels of the first line and had so disordered the attack that great confusion ensued on the entire left side of the field. Seeing their comrades on the verge of collapse under the weight of the Highland assault, the three flanking regiments began firing into the onrushing Jacobites. All along Charles's left, officers scrambled through the clan units trying to halt the warriors. They feared that their men had charged into an ambush and thus ordered a quick retreat across the ravine to the high ground to await reinforcements from the right wing. The critical moment of the battle passed and the routed enemy foot fled toward Falkirk.[40]

The failure of the attack on the Jacobite left was due not only to poor leadership and organization, but also to the disorder that prevailed on the right and center of the line. Because of the undulating hills along the battlefield, neither wing could observe what transpired on the other. Murray's MacDonald regiments could not be rallied after chasing away the dragoons and thus drifted from the field as darkness approached. Their absence, coupled with the movements of the second line, left a gaping hole in the center of Charles's formation. Charles belatedly employed most of his reserves, mainly the Irish piquets, to cover the left flank of the attacking regiments, but the move was too little, too late. By the time the Irishmen reached the left side of the field, Hawley's infantry were making a rapid retreat covered by the three infantry regiments on their flank and the remainder of the dragoons. Had Charles despatched the reserves to fill the gap in the center of the line, thereby providing a link between Murray and the clans on the left, he perhaps would have been able to stage another attack that surely would have crushed the fleeing enemy. Seeing no units to their left, however, Murray and the few troops he had managed to rally had no way of knowing the situation on the far left wing. Murray brought forward the Atholl regiment from the second line to shore up the center. When he moved to the left, he saw the confusion in the ranks of the retreating enemy and made one last attempt to bring the scattered MacDonalds to action. If Murray, with the Athollmen and MacDonalds, had been able to advance against the left flank of the retreating enemy, he probably could have blocked their route to Falkirk and allowed the left wing of Charles's army to regroup and carry out a final assault. But Murray, still operating on foot, failed to regroup the MacDonalds; he thus attacked with only 600 Athollmen and could not keep Hawley from reaching Falkirk. The battle of Falkirk ended with Murray's failed attempt at complete victory.[41]

Casualty figures reveal that Falkirk, despite the many battlefield blunders of Charles and his officers and chiefs, was a Jacobite victory. Hawley's heavy losses confirmed the superiority of the Highland way of war practiced under favorable conditions. Even though the clan regiments were unable to stage the traditional Highland charge, they killed or wounded between 500 and 600 enemy troops and captured several hundred as well. Jacobite losses were much lighter: about fifty killed and from sixty to eighty wounded.[42] Besides the personnel losses inflicted on the government army, the Jacobites ransacked Hawley's camp and took possession of several pieces of artillery, hundreds of muskets, and great amounts of shot and powder. What they could not carry away, they burned. In terms of manpower and material losses, Charles had soundly whipped his opponent.[43]

Falkirk was not the decisive triumph that it might have been because the tactical advantages held by the Highland regiments at the outset of the battle were not realized during the actual fighting. Murray was the only high-ranking officer who exhibited any sort of tactical brilliance with his repulse of the enemy dragoons; however, he was rightly criticized by a fellow officer for subordinating his proper role as a commanding general to that of a foot soldier: ' . . . [a] generals business in a battle is more to command than to fight as a common soldier'.[44] Instead of commanding their troops, Murray and many other Jacobite officers, in the traditional Celtic manner, personally led them into battle on foot with broadsword and target. When they were able to instruct their men in the heat of battle, as on the left flank, it was only to call them to a halt, which did nothing to abate the confusion. To turn loose an impetuous and undisciplined army with no specific orders or effective means by which to communicate with it during battle was irresponsible enough in itself, but to then attempt to call it back in the excitement of combat was even more foolhardy. A Jacobite officer wrote:

> It is often more dangerous to stop the fire and impetuosity of soldiers, of whom the best are but machines, and still more of undisciplined men, who do not listen to any orders, than to let them run all the risks in order to carry every thing before them.[45]

The weather had favored the Jacobites as well. The storm that blew in rendered many of the enemy's muskets inoperable and deprived the British of their main strength.[46] After the battle Murray realized that the Jacobites had let slip away an opportunity for complete victory: ' . . . the nearness of the attack, the descent of a hill, the strong wind and rain which was . . . directly in the enemy's face . . . ; in a word, the Highland army had all the advantages that nature or art could give them'.[47] The Gaels indeed had held almost every conceivable tactical advantage at Falkirk, but they did not destroy the enemy as their forebears had done in earlier campaigns. In 1746 it became clear that the old tactics alone could no longer overwhelm a regular army, regardless of the conditions under which they were practiced.

The battle of Culloden (16 April 1746) not only ended the 'Forty-five, but also witnessed the ascendancy of modern conventional British tactics and weaponry. The road to Culloden had begun, from a tactical standpoint, a century earlier with the alliance of MacColla and Montrose and the subsequent introduction of the Highland charge into Scotland. Since the 1640s the clans had experienced a true military 'golden age'. They had proved themselves to be masters of the battlefield time and time again against enemy armies that, on paper at least, should have given them a good fight. On all but a few occasions the Highlanders swept away the opposition with relative ease. From Inverlochy to Prestonpans and Falkirk, the wild, unbridled clansmen had refused to change their tactics even though the British army slowly had evolved into a formidable opponent and by 1746 was no longer unfamiliar with or overawed by the Highland charge. But even then, improvements in British tactics and weaponry alone could do no more than diminish some of the shock of the charge if it was carried out under irregular battlefield conditions. To blunt it effectively required something more — a conventional scenario in which the two armies faced one another across ground favorable to the employment of cavalry and artillery. At Culloden the Highlanders' very serious strategic mistake led them finally to give battle under circumstances that negated every tactical advantage they had ever enjoyed. Culloden, like Kinsale a century and a half earlier, pointed up the Gaels' most telling weakness — their inability to adapt to the dictates of modern tactical warfare.

When Prince Charles decided on the morning of 16 April to fight on Culloden Moor, the Jacobites could only await the enemy's approach and then array themselves in response to the Duke of Cumberland's alignment. At about 10:30 the British army marched into sight about two miles east of the Jacobite camp. There Cumberland formed his troops up in two lines, with most of his cavalry on the left, and then resumed his advance. At that point it was too late for the Jacobites to make any major adjustments in their position. They were so fatigued from their abortive night march that they were not able to move eastward to the area they had occupied the day before; therefore, they were forced to draw up a mile farther to the west on unfamiliar ground. On their right stood a stone enclosure which could have served to protect the clan regiments on that flank. To hold the enclosure, however, would have required a large number of Charles's men to be detached from the main body and arrayed in a defensive alignment — a move that would have weakened the Jacobites' offensive strength. Lord George Murray proposed that the enclosure's walls be pulled down. The officers debated that course of action but realized they were out of time. With the enemy only a mile away, the Jacobites attempted to put their regiments into some sort of fighting order before it was too late.[48]

Once Charles became aware of the size and disposition of Cumberland's army, he took measures to align his own forces as advantageously as possible. According to the muster rolls, the Jacobites had about 8,000 men on the day of the battle; however, of this total only about 5,000 to 6,000 were available to take the field. The army was drawn up in two lines, with the few cavalry troops in the rear on either flank and the dozen or so pieces of artillery in the center and on either end of the front line. The front line numbered about 3,000 to 3,500 clansmen, while the rear echelons contained some 1,500 to 2,000 foot and about 200 horse. As a precaution against a flank attack from the enclosure, Murray had moved a small body of foot and a few horse to cover the right side of the entire formation.[49]

Considering the short time they had to put their troops in line of battle, the Jacobite officers did a commendable job; when the composition of the Jacobites' alignment is scrutinized, however, it is apparent that something was amiss: the MacDonalds did not hold their traditional post on the right wing of the front line. The slight put the proud men of Clan Donald into a sullen mood, but Murray refused to concede the honor that he claimed Montrose had bestowed on the Athollmen a century before. Now, instead of concentrating on the enemy, the clansmen quarreled among themselves. Charles had no knowledge of the dispute,[50] but Murray, who had perpetuated the split between the MacDonalds and his Athollmen, must have remembered Clan Donald's occupation of the right wing at Prestonpans and Falkirk. He himself had commanded the MacDonalds on the right of the line at Falkirk! He apparently saw that the right wing at Culloden, which was flanked by the enclosure, would be the most critical area of the field, and he probably wanted to command there because he believed no one else could be trusted to oversee operations at such an important point.

While the Jacobite officers struggled to settle the argument concerning the post of honor, Cumberland's regiments moved steadily forward to take their final positions for the impending battle. The government army, between 7,000 and 8,000 strong, was divided into fifteen regiments of infantry and three regiments of dragoons. Cumberland drew up his army in two lines and, because of his numerical superiority, outflanked the Jacobites on both wings. He kept the lines about fifty yards apart. Then, if the Highlanders broke through the advance regiments, the second-line units would have ample time to respond to the attackers. Cumberland's intent was to provide a true defense in depth to stop the Highland charge.[51]

Cumberland's army advanced in line formation and looked as though it would reach the battlefield in good fighting order; however, when it came within 600 yards of the Jacobites' front line, the artillery train got stuck in a bog. Cumberland halted while his soldiers threw down their muskets and wrestled the cannon from the mud. This delay broke the rhythm of the advance and disordered the infantry regiments. More importantly, it rendered temporarily harmless the most potent weapons in Cumberland's army.[52] The Highlanders might have attacked the enemy before they regrouped and negated Cumberland's overbearing military strength in artillery and musket firepower, but they made no move. The ill feeling and confusion within their own ranks perhaps kept the Highlanders from attacking at this critical juncture. At any rate, the Jacobites lost an opportunity to take on the enemy on the flat moorland under the most advantageous circumstances.

Once the government army had extracted the artillery from the bog and the moment of danger had passed, Cumberland re-formed his lines and advanced to his final position about 400 yards from the Highlanders. The left flank was covered by two dragoon regiments and the eastern section of the park enclosure, while the right was protected by a small morass. Cumberland posted his sixteen pieces of artillery along the front line. As his officers checked their regiments to make certain they were battle-ready, Cumberland must have known that he had the Highlanders where he wanted them. The clansmen were not only outnumbered, outgunned, and outflanked on ground ideal for conventional tactics, but they would also have to fight with sleet and rain blowing hard into their faces. The Jacobites appeared to be disorganized and uncharacteristically hesitant to move forward from their posts. As Cumberland's gunners prepared their pieces and his infantry and cavalry steeled themselves for the coming battle, he could not have envisioned the effect that his preponderance of firepower would have on the previously almost invincible Highlanders.[53]

It was too late for Charles and his lieutenants to do anything but fight. Under less than ideal circumstances the Jacobites had done all that they could to prepare themselves tactically for the most important contest of their lives. The clansmen were to stage the traditional Highland charge. They had been instructed to stand their ground until ordered to attack; there was to be no repeat of the confusion that had cost them a complete victory at Falkirk. As they awaited the signal to advance, the Highlanders must have sensed that the battlefield scenario was unlike any that they had seen before. Cumberland's well-ordered infantry and dragoon regiments and his ominous artillery batteries stood poised across the moor. The relentless wind blew sleet and rain into the Jacobites' faces, and the clansmen waited to execute an attack that many of them perhaps feared would be their last.[54]

Charles's artillery began the battle at about one o'clock with a barrage that was intended to bring on an enemy attack. He apparently believed that Cumberland would launch an assault since the wind was at his back, but the Jacobites' inaccurate fire was answered only by a steady and effective report from the enemy artillery.[55] The solid shot from Cumberland's guns ' ... did great execution, making lanes through the Highland regiments'.[56] Cumberland hoped that the effect of his cannonade would force the Highlanders to stage a disorganized attack where he could then stage a counterattack. As he witnessed the devastation caused by the artillery, however, Cumberland realized that he need not move at all. If he could keep up the barrage until the clansmen were cut to pieces and fled from the field, he could win an inexpensive victory. In the first few minutes of the artillery duel the Highlanders indeed suffered tremendous casualties. Many threw themselves to the ground in desperation, all the while awaiting the signal that would allow them to rush ahead and silence their tormentors. It finally became clear to Charles that the clan regiments must attack immediately or they would be destroyed where they stood.[57]

Before the charge could be staged, however, the Jacobites had to secure their right flank. When the cannonading began, Murray noticed a squadron of enemy cavalry and a large body of Campbells moving from the left wing down toward the river Nairn. Presently, these forces came upon Murray's flank. The Campbells threw down the park walls to allow Cumberland's dragoons passage to the rear of the Jacobite ranks. Murray had already taken precautions against just such a move, so he was able to frustrate the enemy's intentions.[58] However, the few minutes spent in further securing the right flank delayed Charles's attack and allowed Cumberland's artillery to continue its deadly fire. When Charles was assured that his flank had been covered adequately, he sent word for Murray to begin the attack. Murray, however, delayed, believing that the Highlanders ' ... were as yet at too great a distance, and that what vigour the men had left would be spent before they could reach the enemy'.[59] Murray apparently also feared that the Campbells lying behind the enclosure walls would put up a strong flanking fire and reasoned that it would be best to wait until Cumberland advanced past that point before risking an attack. Each minute that Murray waited, the clansmen grew more impatient. Old Cameron of Lochiel left his regiment and hurried to Murray to ascertain the reason for the delay. Murray despatched a runner to Charles, who again urged his officers to attack at once. Amid all the confusion and noise the

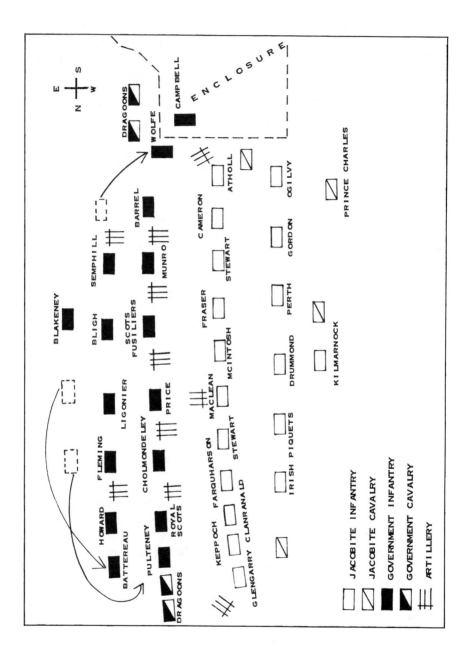

MAP 23. CULLODEN 1746

Jacobites finally were set to launch what they hoped would be a coordinated charge. Murray received word that the attack should begin with an advance by the MacDonalds on the left (as they were the farthest regiments from the enemy), but he looked ahead and saw the MacIntosh regiment in the center of the line lurch forward. The weary Highlanders had taken all the punishment they could bear. Now they took matters into their own hands without waiting for orders.[60]

The attack by the Highlanders on the right wing ran into difficulty at once because of the close proximity of the enclosure. A strong body of Campbells was posted behind the walls, but just before the attack got underway, Cumberland moved the infantry regiment on his extreme left to a position at right angles to the rest of the front line.[61] From this position they fired volley after volley into the unprotected flank of the Highlanders as they advanced across the 400 yards of open terrain that separated them from Cumberland's front. To add to the clansmen's misery, the British artillerymen began loading their pieces with grapeshot, which had a deadly effect on their line. The enemy artillery fire forced the clan regiments in the center of the field to veer sharply to the right and push the already crowded Athollmen, Camerons, and Appin Stewarts nearer to the enclosure and to the enemy musket fire.[62] Murray, however, doggedly pressed home the charge, prompting an enemy officer to note that 'Nothing could be more desperate than their attack ... '[63]

Despite the heavy and accurate musket and artillery fire from the enemy regiments on the Jacobite right, Murray's Highlanders rapidly closed in on Cumberland's front. As the clansmen drew nearer, however, the English quickened their fire to the point that it ' ... was so terrible, that it literally swept away, at once, whole ranks'.[64] Cumberland's infantry then began a slow and orderly advance to meet the Highlanders, who, seeing the enemy coming, fired their traditional volley, threw down their firearms, and drew their broadswords. Murray's troops had such a narrow track over which to carry out the Highland charge that the speed of their advance was affected. The clansmen were within thirty yards of the enemy infantry when they received a particularly heavy hail of musket, grape, and cannister. Those who escaped death or injury now would reach Cumberland's troops before they could reload; thereafter the outcome on the Jacobite right was determined by the sword and the bayonet.[65]

Jacobite chances of victory depended upon reaching Cumberland's front line with enough strength to employ the broadsword and target at close quarters. The clansmen were not the only ones to understand this: Cumberland and his officers did as well. Besides positioning the regiments for defense in depth, Cumberland had trained his troops in the proper manner of dealing with the Highland broadsword in hand-to-hand combat. British soldiers previously had been easily defeated by the Highlanders using blade weapons. If the Highland charge could not be broken, the enemy had virtually no chance of survival. Cumberland would take no such chances. He would do what he could to destroy the clan regiments before they reached his line; and, if the fighting became confined to close quarters, as it almost certainly would, Cumberland's men had been instructed not to take on the Highlander immediately before him, but to thrust with their bayonets toward the clansman to their right. The Highlanders were expert at absorbing a bayonet thrust with their targets on their left forearm, extending that arm to the side, and then slashing with the broadsword in their right hand at the unprotected British soldier. By focusing attention on the clansman on the right, Cumberland's infantry-men would render useless the target and wound the Highlander in his right side with the bayonet. While it is difficult to assess the frequency or effectiveness of this particular tactic at Culloden, the performance of the British infantry in standing firm before the Highland charge suggests that their level of training and discipline far surpassed that of their predecessors at Prestonpans and Falkirk.[66]

Murray intended to bring the battle to close quarters on the Jacobite right wing before Cumberland's firepower weakened the clan regiments to the point where their shock tactics would lack impact. Murray knew that if the Highlanders did not overpower the enemy with their initial attack all would be lost.[67] With the officers and clan chiefs at the head of the clans, it would be impossible to rally the troops in the event of a repulse. Murray, then, led his men on ' ... with all the bravery imaginable, ... ',[68] fully aware of the consequences should the Highland charge succeed or fail.

As Murray's regiments slammed into the left of Cumberland's front line, the two infantry regiments posted there (Barrel's and Munro's) wavered. Here the most furious action of the day occurred. When the clansmen had come within ten yards of the line, they were met with grapeshot and cannister from a battery of enemy artillery brought forward from the second line. The clansmen nonetheless emerged from the smoke, reached the enemy's bayonets, and literally flung themselves onto their adversaries. The best of Murray's clan regiments, the Camerons, hit Barrel's formation on the extreme left so hard that the British infantry gave way. For a moment it appeared that the charge had enough impact to carry the day, but as the Camerons and the Athollmen waded through the enemy front line, Cumberland's two infantry regiments on the left of the second line advanced some fifty paces in good order, knelt, and poured an accurate volley into the ranks of the Highlanders. The impetus of the charge was broken and the battle on the Jacobite right wing turned into a life and death struggle for the Highlanders. The few who remained standing pressed on toward the second line, but soon found themselves surrounded by the remaining elements of the front-line regiments that had regrouped.[69]

The Highlanders probably would have destroyed the entire left wing of Cumberland's army if he had not provided for defense in depth. Once the front had been pierced, the clansmen could not turn their attention to Barrel's and Munro's regiments because of the hail of fire they received from the second-line units. At that moment Murray realized that he must overwhelm the second line as well if he hoped to win the battle. But by the time he had reorganized his troops, they were set upon by the four enemy infantry regiments to their front and rear. The fighting between the lines was so fierce that a government witness wrote that the battlefield was ' ... bespattered with blood and brains'.[70] The Highlanders' attempt to hack their way through the two enemy lines, either back toward their own comrades or forward through the British regiments, was in vain. Still, many

Highlanders fought on; others fell ' ... spitted with the bayonet ... [or] torn in pieces by the musquetry and grapeshot ....'[71] Cumberland's disciplined regiments and his defense in depth had broken the Highland charge on the right side of the field where most of Charles's warriors were engaged. [72]

While Murray's Highlanders on the right carried out their furious assault on the enemy infantry, the MacDonalds, Farquharsons, and the regiment of John Roy Stewart on the left hesitated until it was too late to execute an effective Highland charge. The left wing of Charles's army was father from Cumberland's front than was the right, so that it should have advanced first. As it was, however, the order to attack did not reach the left wing until after the right had charged ahead; therefore, when Murray's clansmen made contact with the enemy, the MacDonalds and their comrades on the left were just beginning to advance. There was some speculation as to whether the MacDonalds had refused to attack because they had been denied their traditional post on the right wing. Such a contention is utterly ridiculous. Since the 1640s the MacDonalds (along with the Camerons) had been the real fighting strength of the various Highland armies. It is unlikely that they would have allowed an insult to their honor to keep them from doing their part in the battle. On the contrary, they perhaps would have fought even harder than usual to prove to Murray and the others that Clan Donald was indeed the elite element of the army. Their initial hesitation probably resulted from moving across the field to an unfamiliar position on the left end of the line.[73]

The delay of the Jacobite left proved fatal to their cause, and this was noted by one of Charles's officers, who wrote that ' ... the only chance the Prince had for a victory that day, was a general shock of the whole line at once ....'[74] If the MacDonalds and the others on the left had begun the attack, or at least had advanced simultaneously with Murray's regiments, it is entirely possible that Cumberland's front line would have been unable to stand up to the impact of a coordinated Highland charge. Cumberland's left wing had been pierced; had his right been broken at about the same time, the second line might not have had nerve enough to advance and repulse the charging Highlanders. The MacDonalds' late start gave the enemy an opportunity to pick off the Jacobites piecemeal, and the sight of the clansmen being cut down near the enclosure no doubt bolstered the spirits and confidence of the government forces opposite the MacDonalds. Conversely, the same spectacle must have demoralized the Jacobite left wing and impressed upon them the futility of repeating the same scene on their end of the line.[75]

Though the MacDonalds and others on the left finally did advance, they did not carry out the Highland charge. Instead, they moved ahead slowly and cautiously, firing their muskets indiscriminately into the solid ranks of Cumberland's infantry regiments. When the MacDonalds were within fifty to a hundred yards of the enemy front, they halted, swords drawn, and cast nervous glances to their left where they expected to be outflanked and attacked momentarily by a regiment of enemy cavalry. From then until their final retreat from the moor, the MacDonalds vacillated between making an attempt to pierce the British formations and falling back to their starting point. While they wavered, the outcome of the battle was being decided on the right side of the moor. Seeing that decisive action was necessary to prevent a total rout, MacDonald of Keppoch, the chief of his clan, tried to persuade his men to make a mad dash toward the enemy and thus bring on a struggle at close quarters. He bravely advanced with sword and pistol but was immediately wounded by a musket ball. Against the advice of a subordinate, Keppoch pulled himself to his feet and pressed on. He moved ahead a few more yards, was hit again, and fell to his death. With Keppoch's fall the MacDonald regiments left the battlefield demoralized and heavy-hearted. Cumberland now saw both wings of Charles's army in flight and ordered his infantry to advance and take possession of Culloden Moor, while his cavalry rode down and butchered the fleeing Highlanders.[76]

Charles's strategy at Culloden had placed the clan regiments on an ill-chosen field that greatly favored conventional British tactics and weaponry, but the performance of the individual Highlanders might have made up for this disadvantage if they had been given a sound tactical plan and been effectively commanded during the battle. Despite the shortcomings on the part of the Jacobite leadership, the clan rank and file who engaged the enemy gave a good account of themselves. Of the 5,000 to 6,000 Jacobites on the field that day, only about 2,000 ever came to blows with the British.[77] Almost all of the 1,000 to 1,200 casualties that the Jacobites suffered came from the ranks of the front-line Highland troops. When the Jacobite casualty figure is compared to the total number of troops that Charles had on the field, the loss comes to between sixteen and twenty percent killed and wounded; however, if that figure is divided by the total number of Highlanders engaged, the casualty rate jumps dramatically to more than fifty percent.[78] If Charles had found a way to bring the full strength of the army to bear on Cumberland without delay, the Jacobites might still have suffered the same high casualty rate, but a swift and coordinated attack by the entire host of clan regiments would have inflicted much higher losses on the enemy than the 300 or so killed and wounded that the British actually suffered.[79]

The Jacobite front line regiments that engaged Cumberland were not able to carry out the Highland charge largely because Charles and his officers and chiefs delayed the attack and thus permitted their men to be subjected to Cumberland's artillery. During the terrible artillery barrage the Jacobite officers could not keep their undisciplined regiments in the proper alignment to execute the charge. An officer wrote that the Highlanders were eager ' . . . to come up with an enemy that had so much the advantage of them at a distance, . . . ' and consequently they forged ahead ' . . . with the utmost violence, but in such confusion, that they could make no use of their firearms'.[80] Therefore, not only was the general, coordinated advance absent from the Highlanders' attack, but also the musket volley that served to disorder the enemy formations. Also, according to one of Charles's lieutenants, many of the clansmen did not have their targets, which reduced their chances of defending themselves when and if they reached the British infantry.[81] The blame for all of these defects and shortcomings must not be placed on the Highlanders themselves, for they did all that Charles and his officers realistically could have expected them to do.

The Jacobite performance at Culloden was flawed because of a lack of battlefield direction from the commanders. Once the clan regiments were committed to an attack, they could not be called back or redirected. This course had been attempted half-heartedly at Falkirk and resulted in the escape of a significant part of the enemy's army. It is not known whether Charles had forbidden his officers and clan chiefs to issue any orders to their men after the charge had been launched, but it is likely that Charles cautioned them against attempts to issue complicated orders through the noise and confusion. It is known that all of the front-line regiments were led into battle by their officers or chiefs, most of whom fell during the initial stages of the conflicts.[82] It goes without saying that the practice of the captain's personally leading his troops into battle made it almost impossible for a Gaelic army to fight in a coordinated fashion after the attack was under way. If Charles had intended to fight a conventional battle on Culloden Moor, he would have been well advised to provide his officers and men with a well-defined tactical plan. Charles simply turned loose his seemingly invincible Highlanders to win the day as they had done repeatedly over the previous century.

Despite the odds against them, the grim determination of the Highlanders impressed observers of the battle. One noted that ' ... they went on with extraordinary resolution. It's not to be wondered that they were beat at last, but very surprising ... [that] they did not run away much sooner'.[83] Another Jacobite wrote that ' ... our defeat did not at all surprise me; I was only astonished to see [the Highlanders] behave so well'.[84] Indeed, for half an hour the clansmen in the front ranks endured terrible punishment, but they fought on valiantly.[85] The courage they displayed, particularly the right side of the line, was captured by a Scottish historian, who wrote:

> Notwithstanding that the three files of the front line of English poured forth their incessant fire of musketry — notwithstanding that the cannon, now loaded with grape-shot, swept the field as with a hailstorm — notwithstanding the flank fire of Wolfe's regiment — onward, onward went the headlong Highlanders, flinging themselves into, rather than rushing upon, the lines of the enemy .... All that courage, all that despair could do, was done. It was a moment of dreadful and agonising suspense, but only a moment — for the whirlwind does not reap the forest with greater rapidity than the Highlanders cleared the line. Nevertheless, almost every man in their front rank, chief and gentleman, fell before the deadly weapons which they had braved; ... but it was not till every bayonet was bent and bloody with the strife.[86]

The old Gaelic military system was finally overwhelmed by the forces of modern tactical warfare at Culloden, but the Highlanders had shown that the individual fighter still had a valuable tactical role to play on the battlefields of the eighteenth century. Though the musket and bayonet triumphed over the broadsword and target at Culloden and the Highland charge at last was broken by the strength of a modern regular army, the tactics that had served the Highlanders so well for the past century did not die on that fateful day in April 1746. Nor was the fighting spirit of the Gaels that had breathed life into the Highland charge diminished by the Jacobite defeat. The clansmen had exhibited ' ... the habits of

F

warriors, and not those of boors'.[87] British officers who had witnessed the Highlanders in action saw in these raw and undisciplined fighters a military capability and a love of combat that was too exploitable to be ignored. The expansion and protection of the Empire would certainly demand a type of irregular tactical warfare that would suit the temperament and experience of the Gaels. The Highlanders were the epitome of front-line shock troops, and their onslaught was compared to ' . . . a flame, the violence of which is more to be dreaded than the duration'.[88] After Culloden the strengths and limitations of the Gaelic military system were laid bare for all to see. The British had suppressed the uprising and were determined that the Highlanders would never again be permitted to stage another.[89] Though many of the Jacobite leaders had sought refuge in France, what remained of the pro-Jacobite clans had to be held in check. The British reasoned that this could best be accomplished by filling the ranks of their army with the militaristic Highlanders who had not fled to the continent into the service of France. Large numbers of clansmen, many of whom knew little else but making war, gradually came to accept military service for their old enemies as an outlet for their cultural aggressiveness. The Highlanders' tactical prowess indeed assured them of much military action in British (or French) armies in the remaining years of the eighteenth century.

NOTES

1. General Henry Hawley's Description of Highland Warfare, 12 January 1746, quoted in David, Lord Elcho, *A Short History of the Affairs of Scotland in the Years 1744, 1745, 1746*, ed. Evan Charteris (Edinburgh: David Douglas, 1907; reprinted ed., Edinburgh: James Thin, 1973), p. 460.

2. By 1745 British infantrymen were armed almost exclusively with the new firelock or flintlock musket, the socket bayonet, and the steel ramrod. The new musket was a .85-inch caliber weapon about five feet long without bayonet and weighed about eleven pounds. A well-trained soldier could fire a round every thirty seconds at an effective range of sixty yards. Greater rapidity of fire was made possible by the use of pre-packaged paper cartridges that held both ball and powder. The socket bayonet could be attached without sacrificing firepower and provided the soldier with an effective weapon for close-quarter combat. Steel ramrods replaced the old wooden ones that were prone to snap. These improvements made the British infantryman a much more formidable opponent in 1745 than he had been in 1689 or 1715. Peter Young and J. P. Lawford, eds., *History of the British Army* (New York: G. P. Putnam's Sons, 1970; London: Barker, 1970), p. 29; J. W. Fortescue, *A History of the British Army*, 13 vols. (London: MacMillan and Company, 1910–1930), I: 586–87.

3. MacDonald of Lochgarry, 'Lochgarry's Narrative,' in *Itinerary of Prince Charles Edward Stuart from his landing in Scotland July 1745 to his departure in September 1746*, ed. W. B. Blaikie (Edinburgh: Scottish History Society, 1897), p. 115; Andrew Lumisden, 'A Short Account of the Battles of Preston, Falkirk, and Culloden,' in *Origins of the 'Forty-Five and other Papers Relating to that Rising*, ed. W. B. Blaikie (Edinburgh: Scottish History Society, 1916), pp. 405–06; Elcho, *Affairs of Scotland*, pp. 266–67.

4. According to Blaikie, ed., *Itinerary*, pp. 90–91, the Jacobite army numbered 2,580 men, including about fifty horse. John Home, *The History of the Rebellion in the Year*

1745 (London: T. Cadell, 1802), pp. 110–11n, writes that the Jacobites had about 2,400 men. The Chevalier de Johnstone, *Memoirs of the Rebellion in 1745 and 1746*, 2nd ed. (London: Longman, Hurst, Rees, Orme, and Brown, 1821), p. 29, writes that Charles's army numbered only about 1,800 men, a figure that is out of line with other estimates. The weight of evidence suggests that the figure of 2,500 Jacobites is more nearly correct. Estimates as to the size of Cope's army are more varied. Elcho, *Affairs of Scotland*, p. 264, gives a figure of 2,100 regular foot, 300 volunteers, and 600 dragoons. Johnstone, *Memoirs*, p. 21, gives a much exaggerated figure of 4,000 men. John Murray of Broughton, *Memorials of John Murray of Broughton Sometime Secretary to Prince Charles Edward, 1740–1747*, ed. R. F. Bell (Edinburgh: Scottish History Society, 1898), p. 200, estimates Cope's strength at 2,700. James Maxwell of Kirkconnell, *Narrative of Charles Prince of Wales' Expedition to Scotland in the Year 1745* (Edinburgh: The Maitland Club, 1841), p. 41, estimates 2,300 foot and 600 dragoons. George Lockhart, *The Lockhart Papers Containing Memoirs and Commentaries upon the Affairs of Scotland from 1702 to 1715, by George Lockhart, Esq. of Carnwath, His Secret Correspondence with the Son of King James the Second from 1718 to 1728, and his other Political Writings; Also, Journals and Memoirs of the Young Pretender's Expedition in 1745, by Highland Officers in his Army*, 2 vols. (London: William Anderson, 1817), II: 489, writes that Cope had 4,000 troops, again a figure that is out of line with other estimates. Lumisden, 'Preston, Falkirk, and Culloden,' p. 406, estimates about 2,000 foot and 700 horse. Robert Chambers, *History of the Rebellion of 1745–1746* (Edinburgh: W. R. Chambers, 1869), pp. 118–19; and Home, *History of the Rebellion*, pp. 110–11n, both give Cope's strength at just over 2,100 men. Fortescue, *British Army*, II: 129, estimates that the government army numbered about 2,800 men. Finally, Sir John Cope, K. B., *The Report of the Proceedings and Opinion of the Board of General Officers on their Examination into the Conduct, Behaviour, and Proceedings of Lieutenant-General Sir John Cope, Knight of the Bath* (London: W. Webb, 1749), p. 43, gives a total of 1,400 foot and 600 horse, a figure that seems much too low. The weight of the evidence suggests that Cope's army at Prestonpans most likely numbered about 2,500 men and was about the same size as the Jacobite force.

5. Maxwell, *Narrative*, pp. 39–40; Chambers, *History of the Rebellion*, pp. 118–19; Johnstone, *Memoirs*, pp. 32–33; Lockhart, *Lockhart Papers*, II: 489.

6. Johnstone, *Memoirs*, p. 33.

7. Home, *History of the Rebellion*, pp. 115–16; Maxwell, *Narrative*, pp. 39–40; Lumisden, 'Preston, Falkirk, and Culloden,' pp. 406–07; Chambers, *History of the Rebellion*, p. 125; Elcho, *Affairs of Scotland*, pp. 269–72; Johnstone, *Memoirs*, pp. 33–34; Lockhart, *Lockhart Papers*, II: 489–90.

8. Johnstone, *Memoirs*, pp. 33–34; Lumisden, 'Preston, Falkirk, and Culloden,' p. 406; Lockhart, *Lockhart Papers*, II: 489–90; Elcho, *Affairs of Scotland*, pp. 267, 270–71; Andrew Henderson, *The History of the Rebellion, MDCCXLV and MDCCXLVI*, 5th ed. (London: A. Millar, 1753), p. 79.

9. Henderson, *History of the Rebellion*, p. 82; Home, *History of the Rebellion*, p. 118; Elcho, *Affairs of Scotland*, p. 269; MacDonald of Lochgarry, 'Narrative,' p. 115; Johnstone, *Memoirs*, p. 30n; Lumisden, 'Preston, Falkirk, and Culloden,' pp. 406–07; Lockhart, *Lockhart Papers*, II: 490.

10. Home, *History of the Rebellion*, p. 104.

11. James Ray, *A Compleat History of the Rebellion from its first Rise in 1745, to its total Suppression at the glorious battle of Culloden, in April, 1746* (London: James Ray, 1754), p. 35; W. A. S. Hewins, ed., *The Whitefoord Papers Being the Correspondence and Other Manuscripts of Colonel Charles Whitefoord and Caleb Whitefoord from 1739 to 1810*

(Oxford: The Clarendon Press, 1898), p. 91; Samuel Boyse, *An impartial history of the late rebellion in 1745. From authentic memoirs; particularly, the journal of a general officer, and other papers, yet unpublished. With the characters of the persons principally concerned. To which is prefixed, by way of introduction, a compendious account of the royal house of Stuart, from its original to the present time* (Reading: D. Henry, 1748), p. 80; Henderson, *History of the Rebellion*, p. 82; Maxwell, *Narrative*, p. 41; Johnstone, *Memoirs*, pp. 35, 39–40; Lumisden, 'Preston, Falkirk, and Culloden,' pp. 407–08; Elcho, *Affairs of Scotland*, pp. 271–72; Lord George Murray, 'Marches of the Highland Army,' in *Jacobite Memoirs of the Rebellion of 1745*, ed. Robert Chambers (Edinburgh: William and Robert Chambers, 1834), p. 40.

12. General Wightman to Lord President Forbes, 26 September 1745, in *Culloden Papers: Comprising An Extensive and Interesting Correspondence from the Year 1625 to 1748*, ed. H. R. Duff (London: T. Cadell and W. Davies, 1815), pp. 224–25; Home, *History of the Rebellion*, pp. 119–20.

13. Ray, *Compleat History*, pp. 35–36; Hewins, ed., *Whitefoord Papers*, p. 91; Henderson, *History of the Rebellion*, pp. 82–83; Maxwell, *Narrative*, p. 41; Elcho, *Affairs of Scotland*, pp. 271–72; Lumisden, 'Preston, Falkirk, and Culloden,' pp. 407–08; Johnstone, *Memoirs*, pp. 39–40.

14. Home, *History of the Rebellion*, p. 120.

15. Maxwell, *Narrative*, p. 41; Lockhart, *Lockhart Papers*, II: 490; Lumisden, 'Preston, Falkirk, and Culloden,' pp. 407–08; Home, *History of the Rebellion*, pp. 119–20; Boyse, *An impartial history of the Rebellion*, pp. 80–81; Johnstone, *Memoirs*, p. 35; Elcho, *Affairs of Scotland*, pp. 271–72; Henderson, *History of the Rebellion*, pp. 82–83; Hewins, ed., *Whitefoord Papers*, p. 91; Ray, *Compleat History*, pp. 35–36.

16. Boyse, *An impartial history of the rebellion*, pp. 80–81.

17. Rev. Dr. Alexander Carlyle, *Autobiography of the Rev. Dr. Alexander Carlyle, Minister of Inveresk, containing Memorials of the Men and Events of his time*, 2 vols. (Edinburgh: William Blackwood and Sons, 1860), I: 142; Johnstone, *Memoirs*, pp. 36–38; Elcho, *Affairs of Scotland*, pp. 271–73; Hewins, ed., *The Whitefoord Papers*, p. 91; Lumisden, 'Preston, Falkirk, and Culloden,' pp. 407–08; Murray, 'Marches,' p. 40; Home, *History of the Rebellion*, pp. 119–20; Ray, *Compleat History*, pp. 35–36.

18. Elcho, *Affairs of Scotland*, p. 277.

19. Major-General Alexander B. Tulloch, *The '45 From the Raising of Prince Charlie's Standard at Glenfinnan to the Battle of Culloden*, 3rd ed. (Stirling: Eneas MacKay, 1908), p. 51; Lumisden, 'Preston, Falkirk, and Culloden,' pp. 408–09.

20. Johnstone, *Memoirs*, p. 38.

21. Lumisden, 'Preston, Falkirk, and Culloden,' p. 409; Johnstone, *Memoirs*, p. 38; Home, *History of the Rebellion*, pp. 120–21; Boyse, *An impartial history of the rebellion*, pp. 80–81; Murray, 'Marches,' p. 41; Ray, *Compleat History*, pp. 35–36; Elcho, *Affairs of Scotland*, pp. 274–76; Maxwell, *Narrative*, p. 42; Hewins, ed., *The Whitefoord Papers*, p. 59; Lady George Murray to Duke of Atholl, 22 September 1745, in *Jacobite Correspondence of the Atholl Family during the Rebellion, MDCCXLV-MDCCXLVI*, ed. J. H. Burton (Edinburgh: The Abbotsford Club, 1845), p. 22; Katherine Tomasson and Francis Buist, *Battles of the '45* (London: B. T. Batsford, 1962; reprint ed., London: Book Club Associates, 1978), pp. 67–69; List of Killed and Prisoners at the Battle of Prestonpans, 1745, Edinburgh, Edinburgh University Library, Laing MSS.

22. J. T. Findlay, *Wolfe in Scotland in the '45 and from 1749 to 1753* (London: Longmans, Green, and Company, 1928), p. 74; Sir James Fergusson, *Argyll in the Forty-Five* (London: Faber and Faber, 1951), pp. 68–69; Home, *History of the Rebellion*,

p. 178; Elcho, *Affairs of Scotland*, pp. 373–74; Tulloch, *The '45*, p. 52; A. G. Bradley, *Wolfe* (London: MacMillan and Company, 1971), p. 34; Henderson, *History of the Rebellion*, p. 265.

23. Johnstone, *Memoirs*, pp. 28n, 119–20; Maxwell, *Narrative*, p. 27.

24. Murray, 'Marches,' pp. 93–94.

25. John Daniel, 'A True Account of Mr. John Daniel's Progress with Prince Charles Edward in the Years 1745 and 1746, written by himself,' in *Origins of the 'Forty-Five*, ed. Blaikie, p. 194; Chambers, *History of the Rebellion*, pp. 229–30; Blaikie, ed., *Itinerary*, pp. 96–97; Maxwell, *Narrative*, p. 99; Elcho, *Affairs of Scotland*, p. 371; Lumisden, 'Preston, Falkirk, and Culloden,' p. 409.

26. Chambers, *History of the Rebellion*, p. 224; Ferguson, *Argyll in the 'Forty-Five*, pp. 68–69; Lumisden, 'Preston, Falkirk, and Culloden,' p. 411.

27. Home, *History of the Rebellion*, p. 165; Elcho, *Affairs of Scotland*, pp. 372–73; Lumisden, 'Preston, Falkirk, and Culloden,' p. 410; Lockhart, *Lockhart Papers*, II: 500; Oliphant of Gask to his Mother, 17 January 1746, in *Atholl Correspondence*, ed. Burton, pp. 142–43; Maxwell, *Narrative*, p. 99.

28. Duncan Warrand, ed., *More Culloden Papers*, 5 vols. (Inverness: Robert Carruthers and Sons, 1923–1930), IV: 200; Elcho, *Affairs of Scotland*, pp. 372–73; Chambers, *History of the Rebellion*, pp. 227–29; Daniel, 'Progress,' p. 194; Home, *History of the Rebellion*, p. 167; Ray, *Compleat History*, p. 243; Lockhart, *Lockhart Papers*, II: 501; Maxwell, *Narrative*, pp. 100–01; Johnstone, *Memoirs*, p. 121; Lumisden, 'Preston, Falkirk, and Culloden,' p. 411.

29. Oliphant of Gask to his Mother, 17 January 1746, in *Atholl Correspondence*, ed. Burton, pp. 142–43; Lumisden, 'Preston, Falkirk, and Culloden,' p. 411; Lockhart, *Lockhart Papers*, II: 501; Chambers, *History of the Rebellion*, pp. 228–29; Daniel, 'Progress,' p. 194.

30. Hawley's alignment at Falkirk was as follows. On the extreme left were Hamilton's, Ligonier's, and Cobham's dragoons. The first line of infantry, from left to right, were Wolfe's, Cholmondely's, Pulteney's, Price's, Ligonier's, and the Royal Regiment. Manning the second line were Blakeney's, Munro's, Fleming's, Battereau's, and Barrel's regiments. In reserve stood the Argyllshire Highlanders, several hundred volunteer militia, and Howard's regiment. Johnstone, *Memoirs*, p. 121; Ray, *Compleat History*, pp. 241–42; MacDonald of Lochgarry, 'Lochgarry's Narrative,' pp. 118–19; Daniel, 'Progress,' p. 195.

31. Charles's alignment at Falkirk was as follows. On the front line, from left to right, stood the Appin Stewarts (300), Camerons (800), Frasers (300), MacPhersons (300), MacIntoshes (200), Farquharsons (200), and MacDonalds of Glengarry (800), Clanranald (400), and Keppoch (600). The second line consisted of the Drummonds, MacLachlans, Gordons, Ogilvies, Athollmen, and other clan and Lowland units. In reserve were the Irish piquets and a small body of horse under Lord Elcho. Home, *History of the Rebellion*, pp. 167–68; Lumisden, 'Preston, Falkirk, and Culloden,' p. 409; Lockhart, *Lockhart Papers*, II: 501; Murray, 'Marches,' pp. 83–84; Elcho, *Affairs of Scotland*, pp. 372–75.

32. Elcho, *Affairs of Scotland*, pp. 374–75; Maxwell, *Narrative*, p. 101; Murray, 'Marches,' pp. 83–84; Johnstone, *Memoirs*, pp. 121, 129–30n; Home, *History of the Rebellion*, pp. 175–76.

33. Daniel, 'Progress,' p. 195.

34. Johnstone, *Memoirs*, p. 121; Elcho, *Affairs of Scotland*, pp. 374–75; Ray, *Compleat History*, pp. 241–42; Henderson, *History of the Rebellion*, p. 266; Boyse, *An impartial history of the rebellion*, pp. 136–37; MacDonald of Lochgarry, 'Lochgarry's Narrative,' pp. 118–19; Lockhart, *Lockhart Papers*, II: 501; Lumisden, 'Preston, Falkirk, and

Culloden,' p. 411.

35. Daniel, 'Progress,' pp. 195–96; MacDonald of Lochgarry, 'Lochgarry's Narrative,' pp. 118–19; Lockhart, *Lockhart Papers*, II: 501; Ray, *Compleat History*, pp. 241–42; Oliphant of Gask to his Mother, 17 January 1746, in *Atholl Correspondence*, ed. Burton, pp. 142–43; Lumisden, 'Preston, Falkirk, and Culloden,' p. 411; Elcho, *Affairs of Scotland*, pp. 374–76; Henderson, *History of the Rebellion*, p. 266; Boyse, *An impartial history of the rebellion*, pp. 136–37; Home, *History of the Rebellion*, pp. 171–72; Maxwell, *Narrative*, pp. 101–02; Murray, 'Marches,' p. 85; Findlay, *Wolfe in Scotland*, p. 73; Johnstone, *Memoirs*, p. 121.

36. Daniel, 'Progress,' p. 196.

37. Maxwell, *Narrative*, pp. 102–03; Johnstone, *Memoirs*, p. 123; Murray, 'Marches,' p. 84.

38. There was a great deal of confusion as to who actually had been asigned to command on the Jacobite left. Most accounts agree that it was Lord John Drummond's responsibility. Murray wrote that ' ... although it is said in the printed relations of the battle, that ... Drummond commanded the left wing, yet I believe he had no directions to do it, and was not there when the battle began'. Murray, 'Marches,' p. 84.

39. Murray, 'Marches,' pp. 85–86; Maxwell, *Narrative*, pp. 102–03.

40. Lockhart, *Lockhart Papers*, II: 502; Maxwell, *Narrative*, pp. 102–04; Home, *History of the Rebellion*, pp. 170, 172–73; Lumisden, 'Preston, Falkirk, and Culloden,' pp. 411–12; Johnstone, *Memoirs*, pp. 124–25; Murray, 'Marches,' pp. 84–87; Boyse, *An impartial history of the rebellion*, pp. 136–37; Findlay, *Wolfe in Scotland*, pp. 74–75; Henderson, *History of the Rebellion*, pp. 266–67; Elcho, *Affairs of Scotland*, p. 376.

41. Johnstone, *Memoirs*, pp. 125–26; Murray, 'Marches,' pp. 86–87; Lumisden, 'Preston, Falkirk, and Culloden,' pp. 411–12; Maxwell, *Narrative*, pp. 102–04; Home, *History of the Rebellion*, pp. 170, 173–74; Lockhart, *Lockhart Papers*, II: 502; Elcho, *Affairs of Scotland*, pp. 376–77; Murray to Duke of Atholl, 21 January 1746, in *Atholl Correspondence*, ed. Burton, pp. 149–50.

42. Hawley's losses, according to contemporary writers, ranged from 150 to 700 killed, and 600 to 700 captured. Charles suffered between thirty and fifty killed and sixty to 120 wounded. Following are the individual estimates of losses, when available, for both sides. Hawley: 600 killed and 700 captured. Johnstone, *Memoirs*, pp. 127–28. Hawley: 300 to 400 killed; Charles: forty killed, eighty wounded. Home, *History of the Rebellion*, p. 177n. Hawley: 650 killed and 700 captured; Charles: forty killed. Lockhart, *Lockhart Papers*, II: 503. Hawley: 700 killed; Charles: forty killed. Daniel, 'Progress,' pp. 198–99. Hawley: 400 to 500 killed, several hundred captured; Charles: forty killed and sixty wounded. Maxwell, *Narrative*, p. 105. Hawley: 500 to 600 killed, 600 captured; Charles: fifty killed, sixty wounded. Elcho, *Affairs of Scotland*, pp. 278–79. Hawley: 500 killed. Murray to Duke of Atholl, 18 January 1746, in *Atholl Correspondence*, ed. Burton, p. 145. Hawley: 600 killed, 700 captured; Charles: forty-seven killed, 100 wounded. Lumisden, 'Preston, Falkirk, and Culloden,' pp. 412–13. Hawley: 150 killed; Charles: thirty killed. Oliphant of Gask to his Mother, 17 January 1746, in *Atholl Correspondence*, ed. Burton, pp. 142–43.

43. Chambers, *History of the Rebellion*, pp. 236–37; Johnstone, *Memoirs*, pp. 127–28; Lockhart, *Lockhart Papers*, II: 503; Daniel, 'Progress,' pp. 198–99; Elcho, *Affairs of Scotland*, pp. 378–79; Lumisden, 'Preston, Falkirk, and Culloden,' pp. 412–13.

44. Elcho, *Affairs of Scotland*, p. 376.

45. Johnstone, *Memoirs*, p. 126.

46. Winifred Duke, *Lord George Murray and the Forty-Five* (Aberdeen: Milne and Hutchinson, 1927), p. 143; Tulloch, *The '45*, p. 52; Johnstone, *Memoirs*, p. 121; Ray,

Compleat History, p. 243; Boyse, *An impartial history of the rebellion*, p. 138; Lockhart, *Lockhart Papers*, II: 503.

47. Murray, 'Marches,' p. 85.

48. Colonel Ker of Gradyne, 'Colonel Ker of Gradyne's Account of Culloden,' in *Jacobite Memoirs*, ed. Chambers, pp. 140–41; Lockhart, *Lockhart Papers*, II: 520, 530–31; Elcho, *Affairs of Scotland*, pp. 431.

49. Elcho, *Affairs of Scotland*, pp. 423–24; Home, *History of the Rebellion*, p. 332; Gradyne, 'Account of Culloden,' pp. 140–41; Lockhart, *Lockhart Papers*, II: 520, 531–32.

50. Maxwell, *Narrative*, p. 149; Duke, *Murray and the Forty-Five*, p. 187.

51. Lockhart, *Lockhart Papers*, II: 520; Henderson, *History of the Rebellion*, p. 323; Sir Robert Strange, *Memoirs of Sir Robert Strange and Andrew Lumisden*, ed. James Dennistoun, 2 vols. (London: Longman, Brown, Green, and Longmans, 1855), I: 62–63; Elcho, *Affairs of Scotland*, pp. 424–25n.

52. Home, *History of the Rebellion*, p. 230; Chambers, *History of the Rebellion*, p. 289–90.

53. Henderson, *History of the Rebellion*, pp. 325–26; Tulloch, *The '45*, p. 41; Chambers, *History of the Rebellion*, pp. 287–90; Elcho, *Affairs of Scotland*, p. 432; Gradyne, 'Account of Culloden,' p. 141; Lockhart, *Lockhart Papers*, II: 520.

54. Elcho, *Affairs of Scotland*, pp. 431–32.

55. Boyse, *An impartial history of the rebellion*, p. 160; Lockhart, *Lockhart Papers*, II: 520; Strange, *Memoirs*, I: 62–63; Ray, *Compleat History*, pp. 334–35; Elcho, *Affairs of Scotland*, p. 431; Hewins, ed., *The Whitefoord Papers*, p. 78; Suppression of the Rebellion, 22 April 1746, Laing MSS, II. 502.

56. Home, *History of the Rebellion*, p. 230.

57. Elcho, *Affairs of Scotland*, pp. 431–32; Home, *History of the Rebellion*, pp. 230–31; Tulloch, *The '45*, p. 42; Lockhart, *Lockhart Papers*, II: 531.

58. Maxwell, *Narrative*, p. 151; Elcho, *Affairs of Scotland*, pp. 431–32; Fergusson, *Argyll in the 'Forty-Five*, p. 172.

59. Maxwell, *Narrative*, pp. 151–52.

60. Gradyne, 'Account of Culloden,' p. 142; Lockhart, *Lockhart Papers*, II: 521; Maxwell, *Narrative*, pp. 151–52; Home, *History of the Rebellion*, pp. 231–32.

61. Home, *History of the Rebellion*, pp. 230–32; Lockhart, *Lockhart Papers*, II: 531; Chambers, *History of the Rebellion*, p. 296.

62. Peter Anderson, *Culloden Moor and Story of the Battle, with description of the Stone Circles and Cairns at Clava* (Stirling: Eneas MacKay, 1920), p. 64; Elcho, *Affairs of Scotland*, p. 431; Hewins, ed., *The Whitefoord Papers*, p. 78; Maxwell, *Narrative*, p. 152; Lockhart, *Lockhart Papers*, II: 521; Home, *History of the Rebellion*, pp. 231–32.

63. Hewins, ed., *The Whitefoord Papers*, p. 78.

64. Johnstone, *Memoirs*, p. 189.

65. Henderson, *History of the Rebellion*, pp. 327–29; Chambers, *History of the Rebellion*, p. 286; Elcho, *Affairs of Scotland*, pp. 432–33; General James Wolfe to Major Henry Delabene, 17 April 1746, quoted in Findlay, *Wolfe in Scotland*, p. 106; Suppression of the Rebellion, 22 April 1746, Laing MSS, II. 502.

66. Chambers, *History of the Rebellion*, pp. 286–87; Anderson, *Culloden Moor*, p. 56.

67. James Maxwell of Kirkconnell wrote that the Highlanders were ' . . . more impetuous on their first onset than any other troops . . . ' Maxwell, *Narrative*, p. 143.

68. Lockhart, *Lockhart Papers*, II: 521.

69. Ray, *Compleat History*, pp. 338–39; Chambers, *History of the Rebellion*, pp. 296–97; Duke, *Murray and the Forty-Five*, p. 189; Home, *History of the Rebellion*, pp. 232–33;

Lockhart, *Lockhart Papers*, II: 521, 531; Henderson, *History of the Rebellion*, pp. 327–32; Tulloch, *The '45*, p. 43; Suppression of the Rebellion, 22 April 1746, Laing MSS, II. 502; Gradyne, 'Account of Culloden,' p. 142; Lumisden, 'Preston, Falkirk and Culloden,' pp. 418–19; Boyse, *An impartial history of the rebellion*, p. 159; Wolfe to Delabene, 17 April 1746, quoted in Findlay, *Wolfe in Scotland*, pp. 106–07.

70. Suppression of the Rebellion, 22 April 1746, Laing MSS, II. 502.

71. Hewins, ed., *The Whitefoord Papers*, p. 78.

72. Ray, *Compleat History*, pp. 338–39; Chambers, *History of the Rebellion*, pp. 296–97; Lockhart, *Lockhart Papers*, II: 521; Home, *History of the Rebellion*, pp. 232–33; Tulloch, *The '45*, p. 43; Boyse, *An impartial history of the rebellion*, p. 159; Henderson, *History of the Rebellion*, pp. 327–32; Edward Weston to Robert Trevor, 25 April 1746, quoted in Findlay, *Wolfe in Scotland*, pp. 111–12; Elcho, *Affairs of Scotland*, pp. 432–33.

73. Chambers, *History of the Rebellion*, pp. 297–98; Duke, *Murray and the Forty-Five*, p. 189; Johnstone, *Memoirs*, p. 189–90; Maxwell, *Narrative*, pp. 152–53; Lockhart, *Lockhart Papers*, II: 510; John Roy Stewart, 'Another Song on Culloden Day,' in *Highland Songs of the Forty-Five*, ed. John Lorne Campbell (Edinburgh: John Grant, 1933; reprint ed. Edinburgh: The Scottish Gaelic Texts Society, 1984), pp. 179–80.

74. Maxwell, *Narrative*, p. 153.

75. Chambers, *History of the Rebellion*, pp. 297–98; Home, *History of the Rebellion*, pp. 233–34.

76. Ray, *Compleat History*, pp. 334–35; Hewins, ed., *The Whitefoord Papers*, pp. 78–79; Duke, *Murray and the Forty-Five*, p. 189; Henderson, *History of the Rebellion*, p. 326; Johnstone, *Memoirs*, p. 192; Home, *History of the Rebellion*, pp. 233, 235, 239; Lockhart, *Lockhart Papers*, II: 531; Maxwell, *Narrative*, pp. 152–53; Chambers, *History of the Rebellion*, pp. 297–98, 300–01.

77. Tulloch, *The '45*, p. 45.

78. John Prebble, *Culloden* (London: Martin Secker and Warburg, 1961; reprint ed., Harmondsworth: Penguin Books, 1967), p. 112; Peter Young and John Adair, *Hastings to Culloden* (London: G. Bell and Sons, 1964), p. 229; Hewins, ed., *The Whitefoord Papers*, pp. 78–79; Elcho, *Affairs of Scotland*, pp. 434–35.

79. Hewins, ed., *The Whitefoord Papers*, pp. 78–79; Elcho, *Affairs of Scotland*, pp. 434–35; Lumisden, 'Preston, Falkirk, and Culloden,' pp. 418–19; Tomasson and Buist, *Battles of the '45*, p. 178; Home, *History of the Rebellion*, p. 237; Chambers, *History of the Rebellion*, pp. 311–12.

80. Maxwell, *Narrative*, p. 152.

81. Elcho, *Affairs of Scotland*, pp. 433–34.

82. Home, *History of the Rebellion*, pp. 238–39.

83. Maxwell, *Narrative*, p. 156.

84. Johnstone, *Memoirs*, p. 195.

85. Strange, *Memoirs*, I: 65; Boyse, *An impartial history of the rebellion*, pp. 160–61.

86. Chambers, *History of the Rebellion*, p. 296.

87. Johnstone, *Memoirs*, p. 28n.

88. *Ibid.*, p. 190.

89. Suggestions by Duncan Forbes of Culloden, Lord President of the Court of Session after the Rebellion of 1745, c. 1746–1747, Laing MSS, II. 123; Hewins, ed., *The Whitefoord Papers*, p. 79.

9

The Gael in the French and Indian War

In the immediate aftermath of Culloden, not surprisingly, animosities between Gael and Englishman were fueled to a fever pitch. It was reported that ' ... London all over was in a perfect uproar of joy ... ' A contemporary noted that ' ... John Bull ... is as haughty and valiant to-night as he was abject and cowardly on the Black Wednesday when the Highlanders were at Derby'.[1] Indeed, Britain was secured against internal unrest and was in no mood to brook any further disturbance from the tribes of the north: 'If the ... Highlanders who have escaped the dangers of this rebellion are assured of mercy ... the high probability is that they will with great gladness ... embark again on such a project'.[2] A government officer warned the Highlanders that they could ' ... retire to no mountains so barren or so remote ... ' that the king ' ... cannot in person lead and subsist a sufficient force ... ' to crush them again.[3] The proud clansmen, their honor stung by the setback at Culloden and their very lives endangered by repressive government policies designed to root out the clan system, vented their frustrations in song and verse. With the demise of the old way of life and their unwilling entry into the modern age, the clansmen mourned their fate and awaited the prospect of again drawing the broadsword on the field of honor:

> On this age a thousand curses,
> Dang'rous, changeful are our times;
> On us Fortune's wheel has turned,
> We who ne'er feared any foe;
> Now we are dispersed and scattered
> Midst the glens and heathered hills,
> But we'll rally yet our forces
> When to war we can return.[4]
>
> Alexander MacDonald
> 'A Certain Song'

The Highlanders did return to war, but it was not against their former enemy, nor were their native hills and glens the battlefields on which they would shed their blood. After Culloden large numbers of clansmen were drawn into the struggle for Empire on the side of Great Britain to fight against their former French allies in the western hemisphere.

Once tensions between the pro-Jacobite clans and the government had eased, British army officers began recruiting actively among the Highlanders in search of the troops who would be needed to fight the French in North America. In 1747 the government began offering pardons to any former Jacobite who would enlist for service in Canada or the West Indies.[5] At that time there was only one Highland regiment serving in the British army, the Forty-third (which shortly thereafter

157

became the Forty-second), the nucleii of which were the old independent companies collectively known as the Black Watch.[6] In the early 1750s, when a colonial war with France loomed on the western horizon, Major-General James Wolfe, who had witnessed the Highlanders' courage and prowess at Falkirk and Culloden, expressed a viewpoint that soon became standard British policy toward the clansmen:

> I should imagine that two or three independent Highland companies might be of use; they are hardy, intrepid, accustomed to a rough country, and no great mischief if they fall. How can you better employ a secret enemy than by making his end conducive to the common good.[7]

By 1756 and 1757 two new and distinctively Highland regiments had been raised and despatched to North America.[8] The Seventy-seventh (Montgomery's Highlanders), and the Seventy-eighth (Fraser's Highlanders) regiments, along with the Forty-second (Black Watch), were destined to see action at Fort Duquesne, Ticonderoga, Louisbourg, Quebec, and St. Foy. The outstanding contributions that the clansmen made to the British victory in the New World were not wholly unexpected, as 'No men in this island are better qualified for the American war than the Scots Highlanders'.[9]

The French and Indian War demanded of the British fighting men who could stand the rigors of irregular wilderness warfare as well as conventional warfare. Except on a very few occasions, the Highlanders proved themselves capable of contending with the French regulars, French-Canadian provincials, and Indians within the forests, swamps, and hills of North America. The *sauvages d'Ecosse*, as the Highlanders were called by the French, brought with them to America a highly respected martial reputation that was accentuated by their unusual appearance. The various Indian tribes were particularly impressed by the bright, multi-colored plaids and the ominous broadswords and targets and naturally showed a healthy respect for the clansmen.[10] Highland garb initially was considered by the British to be unsuitable for the harsh American climate, and it was decided to provide the Highlanders with breeches to ward off the severe winter cold. The Highlanders, however, protested vehemently against the proposed change of uniform. The outcry was such that the British finally agreed to the continued use of the plaid and tartan, much to the satisfaction of one clansman, who wrote: ' ... we were allowed to wear the garb of our fathers, and, in the course of six winters, showed the doctors that they did not understand our constitutions ... '[11] It is not hard to imagine what unfortunate consequences might have resulted had the clansmen been stripped of their native costume. After all, the strange and forbidding sight of the Highlanders in their plaids and the mobility that they enjoyed from the loose-fitting garb were trademarks of Gaelic warfare as well as valuable components of their way of fighting.

While Highland warfare in many ways was readily adaptable to the exigencies of a wilderness campaign, circumstances arose during the course of the war in North America that were unfamiliar to the clansmen. Except in their inter-clan struggles,

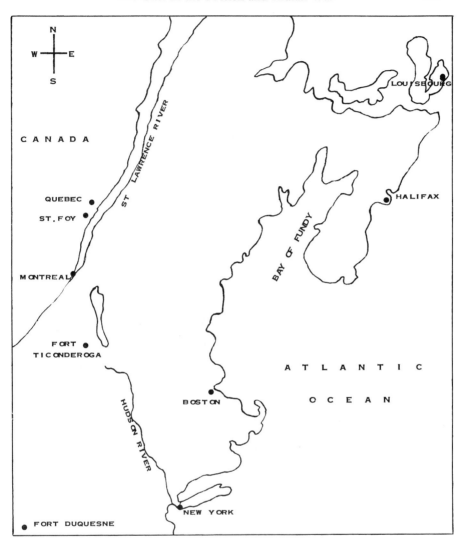

MAP 24.   NORTH AMERICAN THEATER   1756-1763

the Highlanders had not faced an enemy who was as adept in the use of natural surroundings as were the Indians, French-Canadians, and even certain elements of the regular French army. Their early campaigns proved to be valuable, if costly, learning experiences in American forest warfare. In 1758 Montgomery's Highlanders learned their first lesson in wilderness fighting at Fort Duquesne. A detachment of about 800 clansmen and raw American troops was ordered to reconnoitre the French outpost near the shores of the Monongahela and Allegheny rivers. The Highland commander divided his forces and sent forward a party of clansmen accompanied by their pipers, whose rousing skirl alerted the unsuspecting enemy. The French and Indians sallied forth from the fort in much larger numbers than the Scots expected, and a fierce action ensued in which the Highlanders' broadswords and targets were no match for the sharpshooters' muskets on the heavily wooded battlefield. Soon surrounded by a well-concealed enemy, Montgomery's Highlanders managed with a gallant effort to retreat to their main camp. There they were again besieged and the fight continued for another three-quarters of an hour until at last the clansmen fled in a panic. The mêlée cost the Highlanders 231 killed, wounded, and captured and taught them that American warfare indeed was quite different from fighting regular British troops on the hills and open moors of Scotland.[12]

The numerous wilderness forts and outposts throughout the North American theater in some measure determined the nature of the war that the Highlanders fought there. In Scotland there were many fortified castles that Highland armies had found impractical to wrest from the enemy. The clansmen had, therefore, avoided these strongholds, preferring to engage the British in the hills and glens. One reason for the Highlanders' success in wilderness warfare on their native soil was that the British were not experienced in that type of irregular, often improvisational, combat. Not once from 1644 to 1746 did the British attempt to construct any type of earth, stone, or wood defensive works and lure the Highlanders to attack them. Had they thrown up some sort of field fortifications, the British might have afforded themselves enough protection from the Highland charge to have weakened its shock value or to have blunted it altogether. But even though the Highlanders had won most of the battlefield encounters over their tactically inferior enemy, the British had won the wars, and the clansmen's inability to deprive them of strategically placed castles perhaps contributed to the Gaels' eventual defeat. So both the Highlanders and the British during their long series of wars had exhibited glaring weaknesses where fortifications were concerned. In the French and Indian War, however, neither the British nor their Highland allies could afford to repeat those past mistakes. If they were to defeat the French, they had to reduce numerous strongholds that were cleverly constructed and expertly defended. Consequently, from attacks on isolated frontier garrisons in Pennsylvania and New York to the siege of Quebec, British commanders drove their Highland troops to undertake a type of warfare that was unfamiliar to them. In the end it was the Highlanders' persistence and determination in taking on the French, Indians, and French-Canadians who stood behind their battlements that brought victory to British arms in North America.

One of the Highlanders' first attempts to crack a solidly constructed French defensive position came at Ticonderoga in 1758, an extremely bloody affair for the Scots. There the Black Watch was introduced to the harsh realities of American positional wilderness warfare. It faced a series of French defenses that resembled ' . . . a forest laid flat by a hurricane.[13] The French breastworks that defended the approaches to the fort were fronted by hundreds of felled trees, their limbs sharpened and hardened by fire and pointing outward.[14] The British commander intended to take the stronghold with bayonet and broadsword assaults, but time and time again the attacks were repulsed with heavy losses. The determined

Highlanders refused to acknowledge that the defenses were impenetrable and tried repeatedly to hack their way through the tangle of brush. Inspired rather than demoralized by the heavy and accurate enemy fire, the clansmen amazed both ally and enemy with their uncharacteristic tenacity. Indeed, they seemed oblivious to the destruction of their own ranks, and it appeared for a moment that the Highland fury would sweep away everything in its path.[15] A historian of a later day reconstructed the scene:

> The brave Highlanders were there, stubborn and unflinching soldiers, never daunted, never dispirited, always ready to charge. They press on, they force their way through the entanglement of trees; their ranks are thinned by death; but they heed it not; forward! forward! until they are near the entrenchments. A few minutes more and they will force them. For one moment the fate of the day is doubtful.[16]

Despite their bravery the Highlanders were not able to overcome the strong defensive works at Ticonderoga. After four hours of fighting, the clansmen were with great difficulty persuaded to quit the field of battle, leaving behind more than twenty-five officers and half of their rank and file killed or wounded.[17]

The repulse at Ticonderoga certainly impressed upon the Highlanders the difficulty of a conventional attack with broadswords against an enemy who was firmly entrenched in a strong defensive position. An officer in the Black Watch wrote after the battle:

> ... the oldest soldier present never saw so furious and incessant a fire. The affair at Fontenoy was nothing to it. I saw both. We laboured under insurmountable difficulties. The enemy's breastwork was about nine or ten feet high .... But the difficult access to their lines was what gave them a fatal advantage over us .... This [i.e. the felled trees] not only broke our ranks, and made it impossible for us to keep order, but put it out of our power to advance till we cut our way through.[18]

The British attempt to employ the clansmen in a conventional attack against irregular defenses failed not because the Highlanders were unable to fight under such conditions, but because the French were extremely skilled at constructing and defending frontier redoubts. The Highland broadsword was more effective against the breastworks than were the British musket and bayonet, and this suggests how indispensable the clansmen were to the English — in conventional and irregular warfare — in their efforts to drive the French from North America.

The Highlanders fared better in attacking the more conventional, though weaker, French defenses at Louisbourg in 1758. Along the beach where the main British landing under Major-General James Wolfe was to be made, the French had constructed several permanent artillery batteries that were fronted by strong breastworks. These breastworks were similar to those at Ticonderoga in that the French had again used a wall of trees with the branches pointing toward the sea.[19] These defenses, however, were not as thick or as deep, and consequently, were not impenetrable. In addition, the ground of Freshwater Cove near Louisbourg was rocky and undulating, whereas the terrain at Ticonderoga was unbroken by hills or ridges. The lie of the land was thus more familiar to the Highlanders and afforded them a great deal of protection from the French sharpshooters. Once the clansmen of Fraser's Highlanders managed to land, they picked their way through the rocks and timbers and reached a small ridge that offered shelter from the French musketry and cannon. From there the Highlanders rendered the conventional enemy battery entrenchments untenable and methodically cleared them one by one with broadsword assaults aided by the bayonets of the British light infantry. The relative ease with which the 3,000 French defenders were banished from their front-line fortifications demonstrated that the Highlanders could still overwhelm a superior defending force when led by a resolute commander and when operating on the type of terrain they were accustomed to.[20]

While Ticonderoga and the beach fortifications of Louisbourg were representative of the wilderness defensive positions that confronted the Highlanders in North America, the inner defenses of Louisbourg and Quebec (the capital and most formidable citadel of New France) demanded that the clan regiments undertake a type of warfare in which they had failed miserably in the past — the siege. After the Highlanders were integrated into the British army, they began to enjoy the benefits of good organization, logistics, and leadership; therefore, the clansmen's effectiveness at siege warfare improved because of close cooperation with a professional, conventional military force. The Highlanders were given tasks which best suited their abilities and experience during the sieges of Louisbourg and Quebec, while regular British troops carried out most of the typical siege duties. The siege at Louisbourg gave the Highlanders the opportunity to prove their worth in a conventional operation.[21] The clansmen made possible the tightening of the circle around the town by blunting several French attempts to attack the besiegers. More importantly, a body of Fraser's Highlanders took possession of the heights in front of the main fortress and then captured the glacis, exposing the defenders on the parapet and embrasures to deadly musket fire. This coup effectively ended the siege and made the British masters of the strategic harbor of Louisbourg.[22]

Wolfe's spectacular victory on the Plains of Abraham won Quebec for the British, and in the siege Fraser's Highlanders played a crucial role. The siege operations placed several demands on Wolfe's army and on the Highlanders in particular. Firstly, the geography of the Quebec area assured the French commander, the Marquis de Montcalm, of a strong, almost unassailable defensive position. From the Montmorency Falls that emptied into the St. Lawrence River north-east of the city to the Heights of Abraham, which protected Quebec's southern approaches, Montcalm enjoyed a natural barrier that would test the mettle of the ablest tactician and the hardiest and most intrepid troops of the British army in North America. Secondly, Montcalm greatly outnumbered Wolfe and held the interior lines of communication and a vantage point that allowed him to monitor British troop movements — advantages that he believed would forestall any major attack on the city. Thirdly, Montcalm operated in friendly territory; some of the French-Canadian provincials in the area provided him with both supplies and information. These problems, among others, faced Wolfe as he sat before the capital of New France, and it was to the Scottish Highlanders that he turned to negate the strength of Montcalm's defenses.[23]

During the siege of Quebec Fraser's Highlanders' most important task was to overcome the natural defenses that guarded the city. Wolfe's ascent of the Heights of Abraham is one of the most renowned exploits in the annals of military history, British or otherwise, and the Highlanders deserve the credit for the execution of the daring strategem. Rising steeply to a height of some 250 feet above the St. Lawrence, the tree-clad cliffs were considered inaccessible by French and British officers alike. Montcalm himself wrote to a fellow officer: 'We need not suppose that the enemy have wings . . . .'[24] But Wolfe had the Highlanders, and their ability to traverse seemingly impassable terrain gave the British an edge that allowed them to take Montcalm by surprise.

By early September the traditional campaigning season was nearing its end and Wolfe was no closer to capturing Quebec than he had been in the preceding months; therefore, he decided to gamble on a daring attack on the Heights of Abraham. He had located a suitable landing place at the foot of the heights, known locally as the *Anse du Foulon* (later Wolfe's Cove), about one and a half miles from Quebec, where the cliffs could be scaled by a narrow, winding footpath.[25] Montcalm had discussed with his officers the possibility of an ascent of the heights. The French commander believed ' . . . that a hundred men posted there would stop their whole army'.[26] The nature of the terrain indeed made any sort of attack unlikely, but time was running out for Wolfe and he had no other hope of taking the city. Accordingly, he asked for two dozen volunteers to lead the assault, to be followed closely by about 125 of his best soldiers.[27] The advance party was led by Captain Donald MacDonald of Fraser's Highlanders. It is unfortunate that only eight of the twenty-four volunteers can be identified by surname; however, all eight were unmistakably Gaelic.[28]

Wolfe's bold plan was put into action on the night of 12 and 13 September. With some 3,600 men crowded into vessels on the St. Lawrence and 1,200 more waiting on the south bank of the river, Wolfe faced the prospect of encountering double that number of French troops if his ascent of the heights succeeded. The guard that Montcalm had posted on the precipice, however, consisted of only 100 men. As the flat-bottomed boats carrying the advance party of Highlanders and light infantry slipped silently toward the *Anse du Foulon*, they were spotted by the French sentries along the banks. The identity of the small flotilla was kept secret by an alert Highlander who made a quick-witted response in French to the sentries' queries. The volunteers reached their destination and scrambled ashore onto a narrow beach at the foot of the cliffs.[29] Wolfe was there and reportedly said to Captain MacDonald: 'There seems scarcely a possibility of getting up, but you must do your endeavours'.[30] In the next few suspenseful minutes MacDonald and his Highlanders did not disappoint the general.

The swift scaling of the heights took the small French guard by surprise. The ' . . . Highlanders climbed up [the] Steep, Woody, precipice, with unparalleled courage and activity, . . . '[31] and were protected from the fire of the French troops by the darkness. Wolfe had observed the enemy detachment at the top of the heights for several days and correctly reasoned that it could be dispersed rapidly if caught unaware. The guard scattered as the Highlanders reached the top, and the

British foothold was extended gradually throughout the morning of 13 September.[32] The Highlanders had again used their skills at moving over rugged ground to set the stage for a major contest. A historian of the present century wrote that ' ... the battle of Falkirk with its race for the top of the moor ... provided a [good] example of the tactics to be followed ... in the New World ... '[33]

Since his callous remark in 1751 referring to the Highlanders' expendability, Wolfe's attitude toward the clansmen had mellowed. More than a year before the siege of Quebec he wrote: 'The Highlanders are very usefull servicable soldiers, and commanded by the most manly corps of officers I ever saw'.[34] Service in Scotland in the 1740s and early 1750s had familiarized Wolfe with the Highlanders' primitive way of life in the rugged mountains, and he had witnessed the ease with which they moved about in all seasons under extremely adverse conditions. Conversely, no other British general ever gained such a measure of the Highlanders' respect. His gallantry and heroism held the Scots spellbound, and it is little wonder that a French-Canadian historian described Wolfe's temperament as ' ... Celtic rather than Saxon'.[35] The establishment of a strong rapport with the Highlanders assured Wolfe of their unshakeable loyalty. Standing atop the Heights of Abraham on the day of his death in September 1759, Wolfe addressed his men before the battle of Quebec:

> This day puts it into your power to terminate the fatigues of a Siege which has so long employed your courage and patience. Possessed with a full confidence of the certain success which British valour must gain over such enemies, I have led you up ... these steep and dangerous rocks; only solicitous to shew you the foe within your reach. The impossibility of a retreat makes no difference in the situation of men resolved to conquer or die: and, believe me, my friends if your conquest could be bought with the blood of your general, he would most cheerfully resign a life which he has long devoted to his country.[36]

The battle of the Plains of Abraham was the only occasion in the entire war when the Highlanders were able to execute the Highland charge on a grand scale, and they did so under different circumstances. While Fraser's Highlanders, the largest regiment in Wolfe's army at 662 men, did not enjoy the benefits of the rugged, hilly terrain that had enabled their predecessors to defeat stronger regular armies, they were supported by a much heavier weight of firepower than they normally were accustomed to. The field of battle was ideal for a combination of sustained musket fire (as opposed to the single volley of the traditional Highland charge) and the broadsword assault. The mile-wide level plain was interspersed only by fields of grain and occasional stands of scrub and bushes and was bordered on the south by the St. Lawrence, on the north by the St. Charles, and on the east by the city of Quebec. If the French lines were broken by a heavy fire and a determined attack, Montcalm's troops would have almost no chance of escape. The key to a British victory was to move quickly before the enemy could establish a defensive position with their superior numbers and thus lessen the impact of the attack.[37]

The Seventy-eighth Highlanders constituted part of the left wing of Wolfe's front line, which was commanded by General James Murray, under whose leadership the Scots played a crucial role in the British victory at Quebec.

Montcalm's soldiers were unnerved by the shrill tones of the great Highland bagpipe and the sight of the clansmen arrayed for battle in their multi-colored garb, broadswords gleaming in the morning light. The French commander must have known that he had no time to form a defensive position before the British would be upon him, and so he decided to attack. Waves of French troops rushed ahead, firing wildly at the motionless British line. All across the front Wolfe's 3,500 men held their fire as ordered until the enemy was forty yards away. Then the entire British line volleyed with deadly accuracy. The attackers reeled for an instant, continued their advance, and promptly ran into a second and more terrible hailstorm of musketry. Murray then ordered the Highlanders to charge through the smoke and bring the battle to close-quarter combat.[38]

The Highlanders' attack drove the French from the field and crowned the most important British victory of the war. A contemporary witness described the fury of the Highland charge:

> Brigadier General Murray pressed on ... briskly upon the Enemy's center; who not being able any longer to withstand the impetuous fierceness of our small handful of men ... gave way: Upon which Colonel Fraser with his Highlanders rushed in amongst the thickest of their Column with their broad Swords, with such irresistible fury, that they were driven with a prodigious Slaughter into the town .... [39]

The impact of the charge was enhanced further by the traditional musket volley fired while advancing. In previous Highland assaults the use of firearms had been of secondary importance. At Quebec, however, the accurate and sustained volleys of the British front line (including the Highlanders' traditional discharge) broke Montcalm's formation and actually allowed the Highlanders to employ their broadswords against an enemy who was not merely disordered, but in full flight from the battlefield. The Highlanders, therefore, were relieved of the costly task of first breaking the enemy's front ranks with the sword. In effect, then, Wolfe realized an effective melding of the Highland and English ways of war, and that dynamic combination of impetuosity and discipline permitted him to go to his death with full knowledge of the success of his endeavors.[40]

The battle of the Plains of Abraham in numerical terms was a minor encounter when measured by the standards of eighteenth-century warfare; in the light of its consequences, however, it was one of history's most important military encounters, and the Scottish Highlanders more than any other troops in Wolfe's army were responsible for the British victory. Not only did they constitute the largest and most active regiment at Quebec, but the most formidable as well. An observer of the battle echoed the common sentiment:

> The regiments of Lascelles, Kennedy's and Wolfe's grenadiers, did wonders; yet the highlanders, if anything, exceeded them. When these took to their broadswords, my God! what a havock they made! They drove everything before them, and walls could not resist their fury. — Those breechless fellows are an honour to their country. —I cannot do them justice in my description of them; but I have reason to believe that their bravery will meet with approbation, the only reward (except half victuals and cloaths) that a highlander demands being possessed naturally with a kind of martial honour.[41]

The spirit with which the Gaels fought for their former adversaries at Quebec perhaps was best exemplified by the heroics of one Ewan Cameron of Fraser's Highlanders. Cameron reportedly charged across the field, broadsword in hand, where he was hit by a shot that tore off his right arm. Oblivious of his wound, he picked up a bayonet and carried on toward the enemy. He then killed nine French soldiers, including two officers, before taking several musket balls to the chest and throat.[42] Numerous other gallant exploits, both English and Scottish, doubtless went unrecorded that day, and collectively they elicited the praise of Montcalm himself, who reportedly declared just before his death that it was ' ... a great consolation ... to be vanquished by so brave an enemy. If I could survive, I would engage to beat three times the number of such forces as I commanded with a third of British troops'.[43]

In retrospect, Wolfe's victory on the Plains of Abraham virtually sealed the outcome of the French and Indian War; however, its brilliance was overshadowed at the time by the urgency of occupying and holding the city of Quebec. After the death of Wolfe command of the British garrison at Quebec fell on the able shoulders of General James Murray, who was described by an eminent American historian as ' ... a gallant soldier, ... eager for distinction, and more daring than prudent'.[44] Murray's talents were severely tested during the winter of 1759 and 1760, but the real threat to his position at Quebec came the following spring. Toward the end of April he learned of the presence of a large French force (10,000 to 15,000 men) in the nearby village of St. Foy. Murray had three options: to defend the city of Quebec itself; to establish a defensive position on the Plains of Abraham where Wolfe had defeated Montcalm; or to attack the French before they attacked him. In the light of his Scottish (and perhaps Celtic) temperament it is not surprising that Murray chose to attack.[45] One of his subordinates questioned his judgment: ' ... it must appear to every man possessed with the least Share of Reason, to be a Rash enterprize, without any seeming prospect of anything but the total destruction of the whole Army, with the immediate loss of the City'.[46] But Murray would not be deterred.

Murray held Quebec against the enemy's final attempt to recapture the city, and his audacious attack on the would-be besiegers was responsible for his success. If the defense of Quebec had been entrusted to a less impetuous commander than Murray, the French might well have retaken the city and thereby lengthened the war. Murray forced the issue, however, by refusing to stand on the defensive even though he possessed over twenty pieces of artillery and plenty of ammunition. He marched the army out of the city on the morning of 28 April, crossing the same ground on which he had fought beside Wolfe the previous autumn. When Murray had arrayed his army in battle formation, he noticed that the French left wing near Dumont's Mill was having difficulty deploying. Surrounding the mill were several houses along the St. Foy road. Murray determined to strike there before the enemy could occupy the houses and establish a defensive post. Accordingly, he sent forward the right wing of his army, which contained a large number of Highlanders, and drove the French into the forest behind Dumont's Mill. Murray mistook the enemy withdrawal for a general retreat on that side of the field and pressed home the attack. When the Highlanders and English had passed Dumont's Mill, however, they encountered a strongly reinforced French contingent that staged a counterattack. The heaviest fighting raged near the cluster of houses around the mill. Engaged in a fierce hand-to-hand combat, the Highlanders and the French grenadiers struggled for possession of the mill.[47] The Chevalier de Johnstone, one of the few Jacobites in the service of France, described the furious action: ' . . . each of them . . . [took] it and . . . [lost] it by turns. Worthy antagonists! — the Grenadiers, with their bayonets in hand, forced the Highlanders to get out . . . and the Highlanders . . . immediately obliged the Grenadiers to evacuate it . . . with their daggers.' The ' . . . contest would have continued whilst there remained a Highlander and a Grenadier, if both generals had not made them retire . . . .'[48] Finally, however, the weight of French numbers overwhelmed Murray's Highlanders on the right and forced them to withdraw to their starting point.

Though Murray's first attack failed to drive away the French army, it did impress upon the enemy the determination of the smaller British force. The battle continued for two more hours as wave after wave of Fraser's Highlanders attempted to crack the right wing of the French army. Eventually the French were able to advance on Murray's left, despite a heavy fire from the British artillery, and threatened to cut it off from Quebec. Murray ordered a general retreat that was carried out in good order. Highland losses were heavy. Of the 575 men of Fraser's Highlanders who were engaged, over 200 were killed or wounded, including twenty-nine of thirty-nine officers. But their tenacity had forestalled the enemy's attempt to lay siege to the city; the French commander shortly marched his army away, leaving Quebec permanently in British hands.[49]

The battle of St. Foy, from a tactical standpoint, was a British defeat, and Murray's decision to attack the French rather than defend the city has been much criticized. An Englishman who served under him wrote:

> . . . we . . . find [that] no honour could have arisen to General Murray, for such mad, enthusiastic zeal . . . . Indeed it must be confessed that it is the duty of a General commanding an army . . . to exert every faculty for the service of his country; but it may be as readily believed that no State ever yet gave his General Order to throw away the lives of his men without some seeming probability of success . . . . it was therefore . . . Murray's duty to use all possible means to preserve it [i.e. Quebec] and to defend it to the last extremity, and not lavishly to throw away such brave men, on a vain delusion, of gaining to himself great honour.[50]

If Murray's critics had paused to reflect on the nature of Gaelic warfare (if they were even aware of it), they would have better understood what moved the Scot to action. Though he was an officer in the British army, Murray undoubtedly had been immersed deeply in the tactical doctrine of his Highland neighbors. There is no question that he attacked at St. Foy because it was the honorable thing to do; however, it must not be forgotten that he knew the capabilities of his army. Earlier he had seen it destroy a superior French force with broadsword, bayonet, and musket. There was no reason for him to doubt that it could repeat that performance at St. Foy. He was mistaken, but his bold, though costly, offensive clearly was preferable to awaiting the inevitable siege that would have drained both sustenance and spirit from his men. Several months after St. Foy Murray wrote in defense of his actions:

> Did it be asked any soldier if, in my situation, it was right to fight. He will answer without hesitation, 'To be sure' .... Was not the critical moment of attack made use of? Did it succeed? Was not the victory gain'd, had the right wing been as active and as vigorous ... as the left was [on] the 13th of September, 1759? ... Where was the General in this battle [St. Foy]? — Betwixt his own line and that of the enemy — everywhere, where the enemy made a push, animating his own men by his presence.[51]

During the French and Indian War the Scottish Highlanders, in Wolfe's words, ' ... behaved with distinction .... '[52] The active role that they played in the North American campaigns is pointed up by their staggering losses in manpower: at Fort Duquesne Montgomery's Highlanders lost 231 of 400 men engaged, including fourteen officers, a casualty rate of fifty-eight percent; at Ticonderoga casualties within the Black Watch totaled 650 out of about 1,300 combatants, including forty-four officers, a fifty percent loss; at Louisbourg Fraser's Highlanders suffered seventy-four killed and wounded, including seven officers, a casualty rate of six percent; the Battle of the Plains of Abraham cost them 167 out of 662 men employed, including twenty-two officers, a twenty-five percent loss; and at St. Foy they lost 213 troops, including twenty-nine officers, out of 575 engaged, a casualty rate of thirty-seven percent. When the overall Highland casualty rate is calculated for all five battles, it averages nearly thirty-two percent; however, if Louisbourg is omitted, that figure jumps to a staggering forty-three percent. Furthermore, the three Highland regiments lost a total of 116 officers in these five major engagements. The English and American casualty rate for the same five battles was slightly less than nine percent.[53] It is little wonder that the Highlanders' sacrifice has drawn the attention of historians. One wrote: ' ... were records to be searched, the help Scotland gave in actual man-power contributed not a little to that glorious victory for British arms'.[54] Another acknowledged that the ' ... clans had certainly a full share in making that mighty Empire whose foundations may be said to be based on the lives of British soldiers and sailors'.[55]

The Highlanders paid a high price in their service to Britain because they attacked rather than defended in the five major battles under study. Like their forebears the clansmen fought best when they fought offensively. Wolfe and other British commanders must be credited not only for allowing the Highlanders to practice their primitive mode of warfare, but also for providing them with just enough discipline and stability to temper their customary blind rage. A Highland officer, writing more than fifty years after the war, understood the difficulties of integrating the clan regiments into a regular army.

> This impetuosity of Highland soldiers, and the difficulty of controlling them, in the most important part of a soldier's duty, has been frequently noticed and reprobated.

To forget necessary discretion, and break loose from command, is certainly an unmilitary characteristic; but, as it proceeds from very honourable principle, it deserves serious consideration, how far any attempt to allay this ardour may be prudent, or advantageous to the service.[56]

Wolfe's vision of the clansmen dying for the advancement of Empire was perhaps not prompted by a callous disregard for human life, but simply by his understanding of the offensive nature of Gaelic warfare. After all, the Highlander's military traditions demanded that they fight in no less honorable manner than their forebears.

NOTES

1. Rev. Dr. Alexander Carlyle, *Autobiography of the Rev. Dr. Alexander Carlyle, Minister of Inveresk, containing Memorials of the Men and Events of his time*, 2 vols. (Edinburgh: William Blackwood and Sons, 1860), I: 190.

2. Suggestions by Duncan Forbes of Culloden, Lord President of the Court of Sessions, after the Rebellion of 1745, c. 1746–1747, Edinburgh, Edinburgh University Library, Laing MSS, II. 123.

3. W. A. S. Hewins, ed., *The Whitefoord Papers Being the Correspondence and other Manuscripts of Colonel Charles Whitefoord and Caleb Whitefoord from 1739 to 1810* (Oxford: The Clarendon Press, 1898), p. 79.

4. Alexander MacDonald, 'A Certain Song,' in *Highland Songs of the Forty-Five*, ed. John Lorne Campbell (Edinburgh: John Grant, 1933; reprint ed., Edinburgh: The Scottish Gaelic Texts Society, 1984), p. 87.

5. J. MacBeth Forbes, *Jacobite Gleanings from State Manuscripts, Short Sketches of the Jacobites, The Transportations in 1745* (Edinburgh: Oliphant, Anderson and Ferrier, 1903), p. 45.

6. James Browne, *The History of Scotland, Its Highlands, Regiments, and Clans*, 8 vols. (Edinburgh: Francis Nicolls and Company, 1909), VII: 124–52.

7. Wolfe to Captain Rickson, 9 June 1751, quoted in Robert Wright, *The Life of Major-General James Wolfe* (London: Chapman and Hall, 1864), pp. 168–69.

8. Colonel David Stewart, *Sketches of the Character, Manners, and Present State of the Highlanders of Scotland; with details of the Military Service of the Highland Regiments*, 2 vols. (Edinburgh: Archibald Constable and Company, 1822; reprint ed., Edinburgh: John Donald Publishers, 1977), II: 14–23; Browne, *History of Scotland*, VII: 153–54; Wright, *Life of Wolfe*, p. 589n.

9. Wright, *Life of Wolfe*, p. 368n.

10. A. Doughty and G. W. Parmelee, eds., *The Siege of Quebec and the Battle of the Plains of Abraham*, 6 vols. (Quebec: Dussault and Proulx, 1901), III: 52; Wright, *Life of Wolfe*, pp. 442n, 590n; Stewart, *Sketches of the Highlanders*, I: 296n.

11. Quoted in Wright, *Life of Wolfe*, pp. 589n–590n.

12. For a thorough discussion of the near-disaster at Fort Duquesne in 1758, see Francis Parkman, *Wolfe and Montcalm*, 2 vols. (London: J. M. Dent and Company, 1908), II: 96–101; A. G. Bradley, *The Fight with France for North America* (Westminster: Archibald Constable and Company, 1900, pp. 275–78; E. P. Hamilton, *The French and Indian Wars, the Story of the Battles and Forts in the Wilderness* (New York: Doubleday and Company, 1962), p. 257; Louis Antoine de Bougainville, *Adventure in the Wilderness, The American*

Journals of Louis Antoine de Bougainville, 1756-1760, ed. E. P. Hamilton (Norman: University of Oklahoma Press, 1964), pp. 294–95; F. W. Lucas, *Appendiculae Historicae; or Shreds of History Hung on a Horn* (London: Printed for the Author, 1891), p. 75; Stewart, *Sketches of the Highlanders*, I: 312–13.

13. Parkman, *Wolfe and Montcalm*, II: 64.

14. Doughty and Parmelee, eds., *Siege of Quebec*, I: 234; The Abbé H. R. Casgrain, *Wolfe and Montcalm* (Toronto: Morang and Company, 1910), pp. 54–55; Parkman, *Wolfe and Montcalm*, II: 64; Browne, *History of Scotland*, VII: 156; Captain John Knox, *An Historical Journal of the Campaigns in North America for the Years 1757, 1758, 1759, and 1760*, ed. Arthur G. Doughty, 3 vols. (Toronto: The Champlain Society, 1914–1916, I: 191–92.

15. Casgrain, *Wolfe and Montcalm*, pp. 56–58; Parkman, *Wolfe and Montcalm*, II: 67–79; Browne, *History of Scotland*, VII: 156–58; Sir Thomas Dick Lauder, *Legendary Tales of the Highlands*, 3 vols. (London: Henry Colburn, 1841), III: 311–22.

16. Doughty and Parmelee, eds., *Siege of Quebec*, I: 237.

17. Parkman, *Wolfe and Montcalm*, II: 69; Casgrain, *Wolfe and Montcalm*, pp. 57–58; Howard H. Peckham, *The Colonial Wars 1689-1762* (Chicago: The University of Chicago Press, 1964), p. 168; Browne, *History of Scotland*, VII: 159; Stewart, *Sketches of the Highlanders*, I: 302, 305.

18. Letter from Lieutenant William Grant, no date, quoted in Browne, *History of Scotland*, VII: 160.

19. Wright, *Life of Wolfe*, pp. 430–31; Parkman, *Wolfe and Montcalm*, II: 38; Browne, *History of Scotland*, VII: 297; Stewart, *Sketches of the Highlanders*, I: 309–10; Beckles Willson, *The Life and Letters of James Wolfe* (London: William Heinemann, 1909), pp. 372–73; W. T. Waugh, *James Wolfe, Man and Soldier* (Montreal: Carrier and Company, 1928), pp. 159–61.

20. Thomas Pichon, *Lettres et Mémoires pour servir à l' Historie Naturelle, Civile et Politique du Cap Breton dupuis son établissement jusqu' à la reprise de cette Isle par les Anglois en 1758* (La Haye: P. Gosse, 1760), p. 284; Parkman, *Wolfe and Montcalm*, II: 38–39; Wright, *Life of Wolfe*, pp. 430, 432; Doughty and Parmelee, eds., *Siege of Quebec*, I: 105, 107–08; Stewart, *Sketches of the Highlanders*, I: 309–10; Willson, *Life and Letters of Wolfe*, p. 373; Knox, *An Historical Journal*, I; 243.

21. J. T. Findlay wrote that the siege of Louisbourg ' ... was conducted on lines approximating ... those observed on the fields of Flanders ... .' J. T. Findlay, *Wolfe in Scotland in the '45 and from 1749 to 1753* (London: Longmans, Green and Company, 1928), p. 303.

22. Wright, *Life of Wolfe*, pp. 442–43; Stewart, *Sketches of the Highlanders*, I: 310–11; Browne, *History of Scotland*, VII: 297–98; General Jeffery Amherst, *The Journal of Jeffery Amherst Recording the Military Career of General Amherst in America from 1758 to 1763*, ed. J. Clarence Webster (Toronto: The Ryerson Press, 1931), pp. 63–68.

23. Browne, *History of Scotland*, VII: 300–01; Willson, *Life and Letters of Wolfe*, pp. 437–38; A. G. Bradley, *Wolfe* (London: MacMillan and Company, 1917), pp. 144–47; Casgrain, *Wolfe and Montcalm*, p. 96; Extract from a Letter from an Officer in Major General Wolfe's Army, 10 August 1759, in *Military Affairs in North America 1748-1765, Selected Documents from the Cumberland Papers in Windsor Castle*, ed. Stanley Pargellis (London: D. Appleton-Century Company, 1936), pp. 433–35; Stewart, *Sketches of the Highlanders*, I: 326–27; The Chevalier de Johnstone, *The Campaign of 1760 in Canada, a Narrative Attributed to Chevalier Johnstone* (Quebec: Literary and Historical Society of Quebec, 1887), p. 4; The Chevalier de Johnstone, *A Dialogue in Hades. A Parallel of*

Military Errors, of which the French and English Armies were guilty, during the Campaigns of 1759, in Canada (Quebec: Literary and Historical Society of Quebec, 1866), pp. 8–10; Wright, *Life of Wolfe*, p. 568.

24. Montcalm to Vaudreuil, 27 July 1759, quoted in Parkman, *Wolfe and Montcalm*, II: 176.

25. Parkman, *Wolfe and Montcalm*, II: 174–76; Browne, *History of Scotland*, VII: 303; Colonel Malcolm Fraser, *Extract from a Manuscript Journal Relating to the Siege of Quebec in 1759. Kept by Malcolm Fraser, the Lieutenant of the 78th (Fraser's Highlanders,) and serving in that Campaign* (Quebec: Literary and Historical Society of Quebec, 1868), p. 20; 'Journal of Major Moncrief,' in *Siege of Quebec*, eds. Doughty and Parmelee, V: 48–49.

26. Montcalm to Vaudreuil, 27 July 1759, quoted in Parkman, *Wolfe and Montcalm*, II: 176.

27. Wright, *Life of Wolfe*, pp. 576–77; 'Extracts from Journal of the Particular Transactions during the Siege of Quebec,' in *Siege of Quebec*, eds. Doughty and Parmelee, V: 187; Parkman, *Wolfe and Montcalm*, II: 174–75.

28. The eight known surnames of the volunteers are as follows: Fitzgerald, Robertson, Stewart, McAllester, MacKenzie, McPherson, Cameron, and Bell. Knox, *An Historical Journal*, II: 95n; 'Particular Transactions,' in *Siege of Quebec*, eds. Doughty and Parmelee, V: 187.

29. Stewart, *Sketches of the Highlanders*, I: 329; François Gaston, duc de Lévis, *Journal des Campagnes du Chevalier de Lévis en Canada de 1756 à 1760* (Montreal: C. O. Beauchemin et Fils, 1889), pp. 205–07; Casgrain, *Wolfe and Montcalm*, pp. 179–81; Wolfe to Brigadier Townsend, 12 September 1759, quoted in Willson, *Life and Letters of Wolfe*, p. 486; Parkman, *Wolfe and Montcalm*, II: 182–83; Wright, *Life of Wolfe*, pp. 576–77; John Johnson, 'Memoirs of the Siege of Quebec and Total Reduction of Canada in 1759 and 1760,' in *Siege of Quebec*, eds. Doughty and Parmelee, V: 101–02; Knox, *An Historical Journal*, II: 94–95.

30. Quoted in Wright, *Life of Wolfe*, p. 578.

31. Johnson, 'Memoirs,' in *Siege of Quebec*, eds. Doughty and Parmelee, V: 102.

32. Wright, *Life of Wolfe*, pp. 576–78; Parkman, *Wolfe and Montcalm*, II: 177–78; Fraser, *Journal*, p. 20; Browne, *History of Scotland*, VII: 304; Lévis, *Journal des Campagnes*, pp. 206–07; An Account of the Action which happened near Quebec, 13 September 1759, in *Military Affairs in North America*, ed. Pargellis, pp. 437–39.

33. Findlay, *Wolfe in Scotland*, p. 303.

34. Wolfe to Lord George Sackville, 12 May 1758, in *Siege of Quebec*, eds. Doughty and Parmelee, VI: 74.

35. Casgrain, *Wolfe and Montcalm*, p. 71.

36. General Wolfe to his Army, 13 September 1759, quoted in Knox, *An Historical Journal*, III: 336.

37. Wright, *Life of Wolfe*, p. 582; Parkman, *Wolfe and Montcalm*, II: 184, 190n; Fraser, *Journal*, p. 20.

38. Browne, *History of Scotland*, VII: 305–06; Fraser, *Journal*, p. 21; Stewart, *Sketches of the Highlanders*, I: 330; Knox, *An Historical Journal*, II: 100–01; 'Journal of Major Moncrief,' in *Siege of Quebec*, eds. Doughty and Parmelee, V: 53; Parkman, *Wolfe and Montcalm*, II: 186–88; Wright, *Life of Wolfe*, pp. 580–83; Casgrain, *Wolfe and Montcalm*, pp. 191–92.

39. Johnson, 'Memoirs,' in *Siege of Quebec*, eds. Doughty and Parmelee, V: 105.

40. Letter to Mr. J. W., 20 September 1759, in *Siege of Quebec*, eds. Doughty and

Parmelee, V: 23; Parkman, *Wolfe and Montcalm*, II: 188–89; Casgrain, *Wolfe and Montcalm*, p. 202; Wright, *Life of Wolfe*, pp. 583–85; 'Particular Transactions,' in *Siege of Quebec*, eds. Doughty and Parmelee, V: 189; Letter to Captain Calcraft, 20 September 1759, in *Siege of Quebec*, eds. Doughty and Parmelee, VII: 144; Knox, *An Historical Journal*, II: 101–02; *A Journal of the Expedition up the River St. Lawrence; Containing a true and particular account of the transactions of the fleet and army, from the time of their embarkation at Louisbourg 'til after the surrender of Quebec* (Quebec: Literary and Historical Society of Quebec, 1866), pp. 11–12; Fraser, *Journal*, p. 21; Stewart, *Sketches of the Highlanders*, I: 330.

41. Letter of Captain Calcraft, 20 September 1759, in *Siege of Quebec*, eds. Doughty and Parmelee, VI: 146.

42. *Ibid.*

43. Quoted in Wright, *Life of Wolfe*, pp. 588–89.

44. Parkman, *Wolfe and Montcalm*, II: 211. Murray was the son of the fourth Lord Elibank. His ' . . . intrepidity and zeal for the service . . . ' had been recognized by Wolfe at Louisbourg. The ' . . . high opinion which Wolfe entertained of Murray's courage and ability is evident from the fact that he singled him out for the most hazardous experiments of the campaign'. Wright, *Life of Wolfe*, p. 561.

45. Lévis, *Journal des Campagnes*, pp. 259–61; General James Murray, *Journal of the Siege of Quebec, 1759-60* (Quebec: Literary and Historical Society of Quebec, 1871), pp. 30–31; Parkman, *Wolfe and Montcalm*, II: 219–20; Casgrain, *Wolfe and Montcalm*, pp. 253–54; Fraser, *Journal*, pp. 30–31; Johnstone, *Campaign of 1760*, p. 10; Knox, *An Historical Journal*, II: 390–91.

46. Johnson, 'Memoirs,' in *Siege of Quebec*, eds. Doughty and Parmelee, V: 120.

47. Murray, *Journal*, pp. 31–32; Fraser, *Journal*, pp. 31–33; Johnstone, *Campaign of 1760*, pp. 10–11; Lévis, *Journal des Campagnes*, pp. 263–67; Casgrain, *Wolfe and Montcalm*, pp. 256–61; Parkman, *Wolfe and Montcalm*, II: 220–22; Stewart, *Sketches of the Highlanders*, I: 334–35.

48. Johnstone, *Campaign of 1760*, p. 11.

49. Murray, *Journal*, pp. 32–33; Lévis, *Journal des Campagnes*, pp. 263–67; Stewart, *Sketches of the Highlanders*, I: 335; Knox, *An Historical Journal*, II: 393–95; Johnstone, *Campaign of 1760*, pp. 11–13; Fraser, *Journal*, pp. 31–32; Browne, *History of Scotland*, VII: 310–11; Johnson, 'Memoirs,' in *Siege of Quebec*, eds. Doughty and Parmelee, V: 120–21; Casgrain, *Wolfe and Montcalm*, pp. 259–64; Parkman, *Wolfe and Montcalm*, II: 220–23.

50. Johnson, 'Memoirs,' in *Siege of Quebec*, eds. Doughty and Parmelee, V: 122–23.

51. General James Murray to his brother, George Murray, 19 October 1760, in Knox, *An Historical Journal*, II: 395.

52. Wolfe to Sackville, no date, in *Siege of Quebec*, eds. Doughty and Parmelee, VI: 81.

53. Stewart, *Sketches of the Highlanders*, I: 298–336; II: 14–23; Knox, *An Historical Journal*, II: 104, 389; Peckham, *The Colonial Wars*, p. 177; Browne, *History of Scotland*, VII: 289–90, 299, 307, 310–11.

54. Findlay, *Wolfe in Scotland*, p. 306.

55. Major General Alexander B. Tulloch, *The '45 From the Raising of Prince Charlie's Standard at Glenfinnan to the Battle of Culloden*, 3rd ed. (Stirling: Eneas MacKay, 1908), p. 58.

56. Stewart, *Sketches of the Highlanders*, I:302.

10

Conclusion

This book has been limited mainly to the Celts of Ireland and Scotland over a span of nearly two centuries, although Celtic warfare neither began nor ended during that period. The discussion has touched on the Anglo-Saxons and, to a lesser degree, the Americans of the North and South because many of the aspects of continuity earmarked in this book have been detected by Forrest McDonald and Grady McWhiney in similar form in eighteenth and nineteenth-century America. Their 'Celtic thesis' of American history is substantiated by (and consequently, elucidates) the findings of this study. No special effort has been made to resolve all the questions posed by the Celtic thesis or to settle the exact linkage between the European and American Celts. But this work does demonstrate that a link indeed exists.

The large-scale Gaelic and Welsh emigration from 1700 to 1776 brought the Celtic heritage, including military traditions, to the American South. The majority of these immigrants landed in Philadelphia, moved to the Pennsylvania frontier, and gradually pushed south-westward down the Appalachian valleys. The first United States census in 1790 revealed a well-defined ethnic division between the Northern and Southern states. In New England about seventy-five percent of the people were of Anglo-Saxon origin, while Celts outnumbered Anglo-Saxons in the South two to one. Moreover, the frontier regions from western Pennsylvania to Georgia were almost entirely dominated by Celts. Between 1790 and 1850 these Celtic settlers pushed farther westward and populated the interior portions of what would become in 1861 the Confederate States of America. A decade before the American Civil War the South — from Virginia to Texas — was probably three-quarters Celtic.[1]

Far from becoming totally Americanized in the interval between independence and the Civil War, inhabitants of both North and South retained many of their traditional, old-country ways and adapted them to the new environment. The Celtic South, though it lacked the formal clan system and the Gaelic and Brythonic languages, maintained two of the most significant Celtic cultural traits: a livestock economy and a love of things military. The South's rural, pastoral style of life contrasted markedly with the more urban, industrial society of the North. Whereas Southerners were emotional, wasteful, extravagant, hospitable, and leisure-oriented, Yankees were rational, thrifty, frugal, xenophobic, and work-oriented. Southerners cared little for trade and commerce, were technologically backward, and held personal honor in high regard. Conversely, Northerners avidly engaged in commercial activities, revered science and technology, and preferred to settle their personal disputes in the law courts instead of on the dueling field. Ties of extended kinship were (and remain) much stronger in the

H

South than in the North, and this legacy of the clan system perpetuated the practice of 'ancestor worship' among Southerners. Celtic Southerners not only esteemed their ancestors but their military heroes as well. Even today, the most isolated and uneducated backwoods Southerner knows something of the heroic exploits of Robert E. Lee and Thomas 'Stonewall' Jackson.[2]

The cultural dichotomy between North and South was a major cause of the Civil War. Neither section was comfortable when the other controlled the national government. The Celtic South, true to its heritage, could barely tolerate central government even when its own politicians were in power; when control passed to the Republican North in 1861, the South abruptly left the Union to form a separate nation (a task at which Celts, traditionally, have failed miserably).[3] The subsequent war revealed that Southerners had retained most of the military characteristics of their Celtic forebears. With this in mind, the following comparisons of Southern and Gaelic warfare are offered.

First, traditional Celtic warriors and Southerners fought best when they were emotionally motivated rather than rigidly disciplined. From O'Neill's Irish Wars to the American Civil War, Celtic commanders have understood the volatile natures of their men and allowed them to fight in the impetuous, undisciplined manner that suited their temperament. At Yellow Ford, O'Neill and O'Donnell defeated the English by unleashing wave after wave of frenzied Irishmen from the surrounding hills and bogs. Dundee understood Celtic aggressiveness; he knew that to exert too much control over the Highlanders at Killiecrankie would diminish their chance of victory. His ingenious pre-battle plan served to restrain the clansmen until the time was right for the Highland charge. But after the attack began, Dundee realized that it would be unwise to attempt to control the field of battle and temper the Highlanders' furious assault. Emotionalism and a lack of discipline also pervaded Confederate armies during the Civil War. One Yankee noted: 'A Confederate soldier would storm hell with a pen-knife'. A visitor to the South in 1861 found ' ... revolutionary furor in full sway .... Excited mobs ... with flushed faces, wild eyes, screaming mouths [were] hurrahing for 'Jeff Davis' and 'the Southern Confederacy' ... .' 'The Rebels ... fight like Devills ... ,' admitted a Union soldier. 'They outfight us ... in every battle. I admire the desperation [with which they] attack,' wrote another. Besides their emotionalism, the Confederates displayed an aversion to discipline. Southern soldiers ' ... were not used to control of any sort, and were not disposed to obey anybody except for good and sufficient reason'. Robert E. Lee's army in 1862 was described as ' ... an 'Armed mob' ... of undisciplined individuality ... .' Lee himself admitted that 'The great want in our army is firm discipline'.[4]

The Celts' reliance on emotionalism led to their utilization of psychological warfare. Usually at a disadvantage in manpower and material, the Celts unnerved the enemy using their martial reputation, imposing appearance, and a variety of psychological ploys. MacColla and Dundee took advantage of the Celts' ability to overawe their enemies. At Inverlochy and Killiecrankie they positioned their armies so as to demoralize the enemy before the battle began. O'Neill and O'Donnell, too, utilized similar psychological stratagems by shadowing English armies through the forests and bogs of Ulster. The Irish made sure that their presence was known, a tactic that certainly made the enemy soldier ill at ease. By far the most common element of Celtic psychological warfare was the warcry, which was supplemented by the skirl of bagpipes in Highland armies. The Irish, Highland Scots, and Confederates all were noted for the terrifying din that accompanied their charges. The well-known 'Rebel Yell' used by Southern soldiers was an intrinsic part of their attack. A Yankee soldier confessed that the high-pitched cry ' ... made the hair stand up on his head'. Another recalled ' ... that terrible scream and barbarous howling [that was] loud enough to be heard a mile off'. Still another Union soldier described a Rebel attack: ' ... they emerged from their concealment in the woods, and yelling as only the steer-drivers of Texas could yell, charged upon our division'. Colonel James Fremantle, an Englishman, observed that ' ... Southern troops, when charging ... , always yell in a manner peculiar to themselves .... The Yankee cheer is much more like ours'.[5]

Celtic logistics remained primitive throughout the period under study. The Irish armies' march to Kinsale, MacColla's trek out of the Great Glen to Inverlochy, and Prince Charles's campaign into England showed that Celtic troops traveled lightly and quickly. They were hardier than other troops of the period, and their disregard for a complicated logistical system dramatically increased their mobility. The Irishman or Highland Scot usually carried no more than his weapons, a plaid or mantle, and a little meal and whisky. He bore such deprivations manfully, being ' ... inured to fatigue, and of a strong and vigorous constitution, frequently marching six or seven leagues a day ....'[6] Southern troops also paid slight attention to the problem of logistics. They were often ' ... without shoes or proper equipment because they could see no purpose in carrying what they did not need at the moment'. Union General Winfield Scott understood the Celtic penchant for ignoring logistical services: Southerners ' ... will not take care of things, or husband [their] resources .... If it could all be done by one wild desperate dash [then they] would do it, but [they cannot] ... stand the long ... months between the acts, the waiting'. Another observer wrote that the Confederates commonly threw ' ... away their knapsacks and blankets on a long march'. The lack of logistical services and the Rebels' disregard for their equipment allowed Confederate armies to move more rapidly than their Union counterparts; however, Southern armies were defeated partly because they lacked the material resources necessary to fight a protracted war.[7]

Perhaps because of their logistical disadvantage, the Celts were masterful at using the natural environment to offset the enemy's technological superiority. O'Neill's crude but effective field fortifications and the Highlanders' use of the rugged terrain of the homeland frequently neutralized the strength of the enemy's regular forces. Southerners also used the forests, hills, and swamps of the Confederacy as staging points for attacks that often caught the Union forces by surprise. Since the South was a rural, pastoral society, her young men usually were experienced woodsmen who were adept at traversing difficult terrain and making do with the resources that nature offered. When contrasted with the lack of outdoor skill that plagued thousands of Yankee urban dwellers, Southerners' familiarity with their natural surroundings gave them a decided advantage in many battles.[8]

The Highland Scots and Irish were averse to adopting the latest military technology, preferring the broadsword and target to more modern implements of war. The relegation of firearms and artillery to places of secondary importance in their arsenals played a significant role, for better or worse, in their military fortunes. O'Neill's and O'Donnell's Irish armies made effective use of firearms at Clontibret, Yellow Ford, and the Moyry Pass. When these battles reached their critical stages, however, the Irish laid down their muskets in favor of blade weapons. Moreover, though O'Neill had access to artillery, he made almost no use of it. Alasdair MacColla and his successors employed firearms as an integral part of the Highland charge, but the troops cast them away after one volley and resorted to the claymore or broadsword and target. The Highland Scots, like their Irish kinsmen, neglected the use of artillery. At the outset of the American Civil War 'artillery was practically non-existent' in the western Confederacy. The Tennessee state armory contained only four field pieces; Mississippi possessed eight guns but not a single caisson, battery wagon, or forge.[9] The Confederate Army eventually adopted most of the military technological innovations of the day; however, it did not make effective use of them when compared to the Union forces. Later in the war both sides were armed with rifled firearms and artillery. Rifling, however, proved more beneficial to defending armies than to attacking ones. And since the Confederates attacked most of the time during the first two and a half years of the war, they negated the effectiveness of their new weapons. Union armies, secure behind elaborate defensive works, took full advantage of the increased accuracy and rate of firepower. Conversely, attacking Confederate armies found it difficult to fire as often or as effectively as the enemy; the Rebels gave up the benefits of rifling and came to depend upon the bayonet and rifle butt as their main offensive weapons. Such tactics were often successful when Southern troops reached the enemy lines in large numbers. But unlike their Celtic forebears before 1689, they were usually cut down by increased firepower before they could bring the battle to close-quarter combat. The Confederates' Celtic military heritage emphasized the headlong attack over the cautious defensive and thereby ignored the battlefield changes wrought by the new weapons. They continued the use of tactics that were more suitable to the broadsword and target than to modern rifled weapons. This misuse of (rather than aversion to) military technology proved disastrous to the Confederates.[10]

Celtic troops normally lacked tenacity, and consequently they did not follow up their initial attack. If the first charge succeeded, the victory was theirs; if they were repulsed, they often left the field thoroughly disorganized. Kinsale, Culloden, and the action on Mar's left wing at Sheriffmuir illustrated the Celts' lack of staying power when confronted by an enemy who could stand up to their first assault. This characteristic lack of tenacity resulted in part from a lack of discipline and an overabundance of emotional fervor. The Confederate soldier was described as ' ... an admirable fighting man but a poor soldier'.[11] If he was unable to defeat the enemy with his first wild charge, he became discouraged and quit the field. The impetuous nature of Confederate officers and their troops led to great disorder after the attack had begun, a Celtic trait that hindered their ability to regroup and continue fighting in an orderly manner.

The clans of Scotland and Ireland were almost constantly engaged in internecine warfare, a charge often leveled at the American South. The MacDonald–Campbell feud was the most notable feud in Scotland, but throughout the period under study numerous other tribes in Scotland and Ireland fought among themselves, making England's task of subjugation much easier. It was standard English policy to foster discord among the Celts, and the latter's inability or unwillingness to put aside their private quarrels promoted that policy. Throughout the American South similar feuds prevailed before, during, and after the Civil War and contributed to the characteristic fragmentation of Southern society. The strength of the extended family bred close kinship ties, and rural isolation bred a dependence upon force rather than on established laws. When the interests of two families conflicted, they commonly resorted to violence for a redress of grievances instead of settling the issue in a court of law. This sort of behavior resulted in the long-running feuds such as the one between the Hatfields and McCoys.[12] Southern quarrels frequently extended beyond families to emcompass entire counties or even larger geographical areas. With the coming of the Civil War, Winston County, Alabama, refused to secede from the Union, as did areas of eastern Tennessee, because the inhabitants would not subordinate local interests to those of the Confederacy.

Lastly, political fragmentation traditionally has kept the Celts from forming any sort of central government that could compare or compete with the systems of their enemies. After the demise of the Lordship of the Isles in 1493, most Celtic chieftains were unwilling to surrender their local authority to form a modern nation-state. Hugh O'Neill failed in his attempt to unify Ireland in the 1590s because most of his subordinates jealously guarded their local independence and status, based as they were on the traditions of the Brehon law and on the influence of their bards and *seanchaidh*. Chiefs, both Scottish and Irish, refused to abandon local government, even though it proved an ineffective tool for organizing and fighting prolonged military campaigns. Southern localism likewise hindered the attempt to form an efficient national government from 1861 to 1865. The traditions of local independence were rooted in the isolation of the Southern hills and backwoods, and most people south of the Mason–Dixon line had grown accustomed to self-government. It is no surprise that the constitutional doctrine of 'States Rights' came to be associated with the South. The lack of authority vested in the government of the Confederate States of America revealed the degree to which Southerners distrusted the power and intentions of central governing bodies. The weak and disorganized government that sprang from this collective attitude of mistrust was unable to compete with the Union government in prosecuting the war.[13]

Where continuity in Celtic warfare is concerned, there are, of course, exceptions to the rule. At times the Celts could be disciplined, as was evidenced by O'Neill's exertions at the Moyry Pass and by the Highlanders' restraint during the French attack at Quebec. Moreover, the basic mode of attack was not always the full-blown charge. O'Neill's and O'Donnell's success at guerrilla warfare bear witness to this. In fact, upon close consideration, the main break in continuity occurred in the 1640s, when the Highland Scots all but abandoned the guerrilla tactics that had worked well for previous Celtic armies from antiquity to the late sixteenth century. And, though Celtic troops frequently lacked staying power after the initial attack failed, they proved to be extremely tenacious on a few occasions — particularly at Auldearn, Ticonderoga, and St. Foy. If one looks closely, it would no doubt be possible to find many more instances where the continuum of Celtic warfare was broken; however, any such hiatus is of minor consequence when compared with the overwhelming evidence of continuity.

The preceding threads of continuity represent important cultural strengths and weaknesses that affected the Gaelic military system, but all are secondary to the three most crucial elements that forged the continuum of Celtic warfare: defensive strategy, the Gaelic concept of generalship, and offensive tactics. The Celts were most comfortable and most effective when defending the homeland against the Anglo-Saxon invader. O'Neill and O'Donnell sought first of all to defend Ulster and then undertook the ill-advised strategic offensive against Mountjoy at Kinsale. Both Mar and Prince Charles forced their reluctant Gaelic troops to undertake the strategic offensive in England. At no time during the period under study did the Celts succeed when they abandoned the strategic defensive. All of their victories occurred on home territory when they were commanded by men who understood their preference for defending the native soil, rather than taking the war to the enemy. In the American Civil War Southern armies fared best when they too defended their familiar hills and forests. When the war began, Confederate President Jefferson Davis announced that the South was ' ... waging this war solely for self-defense .... '[14] But Davis and most Confederate generals favored offensive over defensive war. Despite their belief in the superiority of offensive warfare, Confederate leaders perhaps did not realize that while the South might make effective use of the tactical offensive, it was not capable of taking the strategic offensive against a technologically better and numerically larger Union enemy. The disastrous defeat at Gettysburg in 1863 made clear the folly of the full-scale campaign into the heartland of the Union. Once again the Celts had attempted to take the strategic offensive and had suffered a major setback from which they could not recover.

The Celtic concept of generalship was a reflection of an honorbound, primitively heroic society. Although the Gaels were not usually the aggressors from a strategic standpoint, their culture was the most violent and militaristic in Europe. The Scottish Highlands and Ireland offered few occupations other than that of herdsman-warrior; therefore, the profession of arms came naturally to most Gaels, although, like their Southern descendants, they were not trained as regular soldiers. They preferred to operate in small, cohesive units — usually clan regiments — that were independent of one another. These close-knit clan units provided one of the most important intangible ingredients of Gaelic warfare — the relationship between warrior and general or clan chief. Each Celtic fighter took it upon himself to uphold the honor of his chief and clan. Conversely, he expected his chief, as the representative of the clan, to be worthy of his sacrifice. The principal role of the Celtic commander, then, was to lead the clan into battle and draw first blood. Similarly, Confederate commanders led their troops into battle, and of the 425 generals who saw action, 235 were either killed or wounded.[15] While generals such as Montrose, Dundee, and Prince Charles were not expected to risk their lives by charging, the true Gaels were expected to lead the front ranks into the fray. The most conspicuous example of the archetypal Celtic commander was, of course, Alasdair MacColla, whose heroics inspired so many songs, poems, and legends. Charged with the emotional electricity produced by the camaraderie between leaders and followers, the Celts won many of their battles through sheer fortitude and determination.

The most important aspect of continuity in Celtic warfare from 1595 to 1763 was the tactical offensive. Of the major battles under study the Celts attacked in all but one — Kinsale — and they would have attacked there if the confusion within the ranks had not allowed the English to take the initiative. The wild, undisciplined broadsword attack was the cornerstone of Gaelic tactical doctrine, and from 1595 to 1689 it dominated the battlefield against regular armies. Most of these victories resulted from an attack carried out under irregular rather than conventional circumstances, permitting the Gaels to escape with relatively few casualties. From 1689 to 1746, however, they slowly bled themselves to death by attacking better trained and equipped British armies under more conventional conditions. Consequently, the attack — or more precisely, the Highland charge — became more of a liability than an asset until Gaelic offensive tactics finally were overwhelmed at Culloden by the forces of modern, conventional warfare. The South also took the tactical offensive frequently in the first two and a half years of the Civil War. By the summer of 1863 the Confederates had suffered over 175,000 casualties — more men than were in arms for the Confederacy in 1861. Thirty-five percent of these losses occurred in only three battles — the Seven Days Battle (20,000), Gettysburg (23,000), and Chickamauga (17,000) — in which the South assumed the tactical offensive.[16] The carnage prompted General Daniel H. Hill to remark: 'It was not war — it was murder'.[17] And indeed it was, for repeated attempts over more than two years to overwhelm the Union with furious assaults so weakened the Confederate military system that its defeat was inevitable after 1863.

Although the French and Indian War occasioned the transfer of the traditional Gaelic military system to the shores of North America, that conflict marked the beginning of the end of an era in Gaelic warfare that had begun in the late sixteenth century. After 1783 and the war of the American Revolution, many of the Gaels who had served in the American wars had settled in the New World. They were relative latecomers when compared with most emigrants from the Celtic world.[18] The vestiges of the old military system that the Celts had brought with them from 1747 to 1783 were destined to be transformed by numerous forces at work in

America. In the colonial wars the Gaels fought for the last time (in America) where they could be recognized as Gaels by sight: with kilt, broadsword, and target. Thereafter, the uniform changed to buckskins and Confederate gray and they fought primarily with musket (or rifle) and bayonet, but their military traditions held on. Though the outward trappings and particular tactics of the Highland charge disappeared, the transplanted Celt's proclivity for the attack remained as the most significant reminder of his heritage.

NOTES

1. At present, Forrest McDonald and Grady McWhiney are engaged in a large-scale study of surnames in the antebellum Southern United States. Their findings thus far indicate that by 1850 the South was overwhelmingly Celtic; furthermore, the Celts came to dominate the culture of the region, thereby making it radically different from the predominantly Anglo-Saxon North. For a discussion of these data and the methodology used to determine them, see Forrest McDonald, 'The Ethnic Factor in Alabama History: A Neglected Dimension,' *Alabama Review*, 31 (1978): 256–65; Forrest McDonald and Ellen Shapiro McDonald, 'The Ethnic Origins of the American People, 1790,' *William and Mary Quarterly*, 37 (1980): 179–99; Grady McWhiney and Forrest McDonald, 'Celtic Names in the Antebellum Southern United States,' *Names*, 31 (June 1983): 89–102. The author is indebted to John Morgan Dederer, 'Afro-Southern and Celtic Southern Cultural Adaptation in the Old South' (unpublished paper, University of Alabama, 1985), for insight into the Celtic influence on Black culture in the antebellum South.

2. Forrest McDonald and Grady McWhiney, 'The Antebellum Southern Herdsman: A Reinterpretation,' *Journal of Southern History*, 41 (1975): 147–66; Grady McWhiney, 'The Revolution in Nineteenth-Century Alabama Agriculture,' *Alabama Review*, 31 (1978): 3–32; McDonald, 'The Ethnic Factor in Alabama History,' *Alabama Review*, 31 (1978): 256–65; Grady McWhiney, 'Saving the Best From the Past,' *Alabama Review*, 32 (1979): 243–72; McDonald and McDonald, 'Ethnic Origins of the American People, 1790,' *William and Mary Quarterly*, 37 (1980): 179–99; Forrest McDonald and Grady McWhiney, 'The Celtic South,' *History Today*, 30 (July 1980): 11–15; Forrest McDonald and Grady McWhiney, 'The South From Self-Sufficiency to Peonage: An Interpretation,' *American Historical Review*, 85 (1980): 1095–1118; Grady McWhiney, 'Jefferson Davis — The Unforgiven,' *Journal of Mississippi History*, 42 (February 1980): 113–27.

3. McDonald and McWhiney, 'The Celtic South,' *History Today*, 30 (July 1980): 11–15.

4. Quotations in this paragraph are taken from Grady McWhiney and Perry D. Jamieson, *Attack and Die: Civil War Military Tactics and the Southern Heritage* (University, Alabama: University of Alabama Press, 1982), pp. 184–85, 188.

5. *Ibid.*, pp. 190–91.

6. The Chevalier de Johnstone, *Memoirs of the Rebellion in 1745 and 1746*, 2nd ed. (London: Longman, Hurst, Rees, Orme and Brown, 1821), p. 104.

7. Quotations from McWhiney and Jamieson, *Attack and Die*, p. 189.

8. McDonald and McWhiney, 'Antebellum Southern Herdsman,' *Journal of Southern History*, 41 (1975): 147–66; McWhiney, 'Revolution in Nineteenth-Century Alabama Agriculture,' *Alabama Review*, 31 (1978): 3–32; McWhiney, 'Saving the Best From the Past,' *Alabama Review*, 32 (1979): 243–72; McDonald and McWhiney, 'The Celtic South,' *History Today*, 30 (July 1980): 11–15; McDonald and McWhiney, 'The South From

Self-Sufficiency to Peonage,' *American Historical Review*, 85 (1980): 1095–1118; Grady McWhiney, 'Continuity in Celtic Warfare,' *Continuity*, 2 (Spring 1981): 1–18.

9. Larry J. Daniel, *Cannoneers in Gray: The Field Artillery of the Army of Tennessee, 1861–1865* (Univrsity, Alabama: University of Alabama Press, 1984), pp. 4, 14.

10. McWhiney and Jamieson, *Attack and Die*, pp. 112–25.

11. *Ibid.*, p. 188.

12. McDonald and McWhiney, 'The Celtic South,' *History Today*, 30 (July 1980): 11–15.

13. *Ibid.*

14. McWhiney and Jamieson, *Attack and Die*, p. 5.

15. *Ibid.*, p. 15.

16. *Ibid.*, pp. 5, 8.

17. *Ibid.*, p. 4.

18. McDonald and McWhiney, 'The Celtic South,' *History Today*, 30 (July 1980): 11–15; McDonald and McDonald, 'Ethnic Origins of the American People, 1790,' *William and Mary Quarterly*, 37 (1980): 179–99; McWhiney and McDonald, 'Celtic Names,' *Names*, 31 (June 1983): 89–102.

Selected Bibliography

Unpublished Primary Sources

Blair Atholl. Blair Castle. Atholl MSS.
Dublin. National Library of Ireland. MS 669.
Edinburgh. Edinburgh University Library. Laing MSS.
Edinburgh. National Library of Scotland. Blaikie Collection.
Edinburgh. National Library of Scotland. MS 3060.
Edinburgh. National Library of Scotland. MS 1672.
Edinburgh. National Library of Scotland. Wodrow MSS.
Edinburgh. Scottish Record Office. Breadalbane Papers.
Edinburgh. Scottish Record Office. Campbell of Stonefield Papers.
Edinburgh. Scottish Record Office. Montrose Muniments.
Edinburgh. Scottish Record Office. Ogilvy of Inverquharity Papers.
Edinburgh. Scottish Record Office. Parliamentary MSS.
London. British Library. Additional MSS.
London. British Library. Egerton MSS.
London. Lambeth Palace Library. Carew MSS.
London. Public Record Office. State Papers. Ireland. Elizabeth.
London. Public Record Office. State Papers. Scotland.
Oxford. Bodleian Library. Carte MSS.
San Marino, California. Huntington Library. Ellesmere MSS.

Printed Primary Sources

Allardyce, Colonel James, ed. *Historical Papers Relating to the Jacobite Period 1699-1750.* 2 vols. Aberdeen: New Spalding Club, 1895.

Amherst, General Jeffery. *The Journal of Jeffery Amherst Recording the Military Career of General Amherst in America from 1758 to 1763.* Edited by J. Clarence Webster. Toronto: The Ryerson Press, 1931.

Armet, Helen, ed. *Extracts from the Records of the Burgh of Edinburgh, 1701-1718.* Edinburgh: Oliver and Boyd, 1967.

Baillie, Robert. *Letters and Journals, 1637-1662.* Edited by David Laing. 3 vols. Edinburgh: Bannatyne Club, 1841-1842.

Balcarres, Colin, Earl of. *Memoirs touching the Revolution in Scotland, 1688-1690.* Edinburgh: Bannatyne Club, 1841.

Blaikie, Walter B., ed. *Itinerary of Prince Charles Edward Stuart from his landing in Scotland July 1745 to his departure in September 1746.* Edinburgh: Scottish History Society, 1897.

———,ed. *Origins of the 'Forty-Five and other Papers Relating to that Rising.* Edinburgh: Scottish History Society, 1916.

Bougainville, Louis Antoine de. *Adventure in the Wilderness, The American Journals of Louis Antoine de Bougainville, 1756–1760.* Edited by E. P. Hamilton. Norman: University of Oklahoma Press, 1964.

Boyse, Samuel. *An impartial history of the late rebellion in 1745. From authentic memoirs; particularly, the journal of a general officer, and other original papers, yet unpublished. With the characters of the persons principally concerned. To which is prefixed, by way of introduction, a compendious account of the royal house of Stuart, from its original to the present time.* Reading: D. Henry, 1748.

Broughton, John Murray of. *Memorials of John Murray of Broughton Sometime Secretary to Prince Charles Edward, 1740–1745.* Edited by R. F. Bell. Edinburgh: Scottish History Society, 1898.

Brown, Hume P., ed. *Early Travellers in Scotland.* Edinburgh: David Douglas, 1891; reprint ed., Edinburgh: The Mercat Press, 1978.

Burt, Captain Edward. *Letters from a Gentleman in the North of Scotland to his Friend in London.* 2 vols. London: Ogle and Duncan, 1822.

Burton, J. H., ed. *Jacobite Correspondence of the Atholl Family during the Rebellion, MDCCXLV–MDCCXLVI.* Edinburgh: The Abbotsford Club, 1845.

Campbell, John Lorne, ed. *Highland Songs of the Forty-Five.* Edinburgh: John Grant, 1933; reprint ed., Edinburgh: Scottish Gaelic Texts Society, 1984.

Campbell, Robert. *The Life of the Most Illustrious Prince John, Duke of Argyll and Greenwich.* London: Charles Corbett, 1745.

Carlyle, Rev. Dr. Alexander. *Autobiography of the Rev. Dr. Alexander Carlyle, Minister of Inveresk, containing Memorials of the Men and Events of his time.* 2 vols. Edinburgh: William Blackwood and Sons, 1860.

Carte, Thomas, ed. *A Collection of Original Letters and Papers Concerning the Affairs of England from the year 1641 to 1660.* 2 vols. London: Society for the Encouragement of Learning, 1739.

Chambers, Robert, ed. *Jacobite Memoirs of the Rebellion of 1745.* Edinburgh: William and Robert Chambers, 1834.

Church of Scotland. General Assembly. *Records of the Kirk of Scotland, containing the acts and proceedings of the General Assembly, from the year 1638 downwards.* Edited by Alexander Peterkin. Edinburgh: J. Sutherland, 1838.

Clarke, Rev. J. S., ed. *The Life of James the Second, King of England, collected out of Memoirs writ by his own hand, together with the king's advice to his son and His Majesty's will.* 2 vols. London: Longman, Hurst, Rees, Orme, and Brown, 1816.

Cope, Sir John, K. B. *The Report of the Proceedings and Opinion of the Board of General Officers on their Examination into the Conduct, Behaviour, and Proceedings of Lieutenant-General Sir John Cope, Knight of the Bath.* London: W. Webb, 1749.

Creichton, Captain John. 'Memoirs of Captain John Creichton, From his own Materials, drawn up and digested by Dr. J. Swift, D.S.P.D.' In Jonathan Swift. *The Works of Jonathan Swift, Dean of St. Patrick's, Dublin, with notes and a life of the author by Sir Walter Scott.* 2nd ed. 19 vols. London: Bickers and Son, 1883.

Daniel, John. 'A True Account of Mr. John Daniel's Progress with Prince Charles Edward in the Years 1745 and 1746, written by himself.' In *Origins of the 'Forty-Five and other Papers Relating to that Rising.* Edited by Walter B. Blaikie. Edinburgh: Scottish History Society, 1916.

Defoe, Daniel. *A Tour through the Whole Island of Great Britain.* Harmondsworth: Penguin Books, 1971.

_____. *Memoirs of a Cavalier.* Edited by James T. Boulton. London: Oxford University Press, 1972.

Diodorus Siculus. *Diodorus of Sicily.* Translated by C. H. Oldfather. London: W. Heinemann, 1933.

Docwra, Sir Henry. *A Narration of the Services done by the Army ymployed to Lough Foyle under the leadinge of me SR Henry Docwra, Knight.* Edited by John O'Donovan. Dublin: The Celtic Society, 1849.

Doughty, A. and Parmelee, G. W., eds. *The Siege of Quebec and the Battle of the Plains of Abraham.* 6 vols. Quebec: Dussault and Proulx, 1901.

Duff, H. R., ed. *Culloden Papers: Comprising An Extensive and Interesting Correspondence from the Year 1625 to 1748.* London: T. Cadell and W. Davies, 1815.

Dundee, John Graham of Claverhouse, Viscount. *Letters of John Grahame of Claverhouse, Viscount Dundee, with Illustrative Documents.* Edinburgh: James Ballantyne and Company, 1826.

Elcho, David, Lord. *A Short Account of the Affairs of Scotland in the Years 1744, 1745, 1746.* Edited by Evan Charteris. Edinburgh: David Douglas, 1907; reprint ed., Edinburgh: James Thin, 1973.

'Extracts from Journal of the Particular Transactions during the Siege of Quebec.' In *The Siege of Quebec and the Battle of the Plains of Abraham.* Edited by A. Doughty and G. W. Parmelee. 6 vols. Quebec: Dussault and Proulx, 1901.

Fraser, James. *Chronicles of the Frasers, The Wardlaw Manuscript.* Edinburgh: The Scottish History Society, 1905.

Fraser, Colonel Malcolm. *Extract from a Manuscript Journal Relating to the Siege of Quebec in 1759. Kept by Malcolm Fraser, the Lieutenant of the 78th (Fraser's Highlanders,) and serving in that Campaign.* Quebec: Literary and Historical Society of Quebec, 1868.

Fraser-MacKintosh, Charles, ed. *Letters of Two Centuries Chiefly Connected with Inverness and the Highlands, from 1616 to 1815.* Inverness: A. and W. MacKenzie, 1890.

Gainsford, Thomas. *The Glory of England.* London: Printed by Edward Griffin, 1618.

Gordon, Sir John. *The Correspondence of Sir John Gordon, Bart. of Invergordon.* Edinburgh: n.p., 1835.

Gordon, Patrick. *A Short Abridgement of Britane's Distemper, from the yeare of God 1639 to 1649.* Aberdeen: The Spalding Club, 1844.

Gradyne, Colonel Ker of. 'Colonel Ker of Gradyne's Account of Culloden.' In *Jacobite Memoirs of the Rebellion of 1745.* Edited by Robert Chambers. Edinburgh: William and Robert Chambers, 1834.

Great Britain. *Accounts of the Lord High Treasurer of Scotland.* Edited by Thomas Dickson and James Balfour Paul. 10 vols. Edinburgh: General Register House, 1902.

_____. *The Acts of the Parliaments of Scotland.* Edited by Thomas Thomson and Cosmo Innes. 12 vols. Edinburgh: General Register House, 1814–1875.

_____. *The Register of the Privy Council of Scotland.* Edited by J. H. Burton *et al.* 38 vols. Edinburgh: General Register House, 1877–1970.

Guthry, Henry. *The Memoirs of Henry Guthry, Late Bishop of Dunkeld.* Glasgow: A. Stalker, 1748.

Hay, John. 'John Hay's Account.' In John Home. *The History of the Rebellion in the Year 1745.* London: T. Cadell, 1802.

Henderson, Andrew. *The History of the Rebellion, MDCCXLV and MDCCXLVI.* 5th ed. London: A. Millar, 1753.

Hennessy, William M., ed. *The Annals of Loch Cé, A Chronicle of Irish Affairs from A.D. 1014 to A.D. 1590.* 2 vols. London: Longmans, Green, and Company, 1871.

Hewins, W. A. S., ed. *The Whitefoord Papers Being the Correspondence and other Manuscripts of Colonel Charles Whitefoord and Caleb Whitefoord from 1739 to 1810.* Oxford: The Clarendon Press, 1898.

Home, John. *The History of the Rebellion in the Year 1745.* London: T. Cadell, 1802.

Jenner, Henry, ed. *Memoirs of the Lord Viscount Dundee, The Highland Clans, and the Massacre of Glenco, and etc.* London: F. E. Robinson and Company, 1903.

Johnson, John. 'Memoirs of the Siege of Quebec and Total Reduction of Canada in 1759 and 1760.' In *The Siege of Quebec and the Battle of the Plains of Abraham.* Edited by A. Doughty and G. W. Parmelee. 6 vols. Quebec: Dussault and Proulx, 1901.

Johnstone, the Chevalier de. *The Campaign of 1760 in Canada, A Narrative Attributed to Chevalier Johnstone.* Quebec: Literary and Historical Society of Quebec, 1887.

_____. *A Dialogue in Hades. A Parallel of Military Errors, of which the French and English Armies were guilty, during the Campaign of 1759, in Canada.* Quebec: Literary and Historical Society of Quebec, 1866.

_____. *Memoirs of the Rebellion in 1745 and 1746.* 2nd ed. London: Longman, Hurst, Rees, Orme and Brown, 1821.

A Journal of the Expedition up the River St. Lawrence; Containing a true and particular account of the Transactions of the fleet and army, from the time of their embarkation at Louisbourg 'til after the surrender of Quebec. Quebec: Literary and Historical Society of Quebec, 1866.

'Journal of Major Moncrief.' In *The Siege of Quebec and the Battle of the Plains of Abraham.* Edited by A. Doughty and G. W. Parmelee. 6 vols. Quebec: Dussault and Proulx, 1901.

Julius Caesar. *The Battle for Gaul.* Translated by Anne and Peter Wiseman. Boston: David R. Godine, 1980.

Keith, James. *A Fragment of a Memoir of Field-Marshal James Keith written by himself, 1714-1734.* Edinburgh: Bannatyne Club, 1843.

Kirkconnell, James Maxwell of. *Narrative of Charles Prince of Wales' Expedition to Scotland in the Year 1745.* Edinburgh: The Maitland Club, 1841.

Knox, Captain John. *An Historical Journal of the Campaigns in North America for the Years 1757, 1758, 1759, and 1760.* Edited by Arthur G. Doughty. 3 vols. Toronto: The Champlain Society, 1914-1916.

Lamont, Sir Norman, ed. *An Inventory of the Lamont Papers, 1231-1897.* Edinburgh: Scottish Record Society, 1914.

Leith, William Forbes. *Memoirs of Scottish Catholics during the XVIIth and XVIIIth Centuries.* 2 vols. London: Longmans, Green and Company, 1909.

Lévis, François Gaston, duc. de. *Journal des Campagnes du Chevalier de Lévis en Canada de 1756 à 1760.* Montreal: C. O. Beauchemin et Fils, 1889.

Lochgarry, MacDonald of. 'Lochgarry's Narrative.' In *Itinerary of Prince Charles Edward Stuart from his landing in Scotland July 1745 to his departure in September 1746.* Edited by Walter B. Blaikie. Edinburgh: Scottish History Society, 1897.

Lockhart, George. *The Lockhart Papers Containing Memoirs and Commentaries upon the Affairs of Scotland from 1702 to 1715, by George Lockhart, Esq. of Carnwath, His Secret Correspondence with the Son of King James the Second from 1718 to 1728, and his other Political Writings; Also, Journals and Memoirs of the Young Pretender's*

Expedition in 1745, by Highland Officers in his Army. 2 vols. London: William Anderson, 1817.

Lochiel, Sir Ewen Cameron of. *Memoirs of Sir Ewen Cameron of Lochiell, Chief of Clan Cameron*. Edited by John Drummond. Edinburgh: The Abbotsford Club, 1842.

Lumisden, Andrew. 'A Short Account of the Battles of Preston, Falkirk, and Culloden.' In *Origins of the 'Forty-Five and other Papers Relating to that Rising*. Edited by Walter B. Blaikie. Edinburgh: Scottish History Society, 1916.

MacBain, Alexander, and Kennedy, Rev. John, eds. *Reliquiae Celticae, Texts, Papers, and Studies in Gaelic Literature and Philology, left by the late Rev. Alexander Cameron, LL.D.* 2 vols. Inverness: The Northern Counties Publishing Company, 1892-1894.

McCrie, Thomas, ed. *The Life of Mr. Robert Blair, Minister of St. Andrews*. Edinburgh: The Wodrow Society, 1848.

MacDonald, John. *Orain Iain Luim, Songs of John MacDonald, Bard of Keppoch*. Edited by A. M. MacKenzie. Edinburgh: The Scottish Gaelic Texts Society, 1964.

MacKay, Major-General Hugh. *Memoirs of the War Carried on in Scotland and Ireland, 1689-1691*. Edinburgh: The Maitland Club, 1833.

McNeill, Charles, ed. *The Tanner Letters, Original Documents and Notices of Irish Affairs in the Sixteenth and Seventeenth Centuries*. Dublin: The Stationery Office, 1943.

MacTavish, Duncan, ed. *Minutes of the Synod of Argyll, 1639-1661*. Edinburgh: Scottish History Society, 1943.

Martin, Martin. *A Description of the Western Isles of Scotland*. 2nd ed. London: A. Bell, 1716; reprint ed., Edinburgh: The Mercat Press, 1981.

Melville, William Leslie, ed. *Leven and Melville Papers. Letters and State Papers chiefly addressed to George Earl of Melville, Secretary of State for Scotland, 1689-1691*. Edinburgh: Bannatyne Club, 1843.

Moryson, Fynes. *An Itinerary Containing his ten Yeeres travell through the Twelve Dominions of Germany, Bohmerland, Sweitzerland, Netherland, Denmarke, Poland, Italy, Turkey, France, England, Scotland and Ireland*. 4 vols. Glasgow: James MacLehose and Sons, 1908.

Murray, Lord George. 'Marches of the Highland Army.' In *Jacobite Memoirs of the Rebellion of 1745*. Edited by Robert Chambers. Edinburgh: William and Robert Chambers, 1834.

Murray, General James. *Journal of the Siege of Quebec, 1759-60*. Quebec: Literary and Historical Society of Quebec, 1871.

O'Clerigh, Lughaidh. *Beath Aodha Ruaidh Ui Dhomnaill, The Life of Aodh Ruadh O'Domhnaill*. Edited by Paul Walsh. Dublin: The Irish Texts Society, 1948.

O'Donovan, John, ed. *Annala Rioghachta Eireann, Annals of the Kingdom of Ireland, by the Four Masters, from the Earliest Period to the Year 1616*. 5 vols. Dublin: Hodges and Smith, 1848.

O'Sullivan, John. 'O'Sullivan's Narrative.' In Alister Tayler and Henrietta Tayler. *1745 and After*. London: Thomas Nelson and Sons, 1938.

Pargellis, Stanley, ed. *Military Affairs in North America 1748-1765, Selected Documents from the Cumberland Papers in Windsor Castle*. London: D. Appleton-Century Company, 1936.

Paton, Henry, ed. *Papers About the Rebellions of 1715 and 1745*. Edinburgh: Scottish History Society, 1893.

Patten, Robert. *The History of the Late Rebellion, with Original Papers and the Characters of the Principal Noblemen and Gentlemen Concern'd in it*. 2nd ed. 2 vols. London: J. Warner, 1717.

Perrott, Sir James. *A Chronicle of Ireland, 1548–1608.* Edited by Herbert Wood. Dublin: The Stationery Office, 1933.

Pichon, Thomas. *Lettres et Mémoires pour servir à Historie Naturelle, Civile et Politique du Cap Breton depuis son établissement jusqu' à la reprise de cette Isle par les Anglois en 1758.* La Haye: P. Gosse, 1760.

Polybius. *The Histories.* Translated by W. R. Paton. London: W. Heinemann, 1922.

Rae, Peter. *The History of the Rebellion, Rais'd against his Majesty George I by the Friends of the Popish Pretender.* London: A. Millar, 1746.

Ray, James. *A Compleat History of the Rebellion from its first Rise in 1745, to its total Suppression at the glorious battle of Culloden, in April, 1746.* London: James Ray, 1754.

Ross, Neil, ed. *Heroic Poetry From the Book of the Dean of Lismore.* Edinburgh: Scottish Gaelic Texts Society, 1939.

Sinclair, John, Master of. *Memoirs of the Insurrection in Scotland in 1715.* Edited by James MacKnight. Edinburgh: The Abbotsford Club, 1858.

Spalding, John. *Memorialls of the Trubles in Scotland and in England, A.D. 1624–A.D. 1645.* 2 vols. Aberdeen: The Spalding Club, 1850–1851.

Spenser, Edmund. *A View of the Present State of Ireland.* Edited by W. L. Renwick. Oxford: The Clarendon Press, 1970.

Spottiswoode Society. *The Spottiswoode Miscellany: A Collection of Original Papers and Tracts, Illustrative Chiefly of the Civil and Ecclesiastical History of Scotland.* Edited by James Maidment. 2 vols. Edinburgh: The Spottiswoode Society, 1845.

Steuart, A. F., ed. *News Letters of 1715–16.* Edinburgh: W. and R. Chambers, 1910.

Strange, Sir Robert. *Memoirs of Sir Robert Strange and Andrew Lumisden.* Edited by James Dennistoun. 2 vols. London: Longman, Brown, Green, and Longmans, 1855.

Stuart, J., ed. *Extracts from the Council Register of the Burgh of Aberdeen, 1643–1747.* Edinburgh: Scottish Burgh Record Society, 1871–1872.

———, ed. *The Miscellany of the Spalding Club.* 2 vols. Aberdeen: The Spalding Club, 1841.

Todd, J. H., ed. *The War of the Gaedhil with the Gaill, or the Invasion of Ireland by the Danes and other Norsemen.* London: Longmans, Green, Reader, and Dyer, 1867.

Turner, Sir James. *Memoirs of his own Life and Times, 1632–1670.* Edinburgh: Bannatyne Club, 1829.

Warrand, Duncan, ed. *More Culloden Papers.* 5 vols. Inverness: Robert Carruthers and Sons, 1923–1930.

Wishart, George. *The Memoirs of James, Marquis of Montrose, 1639–1650.* Edited by A. B. Murdoch and H. F. M. Simpson. London: Longmans, Green and Company, 1893.

Printed Secondary Sources

Adam, Frank. *The Clans, Septs, and Regiments of the Scottish Highlands.* Edinburgh: W. and A. K. Johnston, 1908.

Anderson, Peter. *Culloden Moor and Story of the Battle, with description of the Stone Circles and Cairns at Clava.* Stirling: Eneas MacKay, 1920.

Arnold, Ralph. *Northern Lights: The Story of Lord Derwentwater.* London: Constable, 1959.

Atholl, John, Duke of. *Chronicles of the Atholl and Tullibardine Families.* 5 vols. Edinburgh: By the Author, 1908.

Barrington, Michael. *Grahame of Claverhouse, Viscount Dundee.* London: Martin Secker, 1911.

Barrow, G. W. S. *The Anglo-Norman Era in Scottish History.* Oxford: The Clarendon Press, 1980.

_____. *The Kingdom of the Scots: Government, Church, and Society from the eleventh to the fourteenth century.* New York: St. Martin's Press, 1973; London: Macmillan, 1973.

Baynes, J. C. M. *The Jacobite Rising of 1715.* London: Cassell, 1970.

Beckett, J. C. *A Short History of Ireland.* London: Hutchinson and Company, 1958.

Bottigheimer, Karl S. *Ireland and the Irish, A Short History.* New York: Columbia University Press, 1982.

Boynton, Lindsay. *The Elizabethan Militia, 1558–1638.* London: Routledge and Kegan Paul, 1967.

Bradley, A. G. *The Fight with France for North America.* Westminster: Archibald Constable and Company, 1900.

_____. *Wolfe.* London: MacMillan and Company, 1917.

Breeze, David J. *The Northern Frontiers of Roman Britain.* London: Batsford Academic and Educational, 1982.

Brøndsted, Johannes. *The Vikings.* Translated by Kalle Skov. Copenhagen: Gyldendal, 1960; reprint ed., New York: Pelican Books, 1965.

Brotchie, T. C. F. *The Battlefields of Scotland, Their Legend and Story.* Edinburgh: T. C. and E. C. Jack, 1913.

Browne, James. *The History of Scotland, Its Highlands, Regiments, and Clans.* 8 vols. Edinburgh: Francis A. Nicolls and Company, 1909.

Buchan, John. *Montrose.* London: Thomas Nelson and Sons, 1928; reprint ed., Edinburgh: The Mercat Press, 1979.

Cadell, Sir Robert. *Sir John Cope and the Rebellion of 1745.* Edinburgh: William Blackwood and Son, 1898.

Casgrain, The Abbé H. R. *Wolfe and Montcalm.* Toronto: Morang and Co., 1910.

Chambers, Robert. *History of the Rebellion of 1745–1746.* Edinburgh: W. R. Chambers, 1869.

Childs, John. *The Army of Charles II.* London: Routledge and Kegan Paul, 1976.

Clark, G. N. *War and Society in the Seventeenth Century.* Cambridge: Cambridge University Press, 1958.

Colles, Ramsay. *The History of Ulster from the Earliest Times to the Present Day.* 4 vols. London: Gresham Publishing Company, 1919–1920.

Collingwood, R. G. *The Archaeology of Roman Britain.* London: Methuen and Company, 1930.

Corvisier, André. *Armies and Societies in Europe, 1494–1789.* Translated by Abigail T. Siddall. Bloomington: Indiana University Press, 1979.

Cruickshank, C. G. *Elizabeth's Army.* London: Oxford University Press, 1946.

Curtis, Edmund. *A History of Ireland.* London: Methuen and Company, 1936.

_____. *A History of Medieval Ireland from 1110 to 1513.* New York: The MacMillan Company, 1923; Dublin: Maunsel and Roberts, 1923.

Dalton, Charles. *George the First's Army, 1714–1727.* 2 vols. London: Eyre and Spottiswoode, 1910–1912.

Daniel, Larry J. *Cannoneers in Gray: The Field Artillery of the Army of Tennessee, 1861–1865.* University, Alabama: University of Alabama Press, 1984.

Delbrück, Hans. *History of the Art of War within the Framework of Political History.*

Translated by W. J. Renfroe, Jr. 2 vols. Westport, Connecticut: Greenwood Press, 1975.

_____. *Numbers in History.* London: Hodder and Stoughton, 1913.

Dickinson, W. C. *Scotland from the earliest times to 1603.* London: Thomas Nelson and Sons, 1961.

Duke, Winifred. *Lord George Murray and the Forty-Five.* Aberdeen: Milne and Hutchinson, 1927.

Dunlop, Robert. *Ireland from the Earliest Times to the Present Day.* London: Oxford University Press, 1922.

Dupuy, T. N. *The Military Life of Gustavus Adolphus: Father of Modern War.* New York: Franklin-Watts, 1969.

Edwards, Ruth Dudley, *An Atlas of Irish History.* 2nd ed. London: Methuen and Company, 1981.

Falls, Cyril. *Elizabeth's Irish Wars.* London: Methuen and Company, 1950; reprint ed., New York: Barnes and Noble, 1970.

Ferguson, William. *Scotland's Relations with England: A Survey to 1707.* Edinburgh: John Donald Publishers, 1977.

Fergusson, Sir James. *Argyll in the Forty-Five.* London: Faber and Faber, 1951.

Findlay, J. T. *Wolfe in Scotland in the '45 and from 1749 to 1753.* London: Longmans, Green and Company, 1928.

Forbes, J. MacBeth. *Jacobite Gleanings from State Manuscripts, Short Sketches of Jacobites, The Transportations in 1745.* Edinburgh: Oliphant, Anderson and Ferrier, 1903.

Fortescue, J. W. *A History of the British Army.* 13 vols. London: MacMillan and Company, 1910-1930.

Frame, Robin. *English Lordship in Ireland, 1318-1361.* Oxford: The Clarendon Press, 1982.

Gardiner, S. R. *History of the Great Civil War.* 4 vols. London: Longmans, Green and Company, 1893-1894.

Graham, I. C. *Scottish Emigration to North America, 1707-1783.* Ann Arbor: University Microfilms, 1955.

Grant, I. F. *The Lordship of the Isles, Wanderings in the Lost Lordship.* Edinburgh: The Moray Press, 1935; reprint ed., Edinburgh: The Mercat Press, 1982.

_____. *The Social and Economic Development of Scotland Before 1603.* Edinburgh: Oliver and Boyd, 1930.

Grant, Michael. *The Ancient Historians.* New York: Charles Scribner's Sons, 1970.

Gregory, Donald. *The History of the Western Highlands and Isles of Scotland from A.D. 1493 to A.D. 1625.* Edinburgh: John Donald Publishers, 1881.

Grieve, Symington. *The Book of Colonsay and Oronsay.* 2 vols. Edinburgh: Oliver and Boyd, 1923.

Hamilton, E. P. *The French and Indian Wars, the Story of Battles and Forts in the Wilderness.* New York: Doubleday and Company, 1962.

Hartley, Dorothy. *Lost Country Life.* New York: Pantheon Books, 1979.

Hayes-McCoy, G. A. *Irish Battles.* London: Longmans, Green and Company, 1969.

_____. *Scots Mercenary Forces in Ireland, 1565-1603.* Dublin: Burns, Oates, and Washbourne, 1937.

_____. *Ulster and other Irish Maps, c. 1600.* Dublin: Irish Manuscripts Commission, 1964.

Hechter, Michael. *Internal Colonialism: The Celtic Fringe in British National Development, 1536-1966.* Berkeley: University of California Press, 1975.

Hill, George. *An Historical Account of the MacDonnells of Antrim: Including Notices of some other Septs, Irish and Scottish.* Belfast: Archer and Sons, 1873.

Hutchison, R. E. *The Jacobite Rising of 1715.* Edinburgh: Board of Trustees of the National Galleries of Scotland, 1965.

Johnston, T. B., and Robertson, Colonel James A. *Historical Geography of the Clans of Scotland.* 3rd ed. Edinburgh: W. and A. K. Johnston, 1899.

Jones, Gwyn. *A History of the Vikings.* London: Oxford University Press, 1968.

Keltie, J. S. *History of the Scottish Highlands, Highland Clans and Highland Regiments.* 2 vols. Edinburgh: Thomas Jack, 1887.

Kermack, W. R. *The Scottish Highlands: A Short History, 300–1746.* Edinburgh: W. and A. K. Johnston, 1957.

Kilgour, W. T. *Lochaber in War and Peace.* Paisley: Alexander Gardner, 1908.

Laing, Lloyd. *Celtic Britain.* New York: Charles Scribner's Sons, 1979; London: Routledge and Kegan Paul, 1979.

Lamont, W. D. *The Early History of Islay, 500–1726.* Dundee: Burns and Harris, 1966.

Lauder, Sir Thomas Dick. *Legendary Tales of the Highlands.* 3 vols. London: Henry Colburn, 1841.

Lee, Jr., Maurice. *Government by Pen: Scotland Under James VI and I.* Chicago: University of Illinois Press, 1980.

Lloyd, Joseph. *Alasdair Mac Colla.* Baile 'Ata Cliat: Clodanna do 'Connrad na Gaeoilge, 1914.

Lucas, F. W. *Appendicular Historicae; or, Shreds of History Hung on a Horn.* London: Printed for the Author, 1891.

MacDonald, A. and A. *The Clan Donald.* 3 vols. Inverness: The Northern Counties Publishing Company, 1896.

MacDonnell, John. *The Ulster Civil War of 1641 and its Consequences, with the History of the Irish Brigade under Montrose in 1644–46.* Dublin: M. H. Gill and Sons, 1879.

Mac-Geoghegan, The Abbé. *The History of Ireland, Ancient and Modern, taken from the most authentic records, and dedicated to the Irish Brigade.* Translated by Patrick O'Kelly. Dublin: J. Duffy, 1844; New York: D. and J. Sadler, 1845.

McIan, R. R. *The Clans of the Scottish Highlands.* London: Ackermann, 1845; reprint ed., New York: Alfred A. Knopf, 1980.

MacKenzie, Agnes M. *The Kingdom of Scotland: A Short History.* Edinburgh: W. and R. Chambers, 1940.

MacKenzie, Alexander. *History of the Camerons, with the Genealogies of the Principal Families of the Name.* Inverness: A. and W. MacKenzie, 1884.

————. *History of the MacDonalds and Lords of the Isles.* Inverness: A. and W. MacKenzie, 1881.

MacKenzie, W. C. *The Highlands and Isles of Scotland: A Historical Survey.* Edinburgh: The Moray Press, 1937; reprint ed., New York: AMS Press, 1977.

MacKenzie, W. M. *The Battle of Bannockburn: A Study in Mediaeval Warfare.* Glasgow: James MacLehose and Sons, 1913.

McKerral, Andrew. *Kintyre in the Seventeenth Century.* Edinburgh: Oliver and Boyd, 1948.

MacKie, Euan W. *Scotland: An Archaeological Guide from earliest times to the 12th century A.D.* Park Ridge, N.J: Noyes Press, 1975.

Mackie, R. L. *A Short History of Scotland.* London: Oxford University Press, 1930.

McLynn, F. J. *France and the Jacobite Rising of 1745.* Edinburgh: Edinburgh University Press, 1981.

_____. *The Jacobite Army in England 1745: The Final Campaign.* Edinburgh: John Donald Publishers, 1983.

McNeill, T. E. *Anglo-Norman Ulster, the History and Archaeology of an Irish Barony.* Edinburgh: John Donald Publishers, 1980.

McWhiney, Grady, and Jamieson, Perry D. *Attack and Die: Civil War Military Tactics and the Southern Heritage.* University, Alabama: University of Alabama Press, 1982.

Martin, F. X., and Moody, T. W., eds. *The Course of Irish History.* Cork: The Mercier Press, 1967.

Morris, Mowbray. *Claverhouse.* New York: D. Appleton and Company, 1887; London: Longmans, Green and Company, 1888.

Murray, W. H. *Rob Roy MacGregor, his life and times.* Glasgow: Richard Drew Publishing, 1982.

Myatt, Frederick. *The British Infantry, 1660-1945: The Evolution of a Fighting Force.* Dorset: Blandford Press, 1983.

Napier, Mark. *Memorials and Letters Illustrative of the Life and Times of John Graham of Claverhouse, Viscount Dundee.* 3 vols. Edinburgh: Thomas G. Stevenson, 1862.

_____. *Memorials of Montrose and his Times.* 2 vols. Edinburgh: The Maitland Club, 1848-1850.

Nicholls, Kenneth. *Gaelic and Gaelicised Ireland in the Middle Ages.* Dublin: Gill and MacMillan, 1972.

Notestein, Wallace. *The Scot in History, A Study of the Interplay of Character and History.* New Haven, Connecticut: Yale University Press, 1947.

O'Callaghan, John C. *History of the Irish Brigades in the Service of France.* Glasgow: Cameron and Ferguson, 1870; reprint ed., Shannon: Irish University Press, 1968.

O'Faolain, Sean. *The Irish.* West Drayton: Penguin Books, 1947; New York: Devin-Adair Company, 1949.

Oman, Charles. *A History of the Art of War in the Sixteenth Century.* London: Methuen and Company, 1937.

Otway-Ruthven, A. J. *A History of Medieval Ireland.* London: Ernest Benn, 1968.

Parkman, Francis. *Wolfe and Montcalm.* 2 vols. London: J. M. Dent and Company, 1908.

Peckham, Howard H. *The Colonial Wars 1689-1762.* Chicago: The University of Chicago Press, 1964.

Piggott, Stuart. *The Druids.* London: Thames and Hudson, 1968.

Platt, Colin. *Medieval England: A social history and archaeology from the Conquest to 1600 A.D.* New York: Charles Scribner's Sons, 1978.

Prebble, John. *Culloden.* London: Martin Secker and Warburg, 1961; reprint ed., Harmondsworth: Penguin Books, 1967.

_____. *Glencoe: The Story of the Massacre.* London: Martin Secker and Warburg, 1966.

_____. *The Highland Clearances.* London: Martin Secker and Warburg, 1963.

Quinn, D. B. *The Elizabethans and the Irish.* Ithaca, New York: Cornell University Press, 1966.

Ranelagh, John O'Beirne. *A Short History of Ireland.* Cambridge: Cambridge University Press, 1983.

Rees, Alwyn, and Rees, Brinley. *Celtic Heritage, Ancient Tradition in Ireland and Wales.* London: Thames and Hudson, 1961.

Rogers, H. C. B. *Battles and Generals of the Civil War, 1642-1651.* London: Seeley Service and Company, 1968.

_____. *The British Army of the Eighteenth Century.* New York: Hippocrene Books, 1977.

Rose, D. Murray. *Historical Notes or Essays on the '15 and '45.* Edinburgh: William Brown, 1897.

Salmond, J. B. *Wade in Scotland.* Edinburgh: The Moray Press, 1934.

Salway, Peter. *Roman Britain.* Oxford: The Clarendon Press, 1981.

Scott, Sir Walter. *Tales of a Grandfather, being the history of Scotland from the earliest period to the close of the rebellion, 1745–46.* 2 vols. London: Adam and Charles Black, 1898.

Shearer, John. *The Battle of Sheriffmuir. Related from Original Sources.* Stirling: Eneas MacKay, 1898.

Skene, W. F. *Celtic Scotland.* 3 vols. Edinburgh: David Douglas, 1876–1880.

Smout, T. C. *A History of the Scottish People, 1560–1830.* New York: Charles Scribner's Sons, 1969; London: Collins, 1969.

Stevenson, David. *Alasdair MacColla and the Highland Problem in the Seventeenth Century.* Edinburgh: John Donald Publishers, 1980.

Stewart, Colonel David. *Sketches of the Character, Manners, and Present State of the Highlanders of Scotland; with details of the Military Service of the Highland Regiments.* 2 vols. Edinburgh: Archibald Constable and Company, 1822; reprint ed., Edinburgh: John Donald Publishers, 1977.

Stone, Lawrence. *Social Change and Revolution in England, 1540–1640.* London: Longmans, 1965.

Tayler, Alister N., and Tayler, Henrietta. *1715: The Story of the Rising.* London: Thomas Nelson and Sons, 1936.

_____. *1745 and After.* London: Thomas Nelson and Sons, 1938.

Terry, C. S. *John Graham of Claverhouse, Viscount Dundee, 1648–1689.* London: Archibald Constable and Company, 1905.

_____. *The Rising of 1745 with a Bibliography of Jacobite History 1689–1788.* London: David Nutt, 1900.

Thirsk, Joan, ed. *The Agrarian History of England and Wales, 1500–1640.* Cambridge: Cambridge University Press, 1967.

Tomasson, Katherine, and Buist, Francis. *Battles of the '45.* London: B. T. Batsford, 1962; reprint ed., London: Book Club Associates, 1978.

Tomasson, Katherine. *The Jacobite General.* Edinburgh: William Blackwood and Sons, 1958.

Tullibardine, Marchioness of, ed. *A Military History of Perthshire.* 2 vols. Perth: R. A. and J. Hay, 1908.

Tulloch, Major-General Alexander B. *The '45 From the Raising of Prince Charlie's Standard at Glenfinnan to the Battle of Culloden.* 3rd ed. Stirling: Eneas MacKay, 1908.

Walton, Colonel Clifford. *History of the British Standing Army, A.D. 1660–1700.* London: Harrison and Sons, 1894.

Waugh, W. T. *James Wolfe, Man and Soldier.* Montreal: Louis Carrier and Company, 1928.

Webb, Henry J. *Elizabethan Military Science: The Books and the Practice.* Madison, Wisconsin: University of Wisconsin Press, 1965.

Whittington, G., and Whyte, I. D., eds. *An Historical Geography of Scotland.* London: Academic Press, 1983.

Willcock, John. *The Great Marquess, Life and Times and Archibald, 8th Earl, and 1st (and only) Marquess of Argyll, 1607–1661.* Edinburgh: Oliphant, Anderson, and Ferrier, 1903.

Willson, Beckles. *The Life and Letters of James Wolfe.* London: William Heinemann, 1909.

Wilson, David M. *The Archaeology of Anglo-Saxon England.* London: Methuen and Company, 1976.

Wormald, Jenny. *Court, Kirk, and Community: Scotland 1470-1625.* Toronto: University of Toronto Press, 1981; London: Edward Arnold, 1981.

Wright, Robert. *The Life of Major-General James Wolfe.* London: Chapman and Hall, 1864.

Wright, Thomas, *The Celt, the Roman, and the Saxon: A History of the Early Inhabitants of Britain.* London: Kegan Paul, Trench, Trübner, and Company, 1902.

Young, Peter, and Adair, John. *Hastings to Culloden.* London: G. Bell and Sons, 1964.

Young, Peter, and Lawford, J. P., eds. *History of the British Army.* New York: G. P. Putnam's Sons, 1970; London: Barker, 1970.

Journal Articles

Drummond-Norie, W. 'Inverlochy, 1431-1645,' *Celtic Monthly* 5 (1896-1897): 84.

Hayes-McCoy, G. A. 'Strategy and Tactics in Irish Warfare, 1593-1601,' *Irish Historical Studies* 2 (1940-1941): 255-79.

Lowe, J. 'The earl of Antrim and Irish aid to Montrose in 1644,' *Irish Sword* 4 (1959-1960): 191-98.

McDonald, Forrest. 'The Ethnic Factor in Alabama History: A Neglected Dimension,' *Alabama Review* 31 (1978): 256-65.

McDonald, Forrest, and McDonald, Ellen Shapiro 'The Ethnic Origins of the American People, 1790,' *William and Mary Quarterly* 37 (1980): 179-99.

McDonald, Forrest, and McWhiney, Grady. 'The Antebellum Southern Herdsman: A Reinterpretation,' *Journal of Southern History* 41 (1975): 147-66.

_____. 'The Celtic South,' *History Today* 30 (July 1980): 11-15.

_____. 'The South From Self-Sufficiency to Peonage: An Interpretation,' *American Historical Review* 85 (1980): 1095-1118.

McKerral, Andrew. 'West Highland Mercenaries in Ireland,' *Scottish Historical Review* 30 (April 1951): 1-14.

McWhiney, Grady. 'Continuity in Celtic Warfare,' *Continuity* 2 (Spring 1981): 1-18.

_____. 'Jefferson Davis—the Unforgiven,' *Journal of Mississippi History* 42 (February 1980): 113-27.

_____. 'The Revolution in Nineteenth-Century Alabama Agriculture,' *Alabama Review* 31 (1978): 3-32.

_____. 'Saving the Best From the Past,' *Alabama Review* 32 (1979): 243-72.

McWhiney, Grady, and McDonald, Forrest. 'Celtic Names in the Antebellum Southern United States,' *Names* 31 (June 1983): 89-102.

O'Danachair, C. 'The Battle of Auldearn, 1645,' *Irish Sword* 1 (1949-1953): 128-32.

_____. 'Montrose's Irish Regiments,' *Irish Sword* 3 (1959-1960): 61-67.

O'Domhnaill, Sean. 'Warfare in sixteenth-century Ireland,' *Irish Historical Studies,* 5 (1946-1947): 29-54.

Unpublished Secondary Source

Dederer, John Morgan. Afro-Southern and Celtic-Southern Cultural Adaptation in the Old South. Unpublished paper, University of Alabama, 1985.

Index